Teaching Women's Studies in Conservative Contexts

Women's studies is a field that inspires strong reactions, both positive and negative, inside and outside of the classroom. The field, partly due to its activist origins, is often associated with liberal ideology and is therefore chided by students and others who identify as conservative. The goal of this book is to introduce conservative perspectives into the issues of gender, sexuality, race, and power that are topics of teaching and discussion in women's studies courses. The book also aims to provide examples of pathways by which conservative students and scholars can engage the field of women's studies, not as opponents, but as contributors. Contributors, including administrators, activists, scholar-teachers, artists, and ministers, come together in this collection to engage in writing and responding and to add their approaches to teaching and administering women's studies on their campuses.

Cantice Greene is an assistant professor of English at Clayton State University.

Routledge Research in Gender and Society

For a full list of titles in this series, please visit www.routledge.com

Teaching Women's Studies in Conservative Contexts

Considering Perspectives for
an Inclusive Dialogue

Edited by Cantice Greene

R Routledge
Taylor & Francis Group

LONDON AND NEW YORK

First published 2016
by Routledge

2 Park Square, Milton Park, Abingdon, Oxfordshire OX14 4RN
52 Vanderbilt Avenue, New York, NY 10017

Routledge is an imprint of the Taylor & Francis Group, an informa business

First issued in paperback 2020

Library of Congress Cataloging-in-Publication Data
Names: Greene, Cantice, editor.
Title: Teaching women's studies in conservative contexts : considering
    perspectives for an inclusive dialogue / edited by Cantice Greene.
Description: New York ; London : Routledge, 2016. | Series: Routledge
    research in gender and society ; 48 | Includes bibliographical references and index.
Identifiers: LCCN 2015041380 | ISBN 9781138187108 (hbk. : alk. paper)
Subjects: LCSH: Women's studies. | Conservatism.
Classification: LCC HQ1180 .T384 2016 | DDC 305.4—dc23
LC record available at http://lccn.loc.gov/2015041380

ISBN: 978-1-138-18710-8 (hbk)
ISBN: 978-0-367-59714-6 (pbk)

Typeset in Sabon
by Apex CoVantage, LLC

Contents

Preface

This book assumes that the relationship between women's studies and conservatives is an uncomfortable one. This assumption is based partly on the popular tropes expressed by conservative political talk show hosts, who often include women's studies as chief among the college majors that are useless in the marketplace and that transmit mixed messages to students and the public regarding sexual and platonic relationships, gender, and structural power in and beyond college. This assumption is based on the popular idea that conservative equals sexist, racist, xenophobic, homophobic, Islamophobic, bigot. It is also based on the conservative women and Black women I work with who react uncomfortably to the term feminist, and it is based on the feminist and women's studies journals that rarely, if ever, publish literature that speaks to my experience as a conservative academic engaging reproduction, sexuality, power, and gender issues in my classes.

The assumption that the relationship between women's studies and conservatives is strained is also based on my experience as a conservative who has engaged women's studies uncomfortably for years. In graduate school, when I wanted to focus on women's rhetoric and composition, I was told my area of concentration was feminism. I resisted the term then, but when I read about women negotiating change through literacy and about women's early experiences gaining entry and status in the classroom and the academy, the terms under which I studied no longer mattered. In fact, at times I embrace the term, but other times, an experience reminds me why I've rejected it. I was reminded about the uncomfortable relationship between conservatism and women's studies when I read the responses of the anonymous reviewers of the proposal for this book. One response reverberated in my mind. The reviewer wrote about my chapter in this collection, "I actually questioned if the author of the chapter 'Negotiating Feminism When Color and Credo Trump Gender' really understood what feminism or women's studies was all about." This comment is among those I've heard for years, which underscores a belief that to speak about women's studies, certain (liberal) ideologies have to be upheld as sacred.

Despite the questions and doubts about the book, all along the road to completing it I found new solidarity, first with each of the contributors in the collection, and also with those who agreed to be interviewed for the chapter

"Voices of Administrators." Yet, the encouragement didn't stop there. One notable experience was finding Christine Pohl and her co-edited book *Living on the Boundaries*. Pohl's work on evangelical women, feminism, and the theological academy and her enthusiasm for the project fueled me when I encountered negative reactions that reminded me that conservative sensibilities were not welcomed by some who make their academic home in women's studies. But because enough of us think there's another way to approach the intellectual rift between conservatism and women's studies, this book has reached completion. Enough of us thought of creative ways for these two audiences to talk to each other, starting with upholding a congenial tone when referring to each other. Many of the authors in this collection identify as liberal, and they describe their approaches to teaching women's studies to conservative audiences. Other authors in the text identify as conservatives and express their differences with liberal feminist ideologies. Still some contributors resisted those labels altogether or introduced new ones, such as when Megan Wilson-Reitz describes the feminist religious radical.

Bringing voices to this title required some massaging, presumably because of the strained relationship I mentioned above. After the general call didn't bring a strong representation of conservative voices, I sought out the voices of scholars and teachers who publically identify as conservative and were willing to offer their responses on typically taught themes in women's studies from their related training and experience. I sought these responses to the chapters in order to provide a contrastive viewpoint in anticipation of what our audience might think. When the collection still needed more cohesion, I sought previously published work that fit its theme. The religious, ideological, or cosmological underpinnings that influence thought and activism on these issues emerged as a subtheme of the collection.

The authors of this collection acknowledge the groundbreaking work that has been done by pioneers in the field of women's studies, who dared to ask the question, "Where are the women?" and for pushing that question in directions that now interrogate relationships of power, understandings of gender, race, and sexuality, and the intersectional ways those characteristics can be used by malevolent forces to form an oppressive web against women and others. Yet, we seek to expand the literature and practices common in the field by suggesting that women's studies can attract a larger audience and attempt to reduce the stigma related to the field by considering conservative sensibilities in students, teachers, and scholars. By focusing on conservative sensibilities, we include those who identify as politically moderate, assuming that the line between liberal and conservative is continuous and many issues and factors can cause movement toward one or the other direction.

This book aims to serve as a spotlight on the pathways by which conservatives can engage in the field of women's studies as students—maintaining their authenticity and allegiance to religious, social, and political groups by being honest about points of disagreement, yet engaging strategies of coalition building in the work on behalf of vulnerable groups that speaks deeply to their hearts. For practitioners of women's studies, the book aims to provide a window into the philosophies and religious convictions that preoccupy the conservatives that enter our classrooms each semester, hopefully complicating the simplistic, popular caricatures of conservatives that often pervade academia. The hope is that the ideas articulated here can, in small ways, stand in for and comingle with the ideas of students, who may not yet be adept at articulating their beliefs. Another goal of the collection is to encourage current and future conservative instructors of women's studies to come out from the shadows and join the conversation—to engage in women's studies by learning from voices in the field and incorporating the literature, practices, and strategies they have been using in other environments—church and parachurch ministries, community organizations, and cross-cultural missions to impact the next generation of students. Finally, this book seeks to find solidarity with the few public writings that endeavor to uphold conservative ideas as those worthy of consideration and interrogation. That Beverly Guy-Sheftall in her interview made the statement, "Conservative doesn't mean stupid," points to an assumption that floats in the public psyche. To underscore her words, conservative does not mean unintellectual, and whereas some might be prone to label students as "conservative" because they are unwilling to consider another view of a concept of difference, this book seeks to challenge that practice. Whereas it might have been true in the past that conservative students came to class never having questioned the ideas that shaped their upbringing, and where courses, especially those in women's studies, newly introduced to them secular and liberal ideas, today the opposite may actually be true. To sustain a conservative perspective today is to go against the grain of popular ideas and the majority of academic biases of inquiry. In other words, contemporary thought is so much on the side of secular and liberal ideology that the term "bigot" could readily characterize someone espousing either liberal or conservative ideas.

As an apologist for the term, I am suggesting that conservatism begins with the premise that there is something in the foundation of an idea, concept, or material artifact worth conserving. To be clear, by "conserving," I mean preserving, keeping, safeguarding, or protecting. As I apply the ideology of conservatism to politics, I mean that there is something in our nation's history of governance worth saving. As I apply conservatism to family, I believe that our foundational tenets of a nuclear family beginning with a mother and father are worth saving. In terms of power, that there is an obligation to understand and respect authority (familial, governmental, institutional) could be considered a conservative value. Conservative ideology can be applied religiously as well. The Islamic/Judaic/Christian belief in an all-knowing, all-powerful, benevolent, and just Creator/God who exists outside of nature or earth and who should be worshipped and considered above all human or humanistic ideals and ideas, and that there is infallible literature (or at least, that there are infallible principles in ancient literature) are classified as conservative religious beliefs. It is important to note that contrary to the mainstream belief that conservatives are by default naïve, it takes a critical consciousness and a thoughtful mindfulness to champion age-old virtues in the midst of constantly changing ideas.

Can gender, race, and sexuality be problematized and difference interrogated within a conservative framework? Or, how is a conservative uniquely positioned to engage in conversations about difference, power, sexuality, gender, and race? What can a Black, female conservative add to a conversation about types of belonging? What can an abstinent 19 year old or twenty something college student add to a discussion about sexuality and rape culture? As a field, we should encourage and begin to respect and represent voices of church girls in girlhood studies, without dismissing their stances as only patriarchal. Their stories, experiences, and approaches to engaging difference should be added to our anthologies and policy proposals. In contemporary battles between the power of the state to dictate policies within religious environments, such as Christian-owned businesses, religious clubs in school, and clergy in their performance of marriage, these ideas can be wholly engaged. As those who study and advance theories of difference, it is up to us to recognize the value of ideological difference and to further our approaches by inviting conservatives to enter dialogues and then listen to their voices with a posture of genuine interest. I suggest that our students can benefit from this ideological vision.

In public and intellectual arenas, mainstream thinking can be enriched by a wider variety of viewpoints, including those held by conservatives. Our field, one that has led in the presentation of new ideologies and perspectives, can inspire collaboration in the public sphere by presenting more viewpoints from a wider variety of researchers and practitioners. This book will be a starting point for that collective intellectual growth and practical teaching, beginning with Lihi Ben Shitrit's honest discussion about a secular liberal scholar entering conservative religious spaces in Israel's West Bank to accurately represent little-explored expressions of agency by religious conservatives from a first-person perspective. She seeks to find an apparatus for considering viewpoints that contrast sharply with her own. Her respondents, Meagen Farrell and Megan Wilson-Reitz, offer additional strategies for living and working cross-culturally for the purpose of research and activism.

Judy Isaksen describes her hip hop course at a conservative "boutique" university and the ways she uses hip hop to ask students to interrogate their ideas about race and privilege. In complement, Amena Brown, a spoken word artist, shares her thoughts on what her conservative and moderate-mixed crowds tend to care about, what type of causes they're into, and how she was drawn into hip hop spoken word ministry.

Cecili Chadwick writes about the way she teaches reproductive rights to a conservative (mostly Catholic) classroom by examining the "history of rights" as it relates to reproduction. She critiques the argumentative approaches of the pro-life and pro-choice movements, offering what ends up being a rhetorical analysis that includes conservative texts that her students readily relate to. Within the chapter, she highlights teaching techniques that work well with her students and help her avoid the deadlock along partisan lines that can otherwise tend to ensue.

Offering a different perspective on ways to approach a discussion on abortion, Maria Lastochkina, a freelance scholar, argues that certain secular assumptions about childbearing and sex will not fit the context of the conservative religious women for whom a particular scholar (Erika Bachiochi) purports to speak. Lastochkina's chapter appeared originally in the journal *Christian bioethics*.

I (Cantice Greene) share my experiences in a feminist classroom in a chapter that explains why racial and religious ideologies can sometimes overshadow allegiance to the women's movement within dominant, liberal feminist ideologies. Then, in response, Le'Brian Patrick explains why he is skeptical that a harmony can be reached within a conservative theological position and a liberal one regarding sexuality and marriage.

Jennifer McWeeny interrogates an administrative decision not to amend a Jesuit university's non-discrimination policy to include sexual orientation, and in response, Latona Disher discusses diversity from an administrator's perspective that draws on principles from Christian scripture.

Monica Evans describes her experience growing up in apostolic and conservative churches where girls' and women's voices were subordinated to those of men. That experience informs her call for consciousness-raising groups in conservative churches. Veronica Gravely supports Evans's call for bringing women's voices and experiences to the center of their religious or spiritual experience while offering a critique on the issue of language and gender when appropriating scripture.

Finally, in an effort to advise others who are grappling with the question of developing, growing, or maybe limiting a women's studies offering, a range of administrators offer their experiences of growing and running a program. These voices include Dr. Beverly Guy-Sheftall, founding director of the Comparative Women's Studies Program at Spelman College; Dr. Stanton Jones, provost of Wheaton College, and Dr. Scottie May, associate professor of Christian formation at Wheaton College; and Dr. Julie Hartman-Linck, the coordinator of the women's studies program at Frostburg State University.

The hope of the collection is that, as Dana Bisignani puts it, "it addresses concerns such as: why some women of color and conservative Christians have distanced themselves from feminist movement; how we might separate feminism from 'liberalism'; understanding students' denial of their complicity in systemic violence; the role of individual choice in how we behave/what we believe; and intersectional strategies for complicating single-issue debates and ultimately effecting greater social justice, beginning with our students."[1]

NOTE

1 This quotation is the published summary of a 2013 NWSA panel on the topic of teaching women's studies in conservative contexts. Dana and I were on this panel with Lori Beralt and Minnie Chui.

Acknowledgments

I'm very grateful to Dana Bisignani and the women on the panel at the 2013 National Women's Studies Association (NWSA) conference for serving as the catalysts of this collection, Wanda Scott for connecting me with wonderful Christian activists and writers, Mrs. Edrie Williams for praying for the project, and the staff at Cobb Pregnancy Services (especially Lori Parker and Fran Wiggins), who keep me connected to work that really matters. I'd also like to thank Clayton State University's Creative Activities and Scholarship Enrichment Program (C.A.S.E.) committee for granting me a course release to complete this collection, Dr. Barbara Goodman, Chair of the English department, for supporting my C.A.S.E. proposal, Dr. Sipai Klein, who introduced me to wonderful researchers during this process, Leukisha Akporido of Clayton State's Writers' Studio for reviewing interview transcripts and giving great feedback, and Rae Grabowski, who reviewed the introduction of the book as a participant in the Feminist Scholars Digital Workshop. Special thanks go to Dr. Lynée Gaillet and Dr. Letizia Guglielmo for sharing their experiences navigating a book contract, my husband Darrell Greene for being genuinely excited about the topic, reading many drafts, and making the kids behave, my dad, Robert Payton, for encouraging me in this project, and my mom, Gwendolyn Payton, for continuous support. Finally, I thank the wonderful contributors of this collection. Your perspectives have encouraged me to believe that women's studies is a field where I belong.

Permissions Acknowledgments

Lihi Ben Shitrit's "Practicing Conversations" contains excerpts from her book. Ben Shitrit, Lihi. 2015. *Righteous Transgressions: Women's Activism on the Israeli and Palestinian Religious Right.* Princeton University Press, reprinted by permission of Princeton University Press, and her article: Ben Shitrit, Lihi. 2013. "Women, freedom, and agency in religious political movements: Reflections from women activists in Shas and the Islamic movement in Israel." Indiana University Press, Journals, *Journal of Middle East Women's Studies*, 9:3 (2013), 81–107. (c) 2013. Reprinted with permission of Indiana University Press.

Maria Lastochkina's contribution first appeared in 2013 in the journal *Christian bioethics*, published by Oxford University Press: Lastochkina, Maria. "Remedying Sexual Asymmetry With Christian Feminism: Some Orthodox Christian Reflections In Response To Erika Bachiochi, 'Women, Sexual Asymmetry & Catholic Teaching.'" *Christian bioethics: Non-Ecumenical Studies In Medical Morality* 19.2 (2013): 172–184.

An earlier version of Jennifer McWeeny's contribution appeared in the *APA Newsletter on Lesbian, Gay, Bisexual, and Transgender Issues in Philosophy*: McWeeny, Jennifer. "The Reversibility of Teacher and Student Teaching/Learning Intersectionality and Activism Amidst the LGBTQ Protest." *American Philosophical Association Newsletter on Lesbian, Gay, Bisexual, and Transgender Issues* 10:12 (2011): 5–12.

1 Hip Hop and the Interrogation of Privilege

Judy Isaksen

The year 2014 was an important one for marking the anniversary of one of our society's most progressive advancements. Fifty years prior, President Lyndon Johnson signed the Civil Rights Act of 1964 that addressed racial and sexual inequality and helped to transform America. No longer was it legal to discriminate in matters of employment based on race and sex, and no longer was it legal to segregate people at public locations, including lunch counters, theaters, buses, and clubs. This Act also established the EEOC, providing a watchdog entity to investigate complaints and impose penalties on discrimination. When politicians, activists, musicians, and business leaders gathered for a three-day Civil Rights Summit to celebrate the 50th anniversary, the legacy of the landmark law himself, President Barack Obama, walked onstage to give the keynote address. While Obama acknowledged that racism and sexism in our society is far from eliminated, he rejoiced that "new doors of opportunity and education swung open for everybody," regardless of race, ethnicity, gender, disability, or sexual orientation. "They swung open for you, and they swung open for me. And that's why I'm standing here today."

CONSERVATIVE CAMPUS CONTEXTS

This anniversary, for me, serves as an important landmark and reminder as I continuously frame and reframe my pedagogical work of teaching college-age students about matters of race and gender. But does such an anniversary mean anything to the students we teach? With an African American president and the percentage of women in classrooms across the nation leaning towards 60% or higher, most students see little reason to spend time thinking about matters of diversity, inclusivity, and equality. This societal trend intensifies even more dramatically on my campus, as I teach at a small, Southern, conservative, private liberal arts school with a predominantly White, middle-upper to upper-class student base.

Our so-called "boutique" school, with its pristine and lush campus, feels much more like a country club than a campus, and our student union looks more like a five-star hotel or convention center than a university building. This is a campus where students dress in formal cocktail attire regularly for a variety of sorority and fraternity events. We have free dry cleaning and laundry service, wake-up calls, and valet parking; kiosks around campus offer free food—muffins and hot chocolate in the mornings—as students walk to classes, and we have our own ice cream truck that roams campus, giving away treats. Resort-style pools complete with tiki bars dot the landscape, and never will you see a piece of litter. We also have a rooftop fine-dining steakhouse restaurant on campus that serves as an instructional laboratory for students on all matters of posh and etiquette. The campus is filled with delightful students, nice students, even some quite bright students; they are polished and polite, and most of them are, as you can imagine, also very privileged. And while there are clearly students whose families are making grave sacrifices so their children can attend the school, the university's website indicates that many families are extremely wealthy and quite generous with their prosperity. For example, the school has a Parents Council, with an annual membership fee of $1000. Moreover, the President's Leadership Council, which consists of anonymous donations "comprised of parents of current students," donated $14 million in 2013. I do not denounce or begrudge the students for their sense of privilege; I too am privileged in that I am White, healthy, educated, and gainfully employed. What differs are our nuances around the concept of privilege, and these differences are what fuel my sense of critical social pedagogy. I worked hard over the course of many years, rising up from a working-class position; I am also self-aware of my current sense of privilege. Conversely, for the most part, my students arrived fully privileged and will most likely leave school upon graduation and enter into precisely a similar set of circumstances. Many of our students, as well as our administrators, indulge in what sociologist Allan Johnson calls the "luxury of obliviousness," which is not only having privilege but also having no awareness of that privilege (180). Not surprisingly, the rhetoric of wealth that pervades the campus directly affects matters of academics; in many cases, students' academic engagement does not measure up to their well-honed ability to handle themselves successfully in high-class situations. But in reality, I must sadly admit that being comfortable rubbing elbows with the elite in swanky settings just may serve them better than having a grasp of the arts and humanities.

This rhetoric of wealth quite naturally seeps into the dominant racial discourse on campus; because the administration, faculty, and students are predominantly White, the campus operates, from the top down, with a rhetoric of colorblindness. Discussions of race are generally considered unnecessary primarily because whiteness prevails, so the mere act of giving consideration to matters of race is itself perceived as risky, if not racist. Whereas the perception, given our nation's African American president, is that we now live in a "post-racial" society, I would argue that such a view can be possible only if one has actually spent time and energy thinking critically about matters of race. Only if one is able to make comparisons, pre versus post, based on historical facts can an argument be made that we live in a "post-racial" society. Only if one knows the facts about the residual effects of enslavement, which include economic hardships, educational disadvantages, and racist sexual violence that informs stereotypes about African Americans to this day. Only then can such an argument be made, and honestly, most of our students haven't done that type of intellectual work. Sadly, the campus's racial discourse is not a "post-racial" one; it's not racial at all. As such, this hegemonic discourse keeps matters of race invisible and thereby preserves and sustains the ongoing power of White privilege. The environment on our campus silently serves to reinforce the racial privilege that our predominantly White student body arrives with, packaged comfortably in their very expensive Louis Vuitton bags, to jazz up Peggy McIntosh's knapsack metaphor.

The campus's dominant gender discourse is equally challenging. In terms of faculty, we do have a growing number of female junior faculty, which is hopeful; however, the number of females in positions of administrative power can be counted on two hands, with a few missing fingers. Entering the 2014 academic year, the ratio of males to females in the top tier of administrators, deans, and department heads is 31:6. And much like the national trends, females make up just above 60% of our student body. Yet, despite the large numbers of females on campus, I find it challenging that there is little diversity among the appearances or sensibilities of so many of our female students. The impeccable aesthetic culture on campus and the rhetoric of wealth carry over and inform the gendered performances of female students, most of who also comply with what Naomi Wolf aptly termed the "Beauty Myth." Ever obedient to the demands of the institutional powers of a male-dominated society, the majority of female students perform gender, both in their appearance and behavior, in fairly rigid and subscribed ways—that is, with perfectly coordinated and top-dollar outfits, high heels, hairstyles, and makeup. And most appear completely unaware of the ways in which their submissiveness and attention to beauty are serving the privileged patriarchy.

Discourses surrounding sexuality have been quite interesting, even testy. Dialogue among faculty to start a Safe Space program on campus for our LGBTQ students prompted the university president to voice his concerns about not only our conservative community, but also our conservative parents and board of trustees, thus squelching the program. Joyfully though, the small student PRIDE (People Representing Individuality, Diversity, and Equality) group, oblivious to the concerns of the president, started a Safe Space program that has taken off successfully, supported fully by more than 50% of the faculty, and has not been silenced by the administration. The unwitting success of the student PRIDE group is a healthy indication of several important and hopeful measures: First, that the lines of conservatism are not rigid and static, but evolving and shifting; secondly, that the entire university community can live peacefully together despite wherever one may fall along the continuum from progressivism to conservatism; and finally, that in some respects, the students have greater capacity than the faculty to effect change, and they are putting that agency to good use. So while our campus is physically beautiful and filled with eager and positive students, and while these interstitial discourses give voice to the general sense of entitlement, privilege, and conservatism, the campus culture still has room for small measures of counter-hegemonic movement, which is essential for a critical social pedagogue like myself.

PROGRESSIVE PERSONAL CONTEXTS

My teaching philosophy, which has been developing over two decades, is rooted in the methodology of the intellectual school of thought known as critical pedagogy, as posited by such scholars as Paulo Freire (1970), Henry Giroux (1981; 1983; 1988), Lisa Delpit (1988), and bell hooks (1994). A primary tenet of critical pedagogy posits that education is a vehicle for students not only to improve themselves as individuals, but also to develop into just and productive citizens within our democratic society. Inherent in the project of critical pedagogy is the notion that faculty eagerly partner with students as we all strive to find our voices to explore and analyze systems of power, systems that include both privilege and oppression. Ideally, critical pedagogy works toward learning a variety of tools useful to challenge inequities that are produced by cultural practices and institutions. As a professor who teaches from a critical pedagogy perspective, I find these overlapping and interlocking conservative discourses of race, class, gender, and sexuality that exist on our campus to be quite the challenge. It's hard to challenge oppression when the campus operates with the "luxury of obliviousness."

For critical pedagogues, the classroom is typically a space for disruption, but this site is equally challenged by the makeup of the students in my classroom; it is difficult to have a range of voices and robust dialogue when most everyone has similar and conservative sensibilities. Social and cultural analyst Mary Louise Pratt's notion of the "contact zone," that rich "space where cultures meet, clash, and grapple with each other" (34) is difficult to attain when the homogeneity of students tends to erase the potential for clashing and grappling.

Given the challenges presented by our campus culture and the demographics of our students, I have found, with both time as well as trial and error, that there is one key space that I can turn to for disruption, and that is my curricular choices—namely, what topics I teach and how I rhetorically present them. Not surprisingly, our university's curriculum, for the most part, matches the campus culture. Students are typically accustomed to taking classes that are entrenched in both White and male privilege. However, there are a few pockets across the curriculum where progressive rhetoric and critical pedagogies take place, where courses are rooted in history, critical theory, analysis, and self-reflection. I and a handful of other progressive professors teach these courses, and they naturally draw a particular—and small—audience of progressive students. But what about the other students, those in the majority?

My scholarly and pedagogical work takes place at the provocative intersection of women's studies, gender studies, racial studies, and media, which is a powerful and rewarding challenge. None of these areas can be separated out, for any critique of the hegemony of one is a critique of another. How, then, do I manage to involve my students—students who are predominantly conservative, White, rich, and privileged—in critical analyses of such intersections? By teaching Hip-Hop Culture, a 3000-level undergraduate course that unwittingly captures some conservative and unlikely students into the web of progressive thought.

To unpack the ways that this course has been proven fruitful, the remainder of this chapter will unfold in three parts. First, I will provide a brief overview of hip hop and discuss the value of positioning this musical movement as an intellectual pursuit. Next, using a cultural studies methodology and drawing from the theories of sociology, psychology, social anthropology, communication, and women and gender studies, I will lay out my underpinning theoretical frameworks of White privilege, muted group theory, bringing wreck, and identity construction as they apply to both hip hop and the larger project of disrupting conservative ideologies. Simultaneously, I will also describe the successes I have had in reaching students who, for the most part, have never sought out progressive courses or given critical attention to matters of gender and race.

HIP-HOP CULTURE: WHERE STREET, THEORY, AND PRIVILEGE MEET

At some point during the semester, students typically confess that they signed up for my Hip-Hop Culture course because they like the musical genre and they expected the course to be entertainment-based. Some are surprised, perhaps even disappointed, for I specifically and intentionally design the course to avoid the mainstream Top 40 hip-hop music; rather, our focus is on unraveling hip hop's history and the social, gender, and racial factors that gave rise to this musical movement.

The roots of hip hop were based primarily in oppression. From the movement's earliest days, inner-city youth, primarily males of color, rhythmically called into question and resisted the institutional structures—neglectful governments, police brutality, unequipped schools—that were largely responsible for the racial, social, and economic oppression that colored their lives. Rising from their imaginations and in an attempt to find their voices, this movement consisted of four original elements—DJing/spinning, breaking/

dancing, graffiti art/writing, and MCing/rapping, as well as a variety of derivatives that took shape as hip hop continued to develop. Hip hop was indeed, from its birth, a cultural text. But even more so, it was a cultural text that moved from a subaltern position of the South Bronx ghettos circa the 1970s to one that sought and continues to seek not only agency, but also community. Hip-hop culture includes rap music, but also poetry, spoken word, alternative radio, films, documentaries, journalism, plays, novels, cultural criticism, scholarly books, cyberpolitics, fashion, political organizing, digital productions, language development, entrepreneurialism, consumerism, and more. Hip-hop is a full-blown social movement that via all these various avenues continually explores ongoing racial oppression, gender oppression, and sexual oppression; it's concerned with economic exploitation and cultural colonization. This movement forces us to consider constructions of racial and gender identities and to question our own participation in the reception, consumption, and circulation of these identities; exploring hip hop is a means to understanding one's own identity politics. Along with the beats, hip hop provides a rhythmic but hard-hitting indictment of our social ills. Yes, we are talking about Tupac, Jay-Z and Queen Latifah, Eminem and Nicki Minaj, but we are also talking about Black femininities and masculinities. We are grappling with the intersectionality of race and gender that enables us to better understand the oppressive racial struggles within African American history and culture that gave rise to the hip-hop movement as well as the lyrics that they typically dance to without any analyses. So what better way to bring all of these social ills to the attention of my privileged students and work toward meaningful social change than in the guise of hip hop?

RACIALIZED PRIVILEGE

To contextualize the direction I want to take the course in, I kick-start the semester by asking students to brainstorm privately, for a few minutes, two different lists. The first is about all the ways in which they personally have access to and contact with people of different races from their own. I suggest they consider their neighborhoods, schools, teachers, gyms, doctors, clergy, mail deliverer, friends, their parents' friends, coaches, club leaders. For the second list, I ask them to brainstorm all the ways they came to appreciate hip hop. Was it through TV, advertisements, movies, the radio, friends, particular artists, particular regional styles, or particular dances? When we open the group discussion based on these two lists, we generally find that most White students have very similar experiences: They have little access to people who look different from themselves. In other words, they never cite having an African American doctor or clergyman or neighbor. Yet, most of the White students can all pretty much relate to each other about how they came to enjoy hip hop: Through their love of *The Fresh Prince of*

Bel-Air, a show that went off the air decades ago, or from listening to their local Jamz station, or through hip-hop dance lessons they took along with their ballet and tap, which are always taught to a White dancer. So I ask them to consider why they came to appreciate a Black art form when they had very little access to Black people or culture; I want to see if they can make any connections between these two lists. And typically, most cannot. I frequently witness a stark disconnect between my White students' genuine love for rap music, a decidedly cross-cultural genre, and their connection to and understanding of Black culture. In my experience, I have found that this disconnect often unfolds in either two ways. Either well-meaning White students see their connection to hip hop as completely unconnected to matters of race; that is, their insights of race and hip hop often start and stop with Eminem, and they typically adopt the colorblind sensibility: "He's a dope rapper, so it doesn't matter what color his skin is," they say. Or they defensively spit out endless factoids, demonstrating their keen knowledge of hip hop, as proof that this music has taught them everything they need to know about African American culture. Both are problematic, limiting, and uncritical positions, and the bold confidence with which they hold these positions not only makes my few Black students weary, but also makes the work I attempt to do in this class all the more important.

So with this opening exercise on day one, I am asking them, and for many it may be the first time, to think of race as a concept, as a construct, and as an indicator of social stratification and power. My aim is for students, particularly the White students who make up 98% of the class, to understand their identity *as* White people within systems of institutional racism. Such knowledge will not only help them to understand their connection to the hip-hop movement more thoroughly, but also help them to challenge assumptions of superiority and replace those assumptions with more aware, critical, and equitable racial identities. So we spend time during the first few weeks of the semester reading a blend of racial theorizing alongside the historical birth of hip hop. Jeff Chang's cultural history of the musical movement deals explicitly with the racial foundation of hip-hop. I couple his historical narrative with some readings from psychologist Beverly Daniel Tatum, who is African American, as well as sociologist Allan Johnson, who is White.

Johnson's work on White privilege provides students with foundational knowledge of how racial meaning and racial identity were historically constructed, and he provides personal family stories to show the ways in which his well-meaning ancestors benefited from unearned White privilege, which is passed on from generation to generation, right into his lap (177–79), something most of my privileged students can relate to. Students learn that power and wealth cannot be "uncoupled" from our country's history of race and racism (179). Equally important, Johnson unpacks two key concepts that resonate with students. The first, which I alluded to earlier, is his expression for not only having White privilege, but not even realizing that privilege. He calls it indulging in the "luxury of obliviousness" (180), a useful expression that, in a good semester, we return to time and again. Johnson posits that every system of power has a "path of least resistance" where privileged people typically "accept the organization of social life as just the way things are." By indulging in the "luxury of obliviousness," the privileged class is free to live unaware of what effect they have on those in non-dominant groups (179–80). However, as students learn the origins of this movement—that the birth of hip hop took place in a near necropolis; that politics of abandonment and abject poverty were the roots of the beats they so love; that break dancing was initially a militant gang activity that youth, after burying so many brothers, learned to transform fighting into dancing; that beat boxing and scratching were organic art forms that arose because the denizens of the South Bronx had no money for musical instruments or lessons—as they become aware of the roots of the music they love, their sense of "obliviousness" is impossible to ignore. And recognizing this sense of privilege is only the first step; doing something about it is the second and more important step. Stepping off the path of least resistance and becoming critically conscious about how we construct our own sense of racial identity is the greatest moment of awareness. Johnson argues cogently that none of our racial history had to happen as it did and each of us has the agency to do things differently and construct new racial meaning and identity. As he puts it: "Every social system happens only through the participation of individuals, any one of whom has the potential to change how the system happens by stepping off the path of least resistance" (181). I am aware that there is quite a distance between becoming aware of the "luxury of obliviousness" and "stepping off the path of least resistance," and while I would love for all of my students to make systematic changes, I am quite thrilled when they, through a hip-hop education, are able to simply identify their extreme sense of privilege.

Theorizing by psychologist Beverly Daniel Tatum provides yet another useful tool for students to think about the ways in which they may unknowingly support racist systems without being racist in any personal way. Most Whites—and my students are no different—never want to, in fact, fear being labeled *racist*; this is a word that carries incredible emotional weight. When students discuss topics within hip hop, such as the use of the n-word or the b-word, however, some White students boldly do so without a sense of racist or sexist awareness, which can be extremely frustrating for the more progressive and African American students. Tatum's views, however, help to unpack layers of active and passive racism, which not only prompts students to question their casual comments and think twice about their privileged views, but also provides the African American students with a theoretical framework with which to articulate their views. Tatum uses the analogy of a moving walkway to describe the difference between active and passive racism, stating that:

> Active racist behavior is equivalent to walking fast on the conveyor belt. The person engaged in active racist behavior has identified with

the ideology of White supremacy and is moving with it. Passive racist behavior is equivalent to standing still on the walkway. No overt effort is being made, but the conveyor belt moves the bystanders along to the same destination as those who are actively walking. (163)

Tatum, like Johnson, makes clear that each one of us—regardless of what race we identify with or if we've never committed an active racist act—is responsible for our society's racial constructions. These theorists help the White students to see their own sense of privilege and rethink the ways in which their behavior is, at times, passive racist behavior. Critiquing songs like Macklemore's "White Privilege," in which the Seattle rapper recognizes and explores the implications of being White while fully honoring hip hop's racial history, serves as a nice way to pull the views of Chang, Johnson, and Tatum together. As we move through the semester and the discussions across races become richer and more honest, most of the White students realize that they can make some critical changes in their own life to be actively working against racism rather than passively and obliviously perpetuating the system of racial advantage. And most of the Black students also experience growth in understanding the more nuanced ways of how systems of power and oppression operate; moreover, they are better equipped with theoretical language to articulate the racial pain that they have been experiencing throughout their lives. Most importantly, all of us are learning to talk across lines of race, a skill that needs endless honing.

GENDERED PRIVILEGE

Interstitial to matters of race, and central to the study of hip hop, are matters of gender, male privilege, and sexist oppression. I've noticed repeatedly that when we turn our attention to women in hip hop, most students, both male and female, unless they are hardcore well-schooled hip-hop headz, associate women in hip hop primarily with video hos and being part of a pimp or ratchet culture that sexually serves the patriarchy. I must remind myself that hip hop was a commercialized industry by the time our students were born, so they have seen few other representations of women in their lifetime and are rather desensitized to the denigrating, hypersexualized images and objectifying expressions that saturate mainstream hip hop.

To start to re-sensitize my students and move beyond such representations that blur any individuality within women and openly commodify Black sexuality, I open the discussion by asking students to collectively brainstorm female artists in hip hop. And though the list is never long, it does change over time. Nicki Minaj has been topping the list lately, but students may also give shout outs to Missy Elliott, Lil' Kim, Foxy Brown, Eve, and Lauryn Hill. On the rarest occasion, I hear Salt-N-Pepa, but MC Lyte, no way. Roxanne and Sha-Rock, unheard of. I'm thrilled when someone says Queen Latifah, but that's usually followed by someone quizzically asking, "The actress? The one who does the Cover Girl commercials?" And I usually get a weak, almost apologetic, female voice asking, "Does India Arie count?" and then another hopeful, but equally weak voice may chime in, asking, "How about Alicia Keys?"

I find these unsure, but hopeful, questions about India Arie and Alicia Keys quite telling, because I think this trepidation speaks to the good girl/bad girl dichotomy that so pervades our societal imagination of how women think they should behave in our patriarchy. You're either down with the booty camp of mainstream hip hop, or you're a follower of the conscious neo-soul genre. But what I find is that my students aren't sure how to negotiate the vast terrain between these two extreme ends; they have no voice for doing so because they are muted by the onslaught of problematic representations.

So this is where I turn to muted group theory, a cultural/critical theory that helps to explain some of the ways in which women are muted in and by hip hop. Equally important, the male students can become critically conscious of the ways in which women are being silenced and can recognize their own complicity of silencing by virtue of male privilege.

The muted group theory (MGT) was originated by social anthropologists Edwin and Shirley Ardener, with further development by a variety of critical scholars. MGT asserts that a language system will work well for the dominant group who has established it, which is most typically White men, but less powerful groups—the poor, females, people of color—are often silenced by the very language they are required to use. The theory is based on observations of social anthropologists who would study women's experiences by talking primarily to men; as such, not only do women have to contend with communicating through a language system that doesn't comfortably give voice to their own thoughts, but their experiences are also being represented through a male perspective (Ardener 54). Communication scholar Cheris Kramarae believes that muted group theory is useful "to make gender and race politics more visible" (60), and anthropologist Robin Sheriff argues that the silencing of muted groups is a particular type of silencing in that it is a socially shared phenomenon and fully connects to a question of agency: A "critical feature of this type of silence is that it is both a consequence and an index of an unequal distribution of power" (114).

Such silencing of subordinate racial and gender groups takes place by several interconnected means, and we see these methods operating within the hip-hop world. Trivializing, which is to render the words of women as being unimportant and not worthy of being listened to, occurs alongside of ritualizing, which is the damaging process of repetition—in both acts and images—that serve to normalize the degradation of women. Accompanying trivializing and ritualizing is also the act of controlling, that is, taking over—primarily in decision-making—that renders women as subordinate and therefore silenced (Wall and Gannon-Leary, 1999; West and Turner, 2010).

Once students pinpoint and label these three methods of silencing, we can begin to map such techniques onto women's experiences in hip hop and identify the ways in which an industry controlled nearly entirely by men indeed profits from the trivialization of women. They can easily cite, via any number of hip-hop videos and lyrics, overwhelming evidence that hip hop is an industry that routinely denigrates women as sexual objects for the fantasy pleasure of men. They can conclude that it is no wonder that that same audience of men isn't generally interested in buying the music of female MCs, for women have been so thoroughly trivialized in such a ritualized fashion, that it is doubtful that female artists could have anything of value to spit. They discover that female rappers rarely get the opportunity to express empowering messages because, in order to gain entry into the rap game as performers and to compete with male rappers, female MCs do well to follow the codes set down and controlled by males. This means, for some females artists, embodying the male aesthetic and emulating or appealing to male behavior if they want record producers, who are disproportionately male, to even listen to them. Students also conclude that on the flip side, neo-soul female hip-hop artists are not fully welcomed or given rap status because their positive art is trivialized for attempting to work outside of the controlled ritualization of the male aesthetic, and as a result, such artists are not considered worthy of critical acclaim and therefore suffer financially.

Employing MGT gives students a way to identify the various methods used for silencing women, and then they are able to trace those results to the material reality within the world of hip hop as we know it today. But simultaneously, this theory also opens up the door to discuss the ways in which women's voices are often trivialized, ritualized, and controlled on our campus and in our classrooms; additionally, this theory gives us the tools to analyze the ways in which representations of women in hip hop indeed seep over into our daily lives. Having the support of these easy-to-grasp theoretical concepts empowers students to gain some critical distance so they can begin to see their own lives in a more nuanced light. Female students begin to explore they ways in which they too are silenced, and the male students often can pinpoint their role in such silencing. For example, this notion of muting, along with the ritualized sexualized representations of women, has led to some interesting and honest discussions about the expectations both young men and women have about intimacy and loving. They often admit that the soft pornography that they regularly witness in hip hop tragically serves as their sex education and to replicate what they see has not proven satisfying for either party. They express concerns about the pressure they feel they are under to perform sexually in particular ways. Males openly discuss they ways in which they have certain expectations of the females in their private lives but would be appalled and upset if their younger sister behaved in such ways, ways that they learn from the music they enjoy. In our class discussions, we try to untangle the confusion many women feel when they admit that they love hip-hop music, but they resent being treated disrespect-fully by men in acts and words that sound like the latest music video; when a party starts to feel like the set of a music video, women often feel vulnerable and unsafe. Men sometimes confess that they behave differently depending on who their audience is; they also describe the anxiety they feel to keep up what anti-sexist activist Jackson Katz termed the "tough guise" as well as the fear they feel of being labeled a "wuss." I feel fairly certain that the "feminist sex wars" between anti-porn and sex-positive feminists that has been raging for decades eludes most, if not all, of my students. They are not taking a politic stance and wrangling over the fuzzy definitions and bound-aries of what constitutes porn. Rather, my students, whether progressive or conservative, are struggling with the expected ways in which they feel intimacy should play out in their own lives. That soft porn is a highly visual medium coupled with its ubiquity in all forms of media makes students feel incredibly confused not only about their gender constructions, but also about their sexual appetites. We also discuss how their sexual politics might look once they leave college. Will they continue to enjoy this music once they become parents, and what might be the ramifications of their choices as their children listen and watch such soft porn? Gender politics, indeed, come alive as we bring the trappings of hip hop into our day-to-day lives and disrupt the comfort that they once felt. Finally, students must grapple with the fact that benefiting from White privilege does not seem to protect anyone from the harm of these gender constructions.

BRINGING WRECK

MGT is indeed a provocative and useful theory to help students see some of the limitations involving women within hip hop and how such silencing seeps over into their everyday lives, but as a critical pedagogue, I always aim to counteract problems with possibilities. So we back up a little bit to look at the various ways that women have constructed *themselves* in a variety of posi-tive ways throughout the 40+ year history of hip hop. Whereas historian Jeff Chang does a great job of articulating a full-bodied racial history of hip hop, he sadly does a poor job of articulating the presence of women in the early days. Despite his erasure, when the hip-hop movement was initially emerg-ing, women were a vital part of the early nation-building, and they did have a powerful voice; thankfully, a variety of texts discuss women's participation and power within the movement (Rose, 1994; Good, 1999; Valdés, 1999; Hill Col-lins, 2000, 2006; Morgan, 2000; Perry, 2004; Pough, 2004; Pough et al., 2007). Writer and cultural critic Laura Jamison writes that "[f]emale MCs have tra-ditionally been viewed as interlopers . . . but the fact is, while fewer in number than men, women have been integral to rap since its formative years. Indeed, females have rocked mikes alongside the boys since the beginning" (177). And lest we forget that hip hop's first label, Sugar Hill Records—that launched the 1979 *Rapper's Delight*, often considered rap's first hit record—was started by a woman, Sylvia Robinson. While misogyny within hip hop is a reality that must be addressed, it is equally important that we address the agency that women in hip hop have had and continue to have, and a useful theory to help students understand this positive aspect of hip hop is one called "bringing wreck."

In 1993, Queen Latifah, one of hip-hop's most enduring, successful, and iconic female MCs, blessed the mike with a knock-out line in her Grammy-winning song "U.N.I.T.Y": "I bring wreck to those who disrespect me." Queen Latifah's masterpiece not only spoke out against street harassment, domestic violence against women, and the degradation of women within hip hop, but she also launched a lifelong career of addressing women's empowerment. With her message of bringing wreck—that is, she will not tolerate those who disrespect her, but even more, she will disrupt and actively work against such misogyny—she planted the seeds for theorizing from a hip-hop feminist perspective. Feminist scholar and rhetorician Gwendolyn Pough seized her concept and engaged in theory-building about women, hip hop, and agency. In *Check It While I Wreck It: Black Womanhood, Hip-Hop Culture, and the Public Sphere*, Pough points out that in hip-hop discourse, the phrase *bringing wreck* typically signifies a boastful attitude about one's superior skills and abilities. However, Queen Latifah and, in turn, Pough, are theorizing wreck as a "rhetorical act that can be written, spoken, or acted out in a way that shows resistance" (78). Further, bringing wreck is an act to reshape the "public gaze" so that Blacks, particularly Black females, can be "recognized as human beings—and not to be shut out of or pushed away from the public sphere" (Pough 17). Bringing wreck, then, is a form of hip-hop feminism and it brings wreck to the patriarchal power relations within hip hop, not only disrupting the silence and misogyny that takes place within hip hop, but also opening up ways for women within hip hop to gain agency. Thus, using this theoretical concept as a framework, in the classroom we explore a variety of ways that different female artists bring wreck to hip hop, and then we use these women as models for female students to do the same within their own lives.

African American studies scholar Marlo David Azikwe posits that "Black women bring wreck in a number of critical ways," and it serves us best to critique female MCs with the understanding that the "expressive modes of hip-hop" are "multivocal, interdependent, and intertexual" (351), and that whereas we cannot ignore the sexist, racist, and exploitative aspects of hip hop, we also need to make "space for the gray areas, the ironies, and contradictions that are part of hip-hop and life" (352). This is important for students to realize because as we study a variety of female MCs, we witness a range of ways in which women bring wreck to the industry by very particular and intentional performances of gender. For example, MC Lyte starts off with a masculine approach, but later in her career, she performs gender in more feminine ways. Queen Latifah performs her gender from an

Afrocentric position of strength and self-respect. Salt-N-Pepa were the first MCs to engage sexual imagery within the hip-hop movement, and they did so from a healthy and empowering perspective. Eve, quite conversely, took on masculine characteristics, becoming the sexy gangsta much like Foxy Brown and Lil' Kim, who engage in self-commodification via sexualization. Missy Elliot often uses comedy and street smarts, but also proves herself as not only a rapper, but also a producer. Lauryn Hill celebrates both woman-hood and motherhood in an organic, conscious style. And Nicki Minaj has created an entire cast of alter egos, which enables her to perform gender not only as a female but also as a male, in fact, a gay male. Women in hip hop creatively work against the misogyny within an industry that silences. Some, such as Lil' Kim, Eve, and at times, Nicki Minaj, work within the trappings of the patriarchal system, and some, such as Queen Latifah and Lauryn Hill, work intentionally against the patriarchal system. And regardless of which approach resonates with each listener, students recognize that each of these women bring wreck by individually and intentionally constructing their own female identities.

Exploring these various approaches gives us ample opportunity to dis-cuss concepts of power and authenticity within the roles of women. Just as the MCs are constructing their gender identity, so too are our female students. As conservative and privileged students, many have not thought to examine or speak out against the patriarchy; bringing wreck is some-thing many have never done, in any fashion, yet most have indeed been disrespected. Seeing the bold women of hip hop first being silenced and then bringing wreck prompts students to self-reflexively apply what they are learning and think about their own self-representations. And then they are more prepared to make choices: Does the boldness of Queen Latifah resonate with me? Do I choose to behave in hypersexualized ways within the public sphere, such as Lil'Kim, Foxy Brown, or Nicki Minaj? And if so, why? Is it to reclaim my sexuality and bring wreck to the patriarchy? Or is it because that is what is expected of me *by* the patriarchy? These are the types of questions we discuss and wrestle with, questions that hip-hop culture enables groups of conservative students to unpack, questions that help them to control their own gender performances. These female hip-hop artists provide a powerful critique of both racism and sexism, while offer-ing a variety of models for constructing gender identities that are feminist, progressive, and powerful.

CONCLUSION

By the semester's end, most students who originally fit quite comfortably within a conservative ideology are now delving deeply into the construction of races and the restrictive gender binary of masculinity and femininity; they are also beginning to question their own participation in the reception, consumption, and circulation of these constructions. The female students recognize that despite the protection that our "boutique" campus affords them, they still experience being muted, but now, through an understanding of MGT, they have some skill sets—to recognize that they are being silenced, to understand the underlying power of the patriarchy, to gain confidence, and to acquire their voice—for bringing wreck. And, likewise, the male students, now having a deeper understanding of the patriarchal system and the ways in which they benefit from it, can speak out in solidarity of gender equity.

Critical pedagogy is interested in empowering and transforming students, and teaching Hip-Hop Culture repeatedly proves itself to be fertile territory for beginning this process. Unsuspecting students—students who, for the most part, are not seeking out a progressive course that critically explores matters of gender and race—not only explore dominant racial and sexual discourses in a critical fashion, but they also interrogate and wrestle with their own unearned privilege that they, for the first time, are now recognizing that they have. Word.

WORKS CITED

Ardener, Shirley. "Ardener's 'Muted Groups': The Genesis of an Idea and Its Praxis." *Women and Language* 28.2 (2005): 50–54. Print.

Azikwe, Marlo David. "More Than Baby Mamas: Black Mothers and Hip-Hop Feminism." *Home Girls Make Some Noise: Hip Hop Feminism Anthology.* Ed. Gwendolyn D. Pough, et al. Mira Loma, CA: Parker, 2007. 345–67. Print.

Chang, Jeff. *Can't Stop Won't Stop: A History of the Hip-Hop Generation.* New York: St. Martin's, 2005. Print.

Delpit, Lisa D. (1988). The Silenced Dialogue: Power and Pedagogy in Educating Other People's Children. *Harvard Educational Review* 58.3 (1988): 280–299. Print.

Freire, Paulo. *Pedagogy of the Oppressed.* New York: Continuum, 1970. Print.

Giroux, Henry. *Ideology, Culture and the Process of Schooling.* Philadelphia: Temple UP, 1981. Print.

Giroux, Henry. *Theory and Resistance in Education.* Portsmouth: Heinemann, 1983. Print.

Giroux, Henry. *Teachers as Intellectuals: Toward a Critical Pedagogy of Learning.* New York: Bergin and Garvey, 1988. Print.

Good, Karen R. "Ill Na Nas, Goddesses, and Drama Mamas." *The Vibe History of Hip Hop.* Ed. Alan Light. New York: Three Rivers, 1999. 373–83. Print.

"Join the Parents Council." highpoint.edu. High Point University. 31 Aug. 2014. Web. 31 Aug. 2014. <http://www.highpoint.edu/parents/join-the-parents-council>.

"Office of the President." highpoint.edu. High Point University. 31 Aug. 2014. Web. 31 Aug. 2014. <http://www.highpoint.edu/wanekgift/>.

Hill Collins, Patricia. *Black Feminist Thought: Knowledge, Consciousness, and the Politics of Empowerment.* New York: Routledge, 2000. Print.

Hill Collins, Patricia. *From Black Power to Hip Hop: Racism, Nationalism, and Feminism.* Philadelphia: Temple UP, 2006. Print.

hooks, bell. *Teaching to Transgress: Education as the Practice of Freedom*. New York: Routledge, 1994. Print.

Jamison, Laura. "Ladies First." *The Vibe History of Hip Hop*. Ed. Alan Light. New York: Three Rivers, 1999. 177–85. Print.

Johnson, Allan. G. *The Forest and the Trees: Sociology as Life, Practice, and Promise*. Philadelphia: Temple UP, 2008. Print.

Katz, Jackson. *Tough Guise: Violence, Media, and the Crisis of Masculinity*. Media Education Foundation. 1999. DVD.

Kramarae, Cheris. "Muted Group Theory and Communication: Asking Dangerous Questions." *Women and Language*. 28.2 (2005): 55–61. Print.

Latifah, Queen. "U.N.I.T.Y." *Black Reign*. Motown Records, 1993.

Macklemore. "White Privilege." *The Language of My World*. 2005. MP3.

McIntosh, Peggy. "White Privilege: Unpacking the Invisible Knapsack." *Peace and Freedom Magazine* July/Aug. 1989: 10–12. Print.

Morgan, Jane. *When Chickenheads Come Home to Roost: A Hip-Hop Feminist Breaks It Down*. New York: Simon, 2000. Print.

Obama, Barack. Keynote Address. Civil Rights Summit. LBJ Presidential Library, Austin. 10 Apr. 2014. Web. 10 Apr. 2014. <http://www.c-span.org/video/?318484-1/civil-rights-act-50th-anniversary>.

Perry, Imani. *Prophets of the Hood: Politics and the Poetics in Hip Hop*. Durham: Duke UP, 2004. Print.

Pough, Gwendolyn D. *Check It While I Wreck It: Black Womanhood, Hip-Hop Culture, and the Public Sphere*. Boston: Northeastern UP, 2004. Print.

Pough, Gwendolyn D., Elaine Richardson, Aisha Durham, and Rachel Raimist. *Home Girls Make Some Noise: Hip Hop Feminism Anthology*. Mira Loma, CA: Parker, 2007. Print.

Pratt, Mary Louise. "Arts of the Contact Zone." Modern Language Association's *Profession* 91. 1991: 33–40. Print.

Rose. Tricia. *Black Noise: Rap Music and Black Culture in Contemporary America*. Middletown, CT: Wesleyan UP, 1994. Print.

Sheriff, Robin E. "Exposing Silence as Cultural Censorship: A Brazilian Case." *American Anthropologist* 102 (2000): 114–132. Print.

Tatum, Beverly Daniel. "Defining Racism: Can We Talk?" *The Matrix Reader: Examining the Dynamics of Oppression and Privilege*. Ed. Abby Ferber, Christina M. Jiménez, Andrea O'Reilly Herrera, and Dena R. Samuels. Boston: McGraw, 2009. 159–64. Print.

Valdés, Mimi. "Salt-N-Pepa." *The Vibe History of Hip Hop*. Ed. Alan Light. New York: Three Rivers, 1999. 209–15. Print.

Wall, Celia J., and Pat Gannon-Leary. "A Sentence Made by Men: Muted Group Theory Revisited. *European Journal of Women's Studies* 6 (1999): 21–29. Print.

West, Richard, and Lynn H. Turner. *Introducing Communication Theory: Analysis and Application*. 4th ed. Boston: McGraw-Hill, 2010. 483–500. Print.

Wolf, Naomi. *The Beauty Myth: How Images of Beauty Are Used Against Women*. New York: William Morrow, 1991. Print.

Response

On Hip Hop, Poetry, and the Shared Journey of Womanhood

Amena Brown

Currently

Beautiful lies on the tongues of young women who are unable to speak on behalf of their own confidence

Dissolving in the mouth of never satisfied

X marks the taste of innocence and purity given away in exchange for security in things that will never last

We are just like beautiful

Used to be being used now we've lost our meaning

We have become cliché

We gave beautiful away

In exchange for fine, sexy, fly

We just wanted to be a dime

We just wanted to be worth something

Beautiful is nothing we can put on

Which meant it wasn't ours to give away

Beautiful is a picture developing in the dark room of the wombs of our hearts

Beautiful is a whisper, a longing, a knocking, a glimpse of who we could really be

Beautiful is a piece of the proof God would use to illustrate the power of truth

So God placed a piece of beautiful inside of you

"Beautiful"

I was born in 1980, so hip hop and I basically grew up together. I started writing poetry at 12 years old. I became a big hip hop fan in high school and was especially drawn to the female emcees at that time: Lauryn Hill, Bahamadia, Boss, Rage, Left Eye, and Missy Elliot. I studied their rhyme scheme, lyrics, and metaphors until I learned how to make my own. I couldn't master creating rhymes to the bars of music, so I started creating longer pieces of poetry inspired by Maya Angelou's "Phenomenal Woman." I realized I could combine what I loved about poetry and what I loved about hip hop emcee-ing into the pieces I was writing. I didn't learn this was called spoken word until attending Spelman College in the late 1990s. Hip hop culture, which for me is bigger than the music, influenced my fashion, and worldview and language. I am still a lover and consumer of hip hop culture and I'm glad that hip hop is bigger than the few songs that get played over and over again on the radio . . . that there are still people scribbling rhymes in notebooks, learning to rock on turntables, spraying graffiti, and "keeping it real."

Attending Spelman College gave me the experience of seeing women's studies infused into almost every class I took. Learning about Beverly Guy-Sheftall, reading Alice Walker, and studying historical figures from Hottentot Venus to Angela Davis greatly influenced my perspective on what it means to be a Black woman. This also gave me a great filter through which to see not only how Black women are portrayed in the media and entertainment, but also to begin discovering what I wanted to bring to my work, art, and community as a Black woman. I studied womanist theology and Black writers throughout the diaspora, right alongside Shakespeare and George Eliot.

Since graduating from undergrad, I have left academia, so for the most part, I don't engage in academic discourse in the same way I did when I was in school. Sometimes I miss that because I love engaging new ideas and having intellectual conversations. I applied to grad school with the intent of getting an MFA in poetry, but I was denied by all three of the schools I applied to. A mentor later told me that as an artist, this may have been one of the best things that could happen to me.

When I was in undergrad, we spent a lot of time on exposition, searching for the inherent themes in a piece of literature. I think exposition has its place, but I also think enjoying art, poetry, music, literature for its own sake has its place too. Sometimes after all that exposition, we were trying to surmise what Baldwin, Walker, Hughes, or Brooks meant when they were writing. I think it's just as important to also acknowledge what the art or literature brings up in you as the reader/audience member. That can be even more powerful and may be more of the point of art and literature, not to just pick it apart, but to also dance with it, breathe with it, listen to it, and let our whole selves—mind, body, and soul—experience it.

My perspective on hip hop is the same. I believe it's important to examine culture and art and not to just experience it mindlessly. We should always think about and examine the historical and sociopolitical implications of what we consume and create. But I think it's also important to examine and experience the art we consume and create as work of the soul. There is misogyny and rape culture in some hip hop, and there is also the empowerment of the voices of women in some hip hop. I don't dig the misogyny in hip hop, but one of the things I love about hip hop is that it transcends Top 40 radio or BET music videos. Hip hop is a culture that we have the opportunity to constantly create, and we also have many choices of what kind of hip hop we consume. There are many artists who are adding thoughtful, artful hip hop to the culture that speaks to community, society, and issues of racism, sexism, and socioeconomics. There are also many artists who are making hip hop that is meant to be fun, meant for the party, meant to uplift. These artists range from fashion designers to emcees, dancers, and painters. What drew me to hip hop culture and what still inspires me to be a part of it is that I have an opportunity to add to hip hop culture by creating work I believe in.

My experience in women's ministry has been two-fold: as a speaker/performer and as a participant. As a participant, my most impactful women's ministry experiences have not been at large events, but in homes, small groups, and drinking coffee at coffee shops. I have learned so much from so many women who are vastly different from me in culture, background, occupation, and phase of life. As a speaker/performer, I love that I get to be a part of various women's events of all different denominations. It's been good to see that there are ministries carving out space for women from various phases of life, cultural background, and church experience.

When I speak to women and girls, they need me to BE REAL and talk about issues that women and girls struggle with or are challenged by. As women and girls, many of us struggle with identity, self-image, sexuality, past abuse, and feeling like we aren't enough. Audiences of women and girls need me to be honest about my own past, and to be unafraid to address these topics. I also like to use poetry and humor to address these topics because it creates common ground between us. No matter the age or background of a woman, there are certain experiences that we all have in common, and sharing those experiences reminds us we're not alone. I shared my own past abuse in a workshop for teen girls. Hearing my story encouraged some of the girls to speak to a safe adult about their abuse. This helped them to know that the burden of being a victim of abuse is not something anyone should have to carry alone.

Most of the events where I perform are sponsored by Christian or faith-based organizations, so I'm sure there are a lot of conservatives in those audiences, but there are also people in those audiences who are liberals. There is also a growing number of Christian women who identify as feminist, or, to use the term Sarah Styles Bessey coined in her book of the same title, "Jesus feminists." As a performer, I have the opportunity to meet other leaders as well as members of the audience. A lot of the people I meet in the audience have conservative views about certain things, but it's hard to put everyone in one category because there are so many nuances as to how the pendulum between conservative and liberal views swings in the faith-based audience.

The faith-based audience is increasingly concerned with justice globally. I believe this is a good thing, because justice and caring for the vulnerable is something Jesus stands for. This audience is concerned with victims of human trafficking, orphans, caring for single mothers, prisoners and children of prisoners, and those who are suffering from disease. There are obviously many historical examples of when Christians have gotten it wrong, but I am seeing many examples today of Christians who are getting it right; people who are focusing on how they can let their faith inspire them to help, uplift, and be a positive part of their communities and the world at large.

We need to talk to young women about calling and purpose, about honing in at an early age on what they are passionate about, what they'd like to bring to the world to help make it better. This encourages young women to become engineers, skateboarders, preachers, moms, wives, artists, or whatever it is God calls them to do.

I think we need to talk about sex and sexuality with Christian girls. Not in the limited way we have in the past, but in a way that allows us to empower young women to accept and embrace their whole selves as women. This includes spiritually, physically, and emotionally. I think we need to talk about abuse and the healing process. We need to talk about the choice to abstain from sex or to be celibate and how you do that in today's society. We need to communicate with them so they know they are empowered to choose. Empowerment originates with God, because he gave us free will so we would be empowered to choose.

*Amena's response is based on her answers to the questions below in the order that they appear.

- What is your interaction with hip hop?
- What is your experience in women's studies/women's ministry?
- What are your disagreements/different perspectives on the ideas presented in the chapter?
- When you speak to women and girls, what do those audience need/ want from you?
- Are your audiences conservative? Do they consider themselves feminists? How do you know?
- What are the causes that your audiences are passionate about? Are those causes specific to women or the vulnerable in society?
- Can you suggest new themes that you see a need for based on your work with Christian girls, etc.?

2 Making a Conservative Appeal for Reproductive Rights to a (Mostly Catholic) Student Populace

Cecili Chadwick

"A politics of abstract principle risks missing its aim and indeed producing the opposite of the wished-for result."

Wendy Brown, *Politics out of History*

Teaching reproductive rights to a conservative student body can be difficult because the topic includes a variety of controversial subjects, ranging from the access, availability, and affordability of contraception to abortion rights, sterilization, and eugenics. Having a frank discussion about these topics often stirs up deeply held convictions about the role of morality in politics and unconsidered assumptions about motherhood in modern society. In addition, if a course on reproductive rights is discussion-based, conversations are often derailed by students' competing moral, religious, and political viewpoints (e.g., "a woman's body, a woman's right" or "abortion is morally wrong without question"). Trying to avoid the deadlock requires a carefully crafted syllabus and booklist that explore a conservative approach to reproduction and rights, historical conceptions of reproduction, and an outline of pro-life/pro-choice activism. While this approach is steeped in history and at times only tangentially related to questions of reproductive rights, it provides a new way to see an old problem. Also, because the pro-life movement is well documented as a religious movement, the influence of Christianity on our views about abortion rights ought to be considered. Without exploring these histories and competing philosophies, classroom discussions will likely end up mired in circuitous debates about law, privacy, and freedom of choice.

Philosophies are systems of rationalization. Even if we don't know the philosophy, we still *know the philosophy*. As an example, when someone says, "What's true for you isn't true for me," we know this means that truth is relative to one's experiences—hence, *not actually true*. Similarly, when someone says, "That's just the way the world works," the rationalization is that things are essentially static. If you look closely, both of these catchphrases are products of certain philosophical traditions and contain the paradox of modern, liberal ideology: both everything and nothing are possible. Also, liberalism contains a kind of relativism that champions situated knowledge and personalized "truths," making it hard to establish a moral standard. This is why the use of "big theory" is essential to ground a course on reproductive rights. Knowing what it means to have rights in modern society and understanding the meaning of reproduction frames the class in ways that get beyond the standard rationalizations and philosophic abstractions that can confuse reasonable and situated morality.

Conservative students from Catholic backgrounds in particular are often mistrustful of courses and professors who teach about reproductive rights; however, when you integrate Catholic voices into the discussion, they are more likely to engage in the topic. This is hard to do because with the exception of religious studies courses, we are often trained in the academy to treat matters of faith as somehow off-limits; however, the use of religious voices is a useful tool for discussion. For example, the following quote from Pope John Paul II works well in a lecture about the connections between philosophy and religion:

> Christ taught another way: it is that of respect for human beings; the priority of every method of research must be to know the truth about human beings, in order to serve them and not to manipulate them according to a project sometimes arrogantly seen as better even than the plan of the Creator. (2004)

When Pope John Paul II writes about the "truth," he means a biblical truth, which is offered as an alternative to what might be called "valueless empiricism" (a cornerstone of liberal relativism), and the "project" he refers to could be liberalism itself, with its accent on the *individual* and their pursuit of happiness. It's important to note that the Pope is not discounting scientific methods of research so long as they include an investigation of the truth about human beings as a whole (e.g., political or religious and not only personalized truths). This is also the pursuit of philosophy, broadly defined. This is important because we are in an era characterized by exponential growth in empirical knowledge and "expert" analysis that has pushed the threshold of what we can know about ourselves (stem cell research, cloning, etc.). At the same time, this explosion of knowledge is also creating a radical uncertainty and a narcissistic impulse that is hard to contain. The Pope's conservative principles of the Church are essentially being offered as an alternative.

The work of radical philosopher Slavoj Žižek can be a useful resource to understanding this alternative if presented alongside the teachings of the Pope. Even though Zizek does not explicitly state a position in support of or against abortion rights, his work deals directly with theology and politics. In a talk he gave in the late 1990s at Bard College, he suggests that in our modern, liberal imagination, we prefer the Dalai Lama to Pope John Paul II because the Pope appears old-fashioned and out of touch—even Catholic students have been known to say this in class (not so much about Pope Francis). An example Zizek uses is Pope John Paul II denying abortions to nuns who had become pregnant after being raped in the Bosnian war. While women's groups were outraged at the Church and the Pope for their inflexible position, as Zizek points out, the Pope reminds us that there is "a price to pay for a proper ethical attitude." Interestingly, this price is repeated in the American Constitution, where we've decided to separate politics and religion. In other words, there is a price to be paid for this separation. Zizek makes it clear that he doesn't agree with the Pope, but that the dominant Western view presents itself as being *against* paying a price for an ethical stance. This position represents the desire to "have it your way" as either relativistic or absolutist. In other words, it's an argument without principle. This, for Zizek, is worse than what the Pope is doing with his prohibitive stance against abortion because it endorses either relativism or absolutism as acceptable political positions, which are inherently irreconcilable. Political irreconcilability is dangerous because its only recourse is to violence (from the devastating and depopulating American Civil War to abortion clinic bombings).

A CONSERVATIVE APPROACH TO REPRODUCTIVE RIGHTS

Sometimes it's easier to understand something by describing what it is not. Simply stated, conservatism is anti-relativism and thus vehemently opposed to the values of liberalism and progressivism. If liberals want individuals to be exalted to the point that people can decide for themselves what their version of the "good life" is, traditional conservatives want something different. Whereas some libertarian conservatives might share some of the goals of traditional liberals (freedom for the individual, limited government, personal responsibility, etc.), traditional conservatives believe that men can know what is *good* and that underneath liberal relativism lies an insidious paradox: A self-righteous and censorious moralism.[1]

Liberalism as a philosophy has taken hold of our political sensibilities insofar as most of us identify with its major tenets even if we do not identify as *liberal*. Since the last half of the 20th century, intellectuals across disciplines have struggled to work outside the modern relativist assumptions that disregard certainty, truth, and values; however, these challenges aren't widely read or understood. Instead, most of us have unconsciously adopted a Hobbesian perspective even if we've never actually read Thomas Hobbes, because the scientific framework he provided for thinking about moral and political philosophy is woven into the fabric of our thinking. While Hobbes shared similar goals with Socrates, Plato, Aristotle, and Cicero, he thought the ancients failed to correctly theorize the "good society." For Hobbes, nature made men equal, and because men will only strive for peace if they are on equal grounds, this fact must, at least, be admitted. The social contract was a way to nullify man's natural tendencies towards violence and provide a foundation for peace.

Within liberalism, the social contract is an agreement made explicitly or implicitly between all members of a society. Simply stated, with the social contract, man exchanges obedience for protection and agrees to allow the sovereign power of the state to decide matters of justice. Just as a citizen cannot declare war against a nation, he also cannot declare war against his own neighbor. He gives up this right in order to protect himself, but acquires his own *individual rights* by granting authority to the state to determine matters of life and death. Behind this philosophy is the notion that every man exists independently and on his own in the *state of nature*. With Hobbes, we see the historical beginning of an *equality of rights*. This concept is woven directly into the Declaration of Independence, which famously states, "We hold these truths to be self-evident, that all men are created equal, that they are endowed by their Creator with certain unalienable Rights, that among these are Life, Liberty and the pursuit of Happiness." These values are the cornerstone of modern democracy and are also incorporated into the rhetorical strategies of the pro-life movement.

Whereas liberals lift up the individual out from the institution of the family, conservatives insist that a good political arrangement cannot be maintained without a healthy relationship between communities and families. There is no place for individuals in the conservative utopia because human beings are grounded by their relationships with larger structures and institutions. For conservatives, the good society is maintained through the exaltation of the family, and they believe that happiness can be achieved by living virtuously. Virtue comes from the Latin word *virtus*, which means *manliness*. While we can also understand virtue as being "moral excellence," the Latin roots help us to better understand the conservative idealization of the *gentleman*, and by extension the patriarchal father, as the cornerstone for a good political arrangement. As the philosopher of conservatism Edmund Burke has said, "I love a manly, moral, regulated liberty" (Strauss, 707). This may seem anachronistic, but traditional conservatives emphasize the *gendered* nature of politics because of its connection to other gendered institutions, namely the family. For traditional conservatives and small "r" republicans, the family is at the center of society and all institutions ought to reflect its ideals; however, it's important to note that virtue requires women too, and their relationship to the family is not to be diminished. Feminists discredit conservatives because of their appeals to traditional gendered relations; however, in the functioning of the family, for conservatives, women are honored and protected.

If you want to understand conservative students' viewpoints surrounding the topic of reproductive rights, one must include conservative frameworks and explore this emphasis on the family. When introducing the topic of reproductive rights, it's useful to use the language of conservatism to acknowledge how conservatives view the family as an institution that ought to be protected from what might be considered the arrogant designs of a liberal state. This model can easily be extended to argue that women and men's choices to have children must be honored and maintained within the family and the community and outside the purview of the state. If we consider the decision to have a child as the most personal decision a *family* can make, one can make a conservative appeal to suggest that questions relating to reproduction can and should be answered privately. If you allow the state to determine these matters, you take these choices away from the family, and the supremacy of the state over the family is enshrined. This might not seem like such a dangerous concession for conservatives when it comes to reproduction, but it was certainly the case for religious conservatives when the state took a different view on gay marriage with the 2015 Supreme Court ruling. Whereas this was a landmark victory for liberals, for religious conservatives, the extension of rights is viewed as a threat to the patriarchal family. In this way, the conservative desire to extend "rights" to the fetus may in fact lean into the same trend they are morally opposed to and produce the opposite of what they want: The degradation of traditional family values through the exaltation of the individual.

A principled conservative approach to reproductive issues would accomplish the desired effects of the ennoblement of traditional roles for women and men, the exaltation of the family, and the severe curtailment of consumerist sexualization of women and girls. This could be accomplished by focusing energy and thought on the causes of these things, which are also situated in the political economy and time and space. So, the desired effect of cutting funding to Planned Parenthood (as one example) is decreasing the availability and acceptability of abortion services, but the real effect is that women's dependence on the state is increased. The largest percentage of beneficiaries of welfare benefits in the United States is single women with children. Increased reliance on the state and not the family is the outcome, and the family still deteriorates. Without access to contraception, sex education, and abortions, the state ends up with more children who need more Medicaid, Headstart, rehabilitation programs, and more surveillance—and the costs are enormous. In order to fund them, we need more resources, higher taxes, and more bureaucrats. Philosophically, we arrive back at the tenets of political liberalism when we argue that the fetus is a person. To put it into simple and common political terms, if the preservation of the family or the diminution of abortion are goals for a conservative, then the contingent reversal of claiming fetal rights, the defunding of Planned Parenthood, or abstract arguments for a "right to life" might not be the best ways to accomplish them.

If conservatives want to preserve the family as the center of society, controlling women's reproductive capacities may be more reactionary and less politically salient than affirming the choices women make about who to have children with, when to become pregnant, and how many children to have. In addition, conservatives have historically and routinely denied the existence of natural rights when those claims to rights threaten the existing political and social order prior to capitalist democracy. It's important to remember that slaves, women, and children had no rights at all. With the inclusion of the aforementioned groups in the political and economic order with the validation of rights, conservatives began to embrace the tactic by extending rights to fetuses and abstract persons for the purpose of maintaining tradition. This ideal of proper sexual relations, not to mention proper racial relations, was historically upheld through the management and control of women's reproductive lives. The choice to apply "rights" to fetuses is contingent and not principled, religious, or reasonable. Ironically, religious contingency is the very thing that American conservatives denounce about Islam, because it is explicitly and avowedly anti-secular and fundamentalist.

A principled, conservative approach to questions of reproduction would have to shift the focus from desired effects, which are apolitical and reactionary, to causes of effects, which would introduce political subjects back into political time. This approach would force consideration of the actual costs of raising children for women and the historical, political, and economic oppression of women.

ACTIVITY:

When we talk abstractly about a woman's choice to end an unplanned pregnancy, there's a tendency to see her in stereotypical ways, but when students have an opportunity to hear real-life experiences—as opposed to the framing of those experiences by politicians and academics—they gain an alternative perspective. A great resource to start this conversation is the 1 in 3 Campaign. This movement and website gives women from a variety of backgrounds an opportunity to tell their stories about abortion. There is a short video for students to watch in class on the homepage of the 1in3campaign.org website, and assigning them to read some of the testimonies online for homework is also effective. Having the opportunity to read these stories helps them think about the complexity of abortion, and having them write about their reactions helps them to process their views. Since one out of three women will have an abortion at some point in her life, the students find it easy to relate to these experiences.

Sample Homework Assignment:

Visit the 1in3campaign.org website and read 10–15 testimonials. In addition, watch Leslie Cannold's 2012 TedxCanberra talk entitled, "I Had an Abortion . . . Or Maybe I Didn't." After reading women's stories and listening to Cannold's talk, respond to the following questions in a 2–3 page essay:

1) What are your reactions to the women's stories about abortion?
2) Why don't women talk more publicly about these experiences?
3) Why does abortion carry such a strong stigma?
4) What is the effect of shame on women who have abortions?

PRO-CHOICE/PRO-LIFE MOVEMENTS

In a modern society, the state is tasked with managing and protecting life, and this includes improving (universal healthcare) and policing (judiciary) actual bodies; Michel Foucault calls this *biopower*. That said, it is unsurprising that the modern, liberal state is heavily invested in matters related to reproduction. Most folks who are politically liberal (left-leaning) identify as pro-choice not because they are "pro-abortion," but because they want individuals to be able to decide for themselves their reproductive fate. Most liberals believe that the rights of the fetus (if any) are subordinated to the rights of the woman. Even if a liberal finds abortion to be an egregious act, they remain supportive of a woman's choice to end an unplanned pregnancy because her rights trump the rights of the fetus. Since we can't know the circumstances under which a woman becomes pregnant, we can't determine the fate of the pregnancy. This *truth* is not self-evident for religious conservatives, as they argue ferociously for laws that protect "fetal personhood," but for most liberals, the fetus is not considered to be a person (legally), even though it is alive and human.

For a liberal, what is important about human beings is their capacity for rationality. While there exists the *potential* for rationality within the fetus, this cannot be confused with *actual* rationality. There are in fact conservatives who argue this same point even though we hear it most from liberals, so it works well to use these voices in class. Ayn Rand, in particular, offers support for abortion rights (even though her perspective on this issue isn't widely known) and because she has many followers who are part of the political right, the following passages can open up a fruitful discussion:

> To equate a potential with an actual, is vicious; to advocate the sacrifice of the latter to the former, is unspeakable. Observe that by ascribing rights to the unborn, i.e., the nonliving, the anti-abortionists obliterate the rights of the living: the right of young people to set the course of their own lives. The task of raising a child is a tremendous, lifelong responsibility, which no one should undertake unwittingly or unwillingly. Procreation is not a duty: human beings are not stock-farm animals. For conscientious persons, an unwanted pregnancy is a disaster; to oppose its termination is to advocate sacrifice, not for the sake of anyone's benefit, but for the sake of misery qua misery, for the sake of forbidding happiness and fulfillment to living human beings. ("The Ayn Rand Letter" IV, 2, 3)

For Rand, the fetus has a potential for rationality, but until the child is actually born, there are no rights to be granted. Further, she argues against this notion that human beings have a responsibility or duty to reproduce and advocates for the choice to end an unplanned pregnancy in order to save the woman and her family (along with the state) from the burdens of raising an unwanted child. Radical feminists often make these same points when they write about "compulsory motherhood," but using Rand's work is more effective when teaching the topic to conservative students. Even more forcefully in her book *The Voice of Reason*, Rand states:

> An embryo has no rights . . . A child cannot acquire any rights until it is born. The living take precedence over the not-yet-living (or the unborn). Abortion is a moral right—which should be left to the sole discretion of the woman involved; morally, nothing other than her wish in the matter is to be considered. Who can conceivably have the right to dictate to her what disposition she is to make of the functions of her own body? (p. 58–59)

In this passage, the will of the fetus is subordinated to the will of the mother because of her specific relationship to it. There is, however, a point of departure for traditional liberals. While they agree that the fetus ought not to have rights of personhood because of the potential arrogation of a woman's individual rights, they also don't want any force or motivation (economic, familial, religious, or social) to prohibit a woman from carrying a *wanted* fetus to term. In other words, for the liberal, the state shouldn't prohibit a woman from having an abortion, but the state also shouldn't force a woman to have an abortion if she can't afford to keep her child. This is why liberals often look to the state to ensure that women have enough resources available to have a child regardless of their economic status by advocating higher taxes to fund social services that alleviate the burdens of pregnancy and child rearing. Some of these liberal interventions also push for more government funding for contraception, universal healthcare, and free childcare for women and men working outside the home. In this way, the pro-choice movement in particular does not want to see more abortions, but wants to give women the full decision-making power to decide whether or not to have a child (a matter of life or death) because of her specific relationship to that life and her responsibility to care for it.

To explore this point further, Sister Joan Chittister opens up a critique of the pro-life movement by challenging the limitations of its concerns for women facing an unwanted pregnancy. She supports funding for a range of services and resources for pregnant women and challenges the pro-life movement to do the same when she writes:

> I do not believe that just because you're opposed to abortion, that that makes you pro-life. In fact, I think in many cases, your morality is deeply lacking if all you want is a child born but not a child fed, educated, and housed. And why would I think that you don't? Because you don't want any tax money to go there. That's not pro-life. That's pro-birth.

This passage is useful for class discussion because instead of using feminist theory to challenge the terms of the pro-life movement, Sister Joan is a

Catholic nun offering a critique of the Catholic Church for having a black-and-white policy against abortion while the question about how to care for that child sometimes goes unanswered.

ACTIVITY:

Most students are already familiar with the pro-life/pro-choice debate, so examining the language of the two movements is a good way to start a conversation about their similarities and differences. Assigning students a homework assignment that looks at the literature of three different pro-life organizations and three pro-choice groups is a good start. As one example, National Right to Life (NRL) is one of the largest pro-life movements in the United States, with 50 state affiliates and more than 3,000 local chapters. The organization appeals to its followers by reminding them of the Founding Fathers' emphasis on "unalienable rights," namely, the right to life. As Pope Francis has said, "The right to life is the first among human rights." On the NRL website, they even cite the Declaration of Independence and, in their own words, work to promote "respect for the worth and dignity of every individual human being, born or unborn." When you look closely, you can see the language of liberalism woven into the mission statement of the organization. Another example students can look at is the website of the pro-choice organization, the National Abortion and Reproductive Rights Action League. This organization emphasizes the fight for the right to obtain abortions, contraception, and sex education. Having students look critically for the themes of liberalism within both organizations is a neutral teaching tool that points out the similarities between them.

Sample Homework Assignment:

Visit three pro-life and three pro-choice websites, read the mission statements of these organizations, and consider the following questions to be addressed in class during discussion:

1) How do pro-choice and pro-life groups defend their positions on reproductive rights?
2) If individualism and equality of rights are extended to the fetus, how far should the state go to protect the unborn?
3) From a liberal perspective, why isn't the fetus considered a person?
4) Should the government be responsible for caring for babies born to parents who are without the means to provide for their children?

HISTORICAL VIEWS ON REPRODUCTION

The question about how to properly care for families was considered historically through ancient conceptions of justice and *natural rights*, broadly defined. We can trace the origin of *natural rights* back to the Stoics in the

3rd century BC, who followed the teachings of Socrates and Plato. This school of Hellenistic philosophy was conceptualizing a kind of justice that inhered in the nature of our being and the nature of the universe. For the Stoics, because we can speak and reason, we can and do alter nature. As odd as it seems, this is another way of saying that nature, for the Stoics, wasn't given or static, but achieved. The Stoics explained how natural justice—and thus natural rights—required duties and responsibilities, in a word: Virtue. They were interested in a personal ethic that was publicly oriented and believed that natural justice requires good politics and good politics requires collective action and collective morality. It's important to understand that Stoicism was an orientation to life that recognized life's great difficulties and the slim chance for comfort, happiness, or virtue, but that in the honest recognition of that fact, there was a resoluteness; this determination mandated that individual actions be directed towards some public good. In this view, virtue was exalted because it led to happiness, but it couldn't be imposed (mandated by law), only developed (practiced within a community). In addition, for the Stoics, it was not about what you said, but rather what you did that defined one's character. As Aristotle has said, "We are what we repeatedly do. Not an action, but a habit. Excellence then, is not an act, but a habit." This is very different from the ethos of Western culture in the 21st century, where actions can somehow seem divorced from the person performing them. It's not uncommon to hear someone say, "I know I lied, but I am *not* a liar."

As it relates to reproduction, these personal ethics that were publicly oriented connected women and their reproductive capabilities to the community. In other words, women were encouraged to *have children* or *not have children* depending on the good of the larger community. The choice to have children contained political questions about public health and the public good. Is it good to have more children now? Can we support them? Are there enough resources? It's important to note that children were not viewed as the abstract and limitless possibility for freedom ("every child has a potential"). In antiquity, abortion was not a right, but nor was it prohibited. It was a decision made within a context and community. As an example, if the population growth exceeded the community's capacity to maintain its health—education, moral upbringing, etc.—contraception was promoted, and if the population was too small, families were encouraged to have more children. To make this point clear, the Stoic conception of natural rights was based primarily on the health of communities, and not on individuals except insofar as they were parts of a community.

While it may not be widely known, when it comes to abortion specifically, we often assume that attitudes have liberalized over time, but the opposite is actually the case, so understanding the history is an essential part of a successful course on reproductive rights. Ideological partisans have used the state to impose their private views on women, whether religious or secular, which has set dangerous precedents for overweening governmental power. Looking at recent legislation in regards to fetal personhood is good way to open up a conversation about the proper role of government.

In her book *Is the Fetus a Person?*, Jean Reith Schroedel offers a systematic analysis of fetal personhood through the centuries with reference to religious views and their political applications. As a well-respected political scientist, students respond favorably to Schroedel's work as she outlines the historical rise of Christian opposition to contraception and abortion. As Schroedel describes, in ancient societies, the importance placed on family size in the maintenance of healthy communities led to abortions being widely practiced across the pre-Christian Roman Empire (18). Even in the Old Testament, abortion was not condemned as a capital offense because the fetus was not considered to have a soul. About a hundred years later, the "Teaching of the Twelve Apostles" said abortion was a violation of the Ten Commandments and by the time we got to St. Augustine (4th-5th centuries), the use of birth control, sterilization, abortion, and infanticide was completely denounced (Schroedel 21). Views about the moral acceptability of abortion remained politically unchallenged until the Roman imperial state absorbed Christianity. After this time, Christianity ceases to be a local, community-based moral stance. Only with the rise of tolerance/ liberalism do we talk about tearing these things apart (to the benefit of the community). Schroedel outlines Christian doctrinal perspectives about fetal life starting with the Old Testament and ending with the *Humanae Vitae* written by Pope Paul IV in 1968 (21–22), which is very useful for classroom instruction.

When Christianity was made the official religion of the Roman Empire, as the state religion, it was used as a tool to oppress, control, and extract money and wealth. Religious controversies were thus pretexts for power struggles of every sort. Civil war, genocide, and torture were imbued with religious meaning, corrupting any sense of morality and public good. Religion becomes corrupted in this way by base power struggles, and "public good" loses its meaning. Conversely, the political is corrupted by absolutism. From the institutionalization of Christianity in ancient Rome through the disastrous wars of religion in Europe during the 17th and 18th centuries, the overlap of religion and politics corrupted both. This realization led thinkers like John Locke and many other luminaries of the Renaissance to again separate politics and religion. A revival of republicanism and a turn to history demonstrated that healthy political communities relied less on the uniform enforcement of religious belief, and much more on the coexistence but separation of religion and politics. This allowed for a robust citizenship comprised of a multiplicity of interests, where different groups and communities could maintain autonomy in the practice of their beliefs. Such practice required duties, patriotism, freedom of conscience, freedom of assembly, freedom from state imposition, and freedom of speech—which are all now written into the Bill of Rights, a product of the demands of local communities asserting their rights to be free from religious coercion.

In conclusion, a successful course on reproductive rights will challenge both secular and religious students to understand better their political positions through an understanding of liberal and conservative frameworks. The "rights in history" approach is also a great way to get students to think about concepts often taken for granted in modern democracy. If educators can get through these topics and explore these histories, understanding the language of the pro-life and pro-choice movements becomes more scientific and less emotionally charged. When you look specifically at the rhetorical strategies of these movements alongside the rise of liberalism, you can see how *both* arguments stem from a liberal, consumerist political arrangement and ideological discourse. As such, they rather falsely challenge each other. This strategy also helps to avoid some of the impasses that arise on partisan grounds, whether religious or secular, Republican or Democrat.

NOTE

1   As Slavoj Žižek writes in *Living in the End Times*: ""For liberalism, at least in its radical form, the wish to submit people to an ethical ideal held to be universal is the "crime which contains all crime," the mother of all crimes—it amounts to the brutal imposition of one's own view onto others, the cause of civil disorder. Which is why, if one wants to establish peace and tolerance, the first condition is to get rid of "moral temptation": politics should be thoroughly purged of moral ideals and rendered "realistic," taking people as they are, counting on their true nature, not on moral exhortations"" (35–36).

WORKS CITED

Brown, Wendy. *Politics Out of History*. Princeton: Princeton UP, 2001. Print.
Chittister, Joan. Interview by Bill Moyers. NOW Transcript. PBS, 12 Nov. 2004. Web. 27 Aug. 2015. <http://www.pbs.org/now/transcript/transcript346_full.html>
Hobbes, Thomas. *Leviathan*. Chap. xiii, 103–104.
"Human Rights and Its Discontents" November 16, 1999 Olin Auditorium, Bard College. *Slavoj Zizek*. Web. 10 July 2015.
"John Paul II's Message to the Meeting 2004." *John Paul II's Message to the Meeting 2004*. Web. 1 July 2015.
"NARAL Pro-Choice America." *NARAL Pro-Choice America*. Web. 9 July 2015.
Rand, Ayn. *The Ayn Rand Letter*. Oceanside, CA: Second Renaissance, 1971. Print.
Rand, Ayn, and Leonard Peikoff. *The Voice of Reason: Essays in Objectivist Thought*. New York: New American Library, 1989. Print.
Schroedel, Jean Reith. *Is the Fetus a Person?: A Comparison of Policies across the FiftyStates*. Ithaca, NY: Cornell UP, 2000. Print.
Strauss, Leo. *History of Political Philosophy*. 3rd ed. Chicago: U of Chicago, 1987. Print.

WORKS CONSULTED

"Abigail Adams Asks Her Husband to 'Remember the Ladies'." *History.com.* A&E Television Networks. Web. 9 July 2015.

Lord, Carnes. *The Politics.* Chicago: U of Chicago, 1984. Print.

"National Right to Life | The Nation's Oldest & Largest Pro-life Organization." *National Right to Life.* Web. 9 July 2015.

Rand, Ayn. *Philosophy, Who Needs It.* Indianapolis: Bobbs-Merrill, 1982. Print.

Roberts, Dorothy E. *Killing the Black Body: Race, Reproduction, and the Meaning of Liberty.* New York: Pantheon, 1997. Print.

Solinger, Rickie. *Reproductive Politics: What Everyone Needs to Know.* Oxford: Oxford UP, 2013. Print.

3   Remedying Sexual Asymmetry with Christian Feminism

Some Orthodox Christian Reflections in Response to Erika Bachiochi's "Women, Sexual Asymmetry, and Catholic Teaching"

Maria Lastochkina

Abortion has become such an indispensable part of contemporary experience that even Christians sometimes find it difficult to oppose. Since taking the life in utero has ceased to be regarded as a grave sin and is not always recognized as an unmitigated evil, those who wish to remain faithful to the Word of God struggle to find ways of speaking against killing of the unborn. Some of them, like Erika Bachiochi, seek to beat modern culture at its own game by representing Catholic teaching on human sexuality as a "right kind" of feminism. However, in her appeal to secular rationality, foregoing the metaphysical commitments of faith and replacing them with consequentialist reasoning and data from scientific research, she thereby renders her alternative unviable and un-Christian. In response to this failure, I would like to present some Orthodox Christian considerations pointing toward a more wholesome and consistent way forward.

I. HUMAN SEXUALITY AND ABORTION

When tying the problem of abortion to the question of human sexuality, Bachiochi is right on target. After all, the modern culture of abortion, unlike its counterpart in the ancient world, is more about the individual freedom of sexual expression than about the welfare of the state, at least if one takes account of the ancient world's ethos of abortion.[1] After Freud and the sexual revolution of the 1960s, the killing of the unborn has gradually become integrated into a worldview that affirms sexual self-determination and self-fulfillment. Abortion has become such an indispensable part of this worldview that even for Christians, it is often difficult to trace the real roots of the practice and form a solid opposition. Since taking a life in utero has largely ceased in the secular, post-Christian culture to be regarded as a grave sin and is no longer even recognized as always being an unmitigated evil, those who wish to remain faithful to the Word of God feel compelled to find new ways of speaking against killing of the unborn that would make sense to the contemporary mindset. Some of them, like Erika Bachiochi, seek to beat modern culture at its own game by representing Catholic teaching on human sexuality in terms of a "right kind" of feminism.

Bachiochi begins her discussion by contrasting two worldviews: A secular feminist one and the Roman Catholic one. Each of these links abortion with contraception, the first endorsing the free availability of the former as a fail-safe for the latter, and the second taking a critical stance against both. The author then affirms what she calls "the Catholic story," a "narrative" she presents as focused on the "ontological status" of the fertilized egg and on the "teleological nature" of sex as oriented toward procreation. Immediately afterward, she claims that ontological status presents a "scientific reality": From the very moment of conception, a new human being comes into existence and is endowed with a dignity that must be legally protected by the state. In spite of these strong introductory claims, Bachiochi then devotes the rest of her essay to the consequentialist arguments pursued by the recent Vatican statements.[2] The object is to convince a secular audience of the fact that disregarding human ontology and teleology is harmful for women.

In order to render her objection to abortion (and contraception) plausible for secular feminists, Bachiochi takes note of their underlying concern for justice and equality between the sexes. Underwriting that concern, she traces the problem back to the biological dissimilarity of the sexes, which gives rise to sexual asymmetry, that is, women being disproportionately affected by the potential consequences of sexual intercourse. She then concentrates on the following:

1. Scientific research showing the free availability of abortion and contraception as further disadvantaging women, rather than promoting their equality, and
2. Catholic moral teaching with its prohibition of abortion and limitation of contraception to natural family planning as offering a superior strategy for implementing justice and equality between the sexes.

In this commentary, I argue that Bachiochi's attempt to render the Christian opposition to abortion plausible to a secular audience fails on two accounts. On the one hand, her appeal to secular rational arguments remains unsuccessful: Such arguments are insufficient to establish the absolute harmfulness of abortion (and of artificial—as opposed to "natural"—contraception). There is simply no such thing as a single canonical rationality shared by those who affirm Roman Catholic moral teaching (thus subscribing to the idea of such harmfulness) and those of a secular mind (who evaluate harms and benefits differently). There is no universally valid and at the same time sufficiently specific way of deducing moral oughts from biological facts, as Bachiochi's appeal to such facts presupposes. Her invocation of a very particular Roman Catholic rationality (suggesting the preferability of sexual self-restraint over immediate sexual gratification) can therefore be forever countered in terms of other construals of rationality (supporting profoundly different moral conclusions).

On the other hand, her engagement with the secular commitments to equality between the sexes, and to a utility calculus-based rationality (maximization of benefits over harms), fails to offer her audience a genuine Christian alternative. By trying to prove the Roman Catholic moral position (of prohibiting abortion legally and artificial contraception morally) superior in terms of those very commitments, she distorts what Christianity is all about. As a result, her account is ultimately unhelpful even for those secular feminists for whom the evidence she adduces might have alerted to that vision of human flourishing, in the horizon of which the harms and benefits attending women's role as wives and mothers can be properly evaluated.

Bachiochi identifies as the motive behind secular feminism's endorsement of abortion and contraception the wish to equalize the sexes in two respects: First, in separating sex from procreation, women can enjoy sex "like men do," that is, without having to worry about:

- Whether their sex partner might make a good husband and father,
- The health risks to their own bodies from a (continued) pregnancy and birth,
- The poverty risks involved in having to raise a child single handedly,
- The educational and psychological risks for the child growing up without a father.

Second, in being able to avoid (or terminate) unwanted pregnancies, women can enjoy a career "like men do," that is, without having to choose between being a mother and a professional.

Bachiochi then cites studies showing that, with legalized abortion and readily available contraceptives, women end up as losers in both respects. First, they suffer bodily harm from artificial means of contraception and from the abortions that become "unavoidable" when contraception fails. By the same token, women suffer emotionally because their enjoyment of sex depends on lasting relationships, which in turn are harder to secure in a culture that conceptually separates sex from procreation. Second, women's expected enjoyment of a career is affected by their growing realization that, when they finally are "ready" for a family, they can no longer find a suitable husband or have children.

As Bachiochi points out, this culture has sought to equalize the sexual experiences of men and women by allowing the latter to have greater control over their reproductive capacities and affording both sexes an opportunity to enjoy consequence-free sexual pleasures. However, the means engaged for that goal, that is, contraception and the legalization of abortion, she argues, in going against the fundamental reality of gender dissimilarity, have not only failed to achieve such overall equality, but also exacerbated in the long run the inherent "sexual asymmetry." The result, as she points out, is to further disadvantage women instead of liberating them. With sexual intercourse being dissociated from marital commitment and from what had been construed as "compulsory procreation" within marriage, women still continue to experience sexuality differently from men. Bachiochi quotes research in support of her conclusion that, apart from increasing rather than decreasing both unintentional pregnancy and abortion rates, uncommitted sex appears to undermine rather than enhance even women's attendant carnal enjoyment. As she concludes, the natural feminine vulnerability inherent in the particular design of the female body, which throughout history has indeed often triggered male exploitation, now tends to be discounted altogether. But after several decades of women's sexual liberation, that vulnerability still persists. Contrary to the hopes of the pro-choice feminists, women, as much as ever, long to be able to "choose" a deeper and more steadfast relationship. Only the minority is truly and permanently content to forego serious relational and emotional commitment and motherhood. Sadly, so the author continues, the research data and common experience show that it has become harder than ever to achieve such commitment because men, having tasted the freedom of contraceptive ethos, are less willing to offer or secure the necessary depth of connection. More often than not, this tempts women to consent to sexual encounters they do not particularly desire; they then suffer the psychological and physical consequences as male partners come and go, virtually unaffected.

To the extent that Bachiochi adduces evidence questioning the benefits that secular feminists had expected to result from freely available abortion and contraception, her argument may indeed be persuasive to the audience she envisages. But the author then proceeds to recommend the Roman Catholic approach (of prohibiting abortion and artificial contraception) as a superior strategy for fulfilling those very expectations. She argues that biology should be taken seriously and sexual asymmetry remedied not by tampering with female bodies, but by disciplining and transforming male sexual desire. If women are naturally endowed with the joys and burdens of childbearing, then men should be culturally conditioned to acknowledge not only the joys but also the burdens that come with their begetting. In addition to the legal protection of unborn children (i.e., laws against abortion) and the imposition of economic measures (stretching as far as Shari Motro's extravagant "preglimony"),[3] both sexes are called upon to restore a culture of sexual self-restraint both outside and within marriage. The equality that secular feminists had vainly hoped to secure through modeling the female enjoyment of sexuality and a successful career on a male paradigm can be more effectively brought about through conforming the culture in terms of Catholic principles: If only women, individually and collectively, condition sex on marital commitment and then impose male sexual self-discipline within marriage so as to achieve "natural" contraception where required, both sexes would benefit evenly. In all of this, Bachiochi limits herself to appealing to a kind of consequentialist reasoning—how to avoid harms while pursuing the pleasures of sexual intercourse. This approach makes it possible to represent Catholic teaching as better-than-secular social guidance for women in maximizing their well-being, a true feminism—more balanced and therefore more attractive. And this "new feminism," she asserts, can in turn be readily accessible through exercising reason's embrace of a higher human good of love for women, so that men can be persuaded by a conclusive, secular, and sound rational argument to subordinate their sexual desires to female needs. This strategy is problematic in several respects.

II. LIMITED SOCIAL SUCCESS AND UNSUCCESSFUL APPEALS TO RATIONALITY

According to Bachiochi, if contraception and abortion were replaced by chastity and natural family planning, and if those latter practices were, in turn, enforced by a movement of like-minded, bold, and self-possessed women, then, so she claims, a true remedy for the sexual asymmetry would have been found and the cause for sexual equality would finally be complete.[4] First and foremost, such confidence seems overly optimistic. For one thing, even if such a powerful league could be formed, its very existence would raise the market value of uncooperative women. This rise, in turn, would present a powerful incentive for women not to join the league. And their sexual availability will surely compromise the disciplining impact of their sisters' sexual forbearance.

Bachiochi's analysis of how men and women "ought" to deal with their sexuality and procreative capabilities rests on the claim that there is one proper way for humans to respond to the biological givens of their male and female natures. She engages the traditional Roman Catholic appeal to what the secular world accepts as "reasonable," assuming that it also harmonizes with the "natural law" (cf. her note iii), in terms of which Catholic moral teaching is framed. This presupposes the existence of a single canonical rationality, equally accessible to believers and nonbelievers, by which anyone can derive moral "oughts" from biological facts.

But such an assumption is unrealistic. Why, after all, should secularly minded men feel obligated to respect the specific biological makeup of women, if that means suppressing the drives inherent in their own specific biological makeup? What rationally compelling argument could persuade them to sacrifice opportunities for the immediate and diversified pleasures their own nature craves (and go against the evolutionary drive to "spread their genes"), merely in order to satisfy females' natural yearning for long-term commitments and support? On what rational grounds should they shoulder the cultural burden of having to care for a family (and having to continue supporting children after a divorce), when their natural sexual needs can be satisfied more easily? What particular way of ordering values can be presented as universally valid, and why should men abandon, by "the reason's embrace," the good of mutually desirable immediate gratification in favor of "higher human goods, in this case, respect and love for the good of other, the woman" (Bachiochi, 2013, 161)?

Even for women, the evaluation of which way of prioritizing values should be "right for them" is not easy. Bachiochi quotes various research describing the "costs," that is, bodily, emotional, economical, and social harms, that come with a "contraceptive" and "abortion-accepting" life-style. And indeed, some readers may agree with her that the cost imposed on women by delaying marriage and pursuing a career while being sexu-ally active is obviously too high and has its deleterious effects. By the time they are successful, many of them are likely to find out that the men with whom they slept are still able, and will often prefer, to build a family and have children with a younger partner. There is surely much in this state of affairs to leave women bitter and alone. But if one looks at all of this without presuming there is a God, it will be hard to see the full tragedy and consequently to evaluate these circumstances in such a way as to achieve a proper solution. After all, why shouldn't many women find these costs com-paratively more bearable than the ones accruing to them from the Catholic alternative? Why should they not take the pain of sexual self-denial involved in prolonged premarital chastity to be worse than the disappointments that come with changing affairs? Why should they not be more fearful about having to endure a lifelong sex partner who turns out to be no fun at all than about being able to change partners who become unamusing? Why should they be more worried about remaining childless than about the physical and psychological pains and dependencies that come with motherhood? Why should they not prefer the risks involved in aborting a child that threatens to interfere with their professional life to exposing their old age to the pov-erty that typically afflicts women who failed to accumulate pension entitle-ments? Why should they not define "true charity" in terms of sparing a child the fate of having been unwelcome? Whatever a person considers to be bearable or unbearable hinges on his/her general outlook on life. There is no neutral worldview and thus, in particular, no Roman Catholic and secu-lar feminist neutral way of sorting out competing kinds of harms or goods. Even those unmarried, childless career women who will go through bitter times between their forties and fifties may find themselves compensated by a generously endowed retirement blessing in their sixties to nineties. And, going even beyond Bachiochi's range of subjects, who could argue, by refer-ence to purely secular reasons, that a pregnant woman should accept the burdens that come with a severely handicapped child, when preventing its birth could be interpreted as an act of "responsible parenting?" Catholics pursuing such a strategy will often claim that one can rationally establish sound moral guidance by reference to one canonical vision of nature (as God's good creation) while discounting other aspects of "nature," such as the male sexual drive (as representing nature's merely "fallen" state).

But this is tantamount to embracing the rationalist horn of Euthyphro's dilemma, that is, to claiming that the good of chastity and monogamous commitment is accessible to men through their own reason, unaided by revelation, without knowing that "every good gift and every perfect gift is from above, and comes down from the Father of lights" (James 1:17). Indeed, if that were the case, what would one make of the patriarch Abraham, whom Paul calls a "just man," having had not only wives (Genesis 25:1), but concubines (Genesis 25:6)?[5] And how, without Christ's authoritatively Divine restoration of the original meaning of the law (cf. Mk. 10:5–9), would modern men know not to follow his example?

III. UNSUCCESSFUL APPEALS TO "JUSTICE"

Bachiochi also appeals to modern societies' framing of moral commitment to a "justice" that requires benefits and burdens to be distributed equally among members. But even here, it is difficult to offer unambiguous rational grounds for deciding whether the biological differences between the sexes should or should not be accepted as normative givens in the first place. Only if biological differences are normative could Bachiochi's strategy (of leveling out the resulting imbalances between male and female opportunities for human flourishing by imposing compensating handicaps on men) appear compelling. But there are no rational grounds for not viewing matters quite the other way round: Why could those very biological differences, rather than being taken as ontologically relevant, not be construed as a cultural problem instead? Relief, then, would be sought through ways of reducing the impact of those differences. We usually do not interpret the significant differences in male and female life expectancy in ontological terms, thus raising them to the level of becoming morally normative. In fact, with regard to differences in life expectancy, a properly egalitarian society should seek to mitigate this state of affairs by investing considerably more resources in health care for men than for women. In an analogous sense, sexual differences in view of sexuality and procreation are not acknowledged in the secular culture as "ontological." Instead, a sizeable portion of secular feminism claims that these are culture imposed (i.e., alienated, or distorted) and that gender essentialism itself is a suppressive ideology. Within such a perspective, equality must be secured by dissociating sex even more radically from procreation and, further, procreation from child raising: Fertilization here would be increasingly achieved artificially (thus relieving career-minded women from regrets about having missed their reproductive time window), pregnancy would be provided as a professional service, and bringing up the children would increasingly be trusted to public care and educational institutions.

All of this makes it clear that even the *ad hominem* reasoning engaged in by Bachiochi cannot be trusted to achieve its *ad hominem* goal. Unless one is already supplied with a criterion that can claim independent authority (e.g., because it is Divinely revealed), one has no resources for properly evaluating which goods or harms to prefer over competing goods and alternative harms.

IV. THEOLOGICAL DISTORTIONS

In recommending Roman Catholic moral teaching as a more successful strategy for achieving secular feminists' goals, Bachiochi implicitly suggests that these very goals can be accepted as legitimate. But surely, if we are to oppose the contraceptive ethos of our times, human sexuality needs to be addressed within a broader context. For it is not just biologically determined, but Divinely ordained. While sexuality is indeed heavily conditioned through our culture, it remains spiritually significant even in its carnal aspect. If Christian women are to respond in a specifically Christian way to the challenges posed by the mainstream secular feminism, what they really have to advance and defend is a very unfeminist understanding of a sense and purpose of being a female, an understanding that of necessity will encourage women to rediscover their calling to be a "help meet for" a man (Genesis 2:20) and an heir "together of the grace of life" (I Peter 3:7), rather than just equal partners. In this rediscovery, they will also have to discern how to work out their salvation in the contemporary setting through having children and bringing them up to continue "in faith and charity and holiness with sobriety" (I Timothy 2:15).[6] But Bachiochi points in quite another direction by affirming the consequentialism of recent Vatican arguments and thus endorsing the secular ideals of:

- Maximizing goods, that is, placing oneself and one's own worldly happiness at the center of one's strivings,
- Equality between the sexes, assessed in terms of opportunities to experience such worldly happiness, and
- Women's fulfillment through a professional career.

Bachiochi does refer to the desirability of training men to offer a more self-giving love and a greater willingness to sacrifice. Such training could in fact lead them beyond egoistic happiness maximization. She also offers a critical aside in view of society's inculcating into women the need to identify themselves through education and professional engagements rather than through a life as a wife or mother (Bachiochi, 2013). But she does not expand on the theological insights undergirding these hints, being obviously aware of the fact that such self-sacrificial love and such a distinct mission of women would not make sense to secular minds unconcerned with man's Divine design and transcendent fate. In making the secular quest for a justice of worldly fairness in securing resources for worldly happiness her own, Bachiochi radically secularizes what she presents as Roman Catholic moral teaching. She does so in three respects.

Life in Christ

Insofar as she claims her own alternative account to be Christian, it fails to alert her audience to the crucial fact that following Christ is distinguished by the willingness to bear one's cross. She does not seem to recognize sexual asymmetry as one such universal female cross and therefore somewhat conflates remedying the harmful social consequences that can flow from it (abortion among the gravest) with remedying sexual asymmetry itself (Bachiochi, 2013). That conflation, in turn, makes Christian commitment appear to be serving the same secular ends of seeking—as far as possible—worldly pleasure and avoiding—as far as possible—worldly pain, only using different means (cf. Bachiochi, 2013). All of this, on the one hand, fails to show a distinctively Christian way of accepting suffering that sometimes comes with obeying the Divinely offered guidance and, at other times, offers opportunities for repentance, especially in view of one's inability to shoulder such obedience. On the other hand, it leaves no place for the Divine gift of a love that offers supreme happiness precisely at the moment where such happiness is no longer sought.

Marital Ascesis versus Natural Family Planning

Bachiochi's proposal that men turn from self-love to the love of the other, the woman, through considering her well-being, is surely to be commended. She also correctly appreciates that women, being the custodians of the integrity of sexual morality and culture, will need to help men discipline their sexual impulses and orient them within a family and the raising of children. But she makes a mistake in thinking that this can be properly and consistently done outside of a specifically Christian, that is, a metaphysical understanding of carnal union. In such an understanding, "sex is subservient to sanctity" (Harakas, 1990, 126) and turns a man and a woman not just into the responsible sexual partners a marriage requires, but into "one flesh." Such bodily merging is only fully possible when the sacrifice required is not simply for one another's convenience, but offered in submission to God. The final goal is not, as Bachiochi suggests, to make men understand with their bodies what women naturally understand with theirs or to shift more weight of the biological burden to men.[7] The final goal is, instead, to help one another in the struggle to keep natural pleasures from turning into sinful passions.

Here again, the reading of Bachiochi raises a cardinal question for Christians confronting the dominant culture: To what extent can they rely on secular moral philosophy to lead to the same moral conclusions that faith reveals? And is it at all possible to argue the post-Christian world into embracing Christian values without the change of heart the Gospel requires? One might note that the early Christians generally did not argue pagans into a new way of life, but, rather, converted their hearts so that they could no longer continue in the old way.

In endorsing natural contraception as a morally unobjectionable way of avoiding children within marriage, Bachiochi misunderstands the teleology she herself invokes. If Christians understand that women are saved through the raising of faithful children, and if Christ instructed His followers that to accept children is tantamount to accepting Him, then a contraceptive mindset that prioritizes career and lifestyle goals presents a failure, regardless of the natural or artificial means engaged. As Bachiochi herself admits, the intention to avoid pregnancy may be the same whether one is using either medication or natural methods. Considering that both can fail, without trust in God, there is nothing left to guard the couple against aborting. A proper Christian training in sexual self-discipline (for both sexes) is provided not primarily (and surely not exclusively) in view of female's biological cycles, but by the integrity of a couple's liturgical life. Marital abstinence undertaken within the ascetical-liturgical life of the Orthodox Church, as Paul says, "for fasting and for prayer" (1 Corinthians 7:5), turns it into the sexual ascesis integrated into the couple's spiritual life and transforms the union of husband and wife into a "lesser church," an icon of the relationship between Christ and His Church. Ample opportunities for such transformation are offered in the observation of the weekly fasting days (Wednesdays and Fridays, as well as the nights before partaking in Holy Communion) and of the four yearly fasting periods (six weeks before Christmas, 40 days of Lent, and the two shorter fasts before the feasts of Saint Peter and Saint Paul and the Dormition of the Holy Theotokos). Such vision of sexuality and marriage, unlike any secular notions of sacrificial love, is the only enduring bond between male and female, which was "established in paradise and which will be restored to paradise" (Engelhardt, 2000, 246). It is, however, inaccessible outside of the life of faith, because unless in turning to one another, the couple also turns to God, their intentions even in abstinence may fall short of the mark.

Misplaced Endorsement of Equality

In taking as her starting point secular feminists' quest for equality in view of men's and women's social positions, as assessed in terms of opportunities for sexual and career self-realization, and in recommending the Roman Catholic moral teaching as a superior way of securing such social equality, Bachiochi limits her offer of an alternative to a different strategy for realizing that equality. She fails to alert her audience to the fact that, for Christians, proper equality between men and women is limited to the areas of fellowship with Christ in this and the future life (Galatians 3:28), and of equal rights to the enjoyment of marital love (I Corinthians 7:3–5). She fails, in other words, to invite that audience into the realm where the very quest for an additional social equality becomes misguided.

In this life world, women realize that their ontological status is determined by their Divine mission, which points them to their role as "helpers" of their husbands (Genesis 2:20) in the shared task of dominating the earth (Genesis 1:26–28). They also realize that the curse by which the first couple was expelled from paradise refers women to a "yearning for the man," which is meant to keep her from avoiding the "pains" of childbirth imposed as a therapy for misplaced attempts at autonomous God-likeness. They realize that even after Christ restored the one-to-one relationship between the sexes, women still remain under their husbands' authority, even if that authority is now understood by reference to Christ's headship over the Church. By remaining silent on all those theological circumstances contextualizing "equality" between the sexes, Bachiochi also withholds from her readers the fact that women's wishes for a professional career must be placed within the horizon of their opportunities for salvation, as intimately linked with the bearing and raising of children who will (and this renders public childcare problematic) remain in the faith.

V. CONCLUSIONS

Abortion is a complex phenomenon that, apart from being a faulty solution to the problems of sexual asymmetry, is a sign of human sexuality misunderstood and misdirected. Divinely ordained and spiritually significant, the sexual union between a man and a woman has become in the contemporary secular mindset a good in itself and one of the highest on the scale of human values.

In her analysis of the cultural forces that have rendered abortion an acceptable (even if, at times, regretted) part of women's life and in offering a Christian alternative, Bachiochi is committed to opposing the falsehood of mainstream feminism with the authentically "feminist" Roman Catholic moral teaching. However, in doing so, she defeats her own purpose by identifying with the very cultural commitments about female flourishing that undergird the general acceptance of abortion. Her attempt to prove the Christian alternative superior in terms of those very commitments fails on two accounts. On the one hand, her *ad hominem* strategy presupposes that there exists one canonically rational way of drawing moral conclusions from what contemporary social science establishes as the "givens" of female biology and psychology. She also presumes that philosophical reflection can establish a canonical ranking of human goods in which love for another is by default higher on the value scale than sexual pleasure. But the dominant secular culture elevates sexual engagement to the point where both men and women often define themselves in terms of the quantity and quality of their sexual experiences. Whereas initially, contraception and abortion were thought of as a means toward successfully achieving educational and career goals for women, both have gradually become more of a tool in securing a lifestyle of personal fulfillment quite independent of any particular social ambitions. The sexually realized and satisfied self—not family status or public engagement—is now the order of the day. To sacrifice such personal fulfillment, as Bachiochi suggests, for the scriptural virtues of chastity and commitment requires first an understanding of such virtues as a higher good, and second, a change in lifestyle so profound and drastic that it cannot possibly be effected solely by philosophical arguments and economic analogies, or indeed by any amount of verifiable data from the medical and social sciences. Without the Christian revelation and the guidance of the Holy Spirit, none of this can be fully comprehended, much less embraced in contemporary, everyday experiences.

To make a real difference in opposing the secular culture of abortion, the stance Christians take in sexual relationships, as indeed in many other respects, needs to be not just countercultural, but otherworldly. Thus, sexual asymmetry is best addressed not so much by reversing certain sociohistorical patterns as by personal striving to bring sexual forces of the fallen nature into the service of salvation. The practice of ascesis offered by traditional, Orthodox Christianity shows a way in which such striving can be exercised in achieving genuine gender harmony and securing it in the pursuit of holiness.

ACKNOWLEDGMENTS

I would like to thank Corinna Delkeskamp-Hayes for her insightful comments on an earlier version of this chapter.

NOTES

1 John Wyatt (2009), in his historical perspective on abortion and infanticide, concludes that in the classical Greco-Roman world, the value of the fetus was assessed in terms of its potential to make a future contribution to society, and the number of fetuses balanced against the danger of overpopulation.
2 Occasionally, however, she lapses: In appealing to the fact that any "decent" society demands that parents protect their vulnerable offspring, Bachiochi argues for legally prohibiting abortion in a way that suffers from a *petitio principii*. As she herself recognizes elsewhere, secular society does not accept the view that unborn humans are humans in the full sense, that is, of being entitled to respect for their dignity and protection of life. And in claiming that the teleology of sexuality is more phenomenological than normative, she exposes her case to the strong opposition of homosexuals, who by definition separate sex from procreation (cf. Bachiochi's note iv).
3 It is worth noting, though, that such measures, as well as references to "high cost" and "low cost" of sex and the trading of it (even for commitment), along with the other "crude economic analogies" Bachiochi so freely uses, actually distort her message by reinforcing instead of condemning the secular consumerist understanding of sex as a commodity.
4 Though at this point, one is left wondering why, if it were a matter of such an enforced arrangement, didn't the suffragists, whose views Bachiochi frequently engages in support of her argument, succeed back in the 19th century.

5 Neither Abraham's wives nor his concubines have apparently suffered from the sexual asymmetry issues.
6 This is a topic for another article or indeed extended research in its own right that can help establish ways of sustaining the concept of indissoluble marriage under the multitude of modern demands and constraints without, as Helen Alvaré (quoted by Bachiochi in note xvii) points out, falling into the secular feminist tendency of conflating it with limited roles for women.
7 All such measures do actually sound more like punishment than justice.

WORKS CITED

Bachiochi, E. "Women, Sexual Asymmetry and Catholic Teaching." *Christian Bioethics* 19: 150–171.
Engelhardt, H. T., Jr. 2000. *The Foundations of Christian Bioethics*. Salem, MA: Scrivener.
Harakas, S. S. 1990. *Health and Medicine in the Eastern Orthodox Tradition: Faith, Liturgy and Wholeness*. Minneapolis, MN: Light and Life Publishing Company.
Wyatt, J. 2009. *Matters of Life and Death*. Nottingham, UK: Inter-Varsity Press.

4 Negotiating Feminism When Color and Credo Trump Gender

Cantice Greene

As a triumvirate conservative, I have considered walking away from women's studies due to the sense that I just don't belong here. Around my church and with some Christian friends, my activism for and with women has been considered radical. When I mention my teaching to Christian friends, I find the need to stress that I don't personally seek to redefine or reform roles and positions of authority in the home or elsewhere, nor do I centralize a woman's role in the family or society. In contrast, among colleagues, I scarcely find camaraderie or even engagement when I espouse the virtues of traditional family roles, observational forms of birth control, or the benefits of abstinence. My ideas have a way of ending discussions. So sometimes, I have resorted to being silent instead.

But this tension need not exist. I was attracted to women's studies because it allowed me to narrow my focus of study to women—women writers, women's writing practices, and women in history, culture, and society. While women's studies is about more than women, it has historically allowed women and their lives to be a central subject of research. This characteristic should make our field attractive, especially to young, female college students, but it hasn't. Instead, our field is looked at with skepticism and even contempt by most people who don't self-identify as liberal. Most young people don't self-identify as conservative, so they should be storming our classrooms in droves. They are not. Why is that? It stands to reason that we must also be alienating moderate students. Conservatives are not usually the loudest voices when it comes to change, but Christian conservatives have been when it comes to ending human trafficking, championing the rights of the unborn, and preserving observational, eco-friendly forms of birth control. Also troubling the field's reach is the historical alienation of women of color. Black women, due to their history of slavery and segregation, and by extension, women of color, have not enjoyed the privileges of womanhood in the same way as White women, so their struggles have never been the same. Racial segregation and discrimination have tended to trump gender segregation. Beyond those reasons, politics in higher education where women's studies is taught swings sharply left,[1] alienating moderates and conservatives. If practitioners of women's studies can shift their classroom environment such that they focus on making their examples of women's movement more representative of the social, religious, and political activity of moderates and conservatives, and if we focus on approaches to movement, we have a chance of attracting diversity in the field and staying focused on the interests of all women rather than a few.

I was fortunate to have been introduced to women's studies as an undergraduate when I was still politically naïve and religiously apathetic. Since that time, I have solidified my Christian convictions and political allegiances and, more often than not, they place me into conservative camps. Any conservative in academia knows that it takes a strong resolve to remain committed to women's studies when women's studies is most often dismissive of conservative viewpoints. In this regard, as an area of study, it is not unique. Recent protests against conservatives as commencement speakers[2] and heads of technology-based companies[3] underscore the public disdain that conservatives now face. The present climate is the fallout of years of reluctance by conservatives to highlight their consistent presence in intellectual environments such that liberal/progressive thought is considered to be the only thought pattern in the intellectual arena. Not surprisingly, it was primarily my experiences at a women's college that helped me to embrace studies that centralize women's experiences and engage pedagogical approaches that are innovative and that centralize agency as a tool of change. In addition to my women's college experience, my interactions with three practitioners of women's studies helped me stabilize my philosophy of teaching women's studies. These teachers negotiated difference by opening their understanding of inclusion rather than emphasizing a narrow theoretical point of view. This strategy should be adopted as others endeavor to teach women's studies in conservative contexts.

FINDING PARIS'S *BIRTH CONTROL FOR CHRISTIANS*

When I was apprehensive about pursuing graduate study in feminism, my Facebook friend Dr. Jenell Williams Paris reminded me that a feminist classroom is inclusive. She reasoned that I could expect that my beliefs could be aired alongside the dominant liberal ideologies that pervade feminist classrooms. I hadn't anticipated this response from the anthropologist scholar who wrote *Birth Control for Christians*. When Paris wrote the book prior to 2000, she saw the need for a book that paralleled the groundbreaking title, *Our Bodies, Ourselves*. In her forward, she notes that while *Our Bodies, Ourselves* pioneered an approach to gynecological matters in laymen's terms written by and for women, it also included references to procedures, namely abortion or abortifacient drugs, which were not received favorably in religious communities, especially communities of religious conservatives who believe life begins at conception. That was the environment that created the space for *Birth Control for Christians*. In her book, Paris spends time recounting the Church's historical response to birth control and the subsequent acceptability of a wider variety of controversial contraceptive practices. Her historical overview brings into perspective the rapid rate of change in contraceptive ideas in the last 40 years versus the previous 1,700 years. In the text, Paris reconstructs a record of the scriptures and precepts Christian leaders used to guide their positions on matters of reproduction. By providing the history in the text, she also presents the opportunity for her audience to consider how time and events have come together to create the current moment and exigence for her discussion.

Later, Paris went on to write *The End of Sexuality*, a book that asserts that classifying one's identity based solely on sexuality severely minimizes the complexity of identity and enlarges sexuality in our human lives in possibly unhelpful ways. Both books are written for a Christian audience and for readers who seek to break with mainstream canned ideas in relation to contraception and gender, respectively. The books engage contemporary ideologies and offer viewpoints on sexuality that are less typically discussed. In both books, Paris seeks an alternate way to discuss the polarizing topics of sexuality and reproduction. In her approach to defining cultural understandings of the two, she engages a range of social and religious ideologies. Whether intentional or not, it is a way that attempts to ignite rather than extinguish dialogue. While probably not categorized specifically as texts for women's studies, both books treat issues that are central to the field. It was her advice to recognize women's studies as inclusive that set me at ease as I entered classes as a graduate student, beginning with New Directions in Feminism, taught by Layli Phillips.

TAKING CLASS WITH DR. LAYLI PHILLIPS

Lesson 1: The Women's Studies Classroom Should Be Inclusive.

When I entered the feminist classroom taught by Layli Phillips (now Layli Maparyan), I was both apprehensive and confident. I was in my mid-twenties, a working adult with a master's degree, married, and a mother. I was not easily intimidated and was sure about many basic principles of my life and life in general. So while I knew that my ideas about gender, power, and the usual topics of feminism would clash with the majority of the ideas that were sure to be presented, I had no fear of losing my identity. As an undergraduate, I had grown a passion for women-centered education and an appreciation for activism. Unfortunately in the college teaching I received, Christianity was often implicated in discussions of patriarchy and oppression in ways that characterized the religion as problematic. That indictment had sent me on the same journey that most college students take to recreate an identity. Toward the end of that journey, I concluded that the essence of Christianity is what allows me to separate an ideology from an agent and to judge each respectively. Before 9/11, it was harder to reconcile the ways that a religion could carry the scars of its dissident practitioners. Since then, my personal apologetic training and spiritual experiences had prepared me to hold on to the essence of my faith religion, Christ himself, in times of challenge. With that new assurance, I was excitedly curious about new directions in feminism.

In class with Dr. Phillips some of my beliefs were met with frustration, and others were met with silence. Many of my classmates couldn't relate to my life experiences. They couldn't believe that I could make peace with ideologies that placed a husband as the head of a household. I was able to calmly assert my beliefs because I had engaged my opposition long before I settled into the relationship. I had been the head of household and frankly, I welcomed the sabbatical from being the HNIC.[4] I relished the fact that ultimately, he would be answerable to God for how he treated me and our children. After all, his model was Jesus, so I was happy to be with a man aspiring to live up to the highest example. Other women who have had the opportunity to run a house on their own are more settled with the idea of welcoming a spouse who is willing to take on that responsibility in partnership. Understandably, women who have experienced the man in their relationship sabotage a household have reservations about relinquishing the sole control of their personal and social investments. In that class, I asserted the idea that role doesn't equal value, so while roles in the marriage differed, the value of man and woman is equal. I hadn't come up with those theories; they were articulated in scripture. I also knew that the average young adult American student had not seriously studied scripture, and could not determine whether the principles I was communicating could actually be found there. Many teenage churchgoers have been turned off from "religion" after a cursory look at isolated scriptures that seemed to point to a rigid God of machismo, especially as it relates to sexuality and relationships. Worse still, students who manage to enter college having a daily relationship with Christ through prayer, service, and study are challenged by the dominant secular and liberal attitudes expressed by professors of higher education. Jay Budziszewski's *How to Stay Christian in College* noted that a teacher at his university once opened her class by saying, "All of you are too intelligent to be pro-life, right?" (153).

I was not surprised that my declaration of the "freedom in submission" was met in class with quiet repugnance—repugnance, that is, if I accurately read their faces. A few classmates voiced their ridicule outside of class when they thought I was out of earshot. I knew that my beliefs were countercultural in the secular-liberal environment of our classroom. As a younger student, I would have been likely to respond the way they had to my ideas about family and religion. In my choice of undergraduate institutions to attend, I had unknowingly plunged myself deep into the ideology of feminism at a time when feminism was not in vogue in the working-class African American social circles of my adolescence. The president of my college had referred to God by male and female pronouns and often reminded us that having a man was a choice, not a requirement in our lives. In doing so, she was maximizing the political environment of that time. This feminized, new way of seeing God had sent me into a quagmire of emotion, but ultimately, it launched me into a study of my faith that solidified my allegiance to Christianity. After trying on other religions, the God of those other groups didn't feel like the God that I had learned to worship as a thirteen-year-old girl who was excited to get baptized. Once I was convinced that the Christian God was the one for me, I studied the reasons why God is referred to with male pronouns. In a nutshell, I learned that Jesus referred to God this way, so I resolved that if the name Father was good enough for Jesus, then it's good enough for me. Then I studied Christian history, which indeed includes atrocity, but also includes spiritual revolutions that sparked intellectual and cultural revolutions that changed whole societies, liberated women, and gave new freedoms and opportunities to people once oppressed.

Lesson 2: This Women's Studies Classroom Values Discussion and the Teacher May Be Decentralized.

Initially, when my classmates called our professor by her first name, "Layli," it made me question whether she had earned a PhD. At the time, I wasn't connecting it to the Marxist approach of flattening power structures and decentralizing the teacher's authority in the classroom. Power structures and our complicity or non-complicity with them is a theme of women's studies that is familiar to Black women and minorities due to their civil rights struggles. Women of color, even religious ones, don't often wrestle with the theories of the field that suggest that power structures have been complicit in keeping women and people of color out of positions of power. In the class, I didn't attempt to argue the case of autonomy vs. power structure, but to myself, I reasoned that the most important power structure was the elephant in the room. From my point of view, whether as an act of judgment or benevolence, God had allowed power structures to be built and endure. Discussion about supernatural power became a theme within Layli's classroom as transnational feminisms were introduced. I noticed that the third-world cosmologies of Malidoma Patrice Somé's *Of Water and the Spirit* were not completely unfamiliar. They reminded me of the Pentecostal spiritual traditions that I had been exposed to as a very young child. Ironically, the Pentecostal tradition is both empowering and restrictive to women. The emphasis on engagement with the spirit attracts many women and others who favor religious communities that encourage expressivism. At the same time, the Pentecostal denomination has traditionally supported a performance of gender with prescribed limits on women's dress and adornment of jewelry and makeup and also their leadership roles in the church. Somé begins his book by issuing a warning about the West's "sickness of the soul," which is partly a result of the West's "progressive turning away from functioning spiritual values. . ." (1). The book goes on to chronicle Somé's Dagara initiation. For the young men of the Dagara people living in southeast Burkina Faso, the initiation was a month-long journey of physical, spiritual, and emotional elder-guided challenges designed to give the journeyman an understanding of the earth, spiritual truths, and their culture to help them find their relationship among all three. Somé recounts the importance of his initiation: "For me initiation had eliminated my confusion . . . I had come to understand the sacred relationship between children and old people, between fathers and their adolescent sons, between mothers and daughters . . . why a strong, functioning community is essential for maintenance of an individual's sense of identity, meaning, and purpose" (Some 3).

The sickness of the soul that the book warns about, along with the understanding between relationships within communities, is a central concern of womanism. It is a point of difference between feminism and womanism, because womanism is deeply invested in women's wellness as a byproduct of her connection to others—namely the men, children, and other women within her community. In contrast, feminist ideas seem indifferent to whether or not a woman remains connected to men and children, if not encouraging of a fierce individualism that cheers a woman's independence from the two. Women of color have been especially critical of the rugged individualism of feminism.

Lastly, Layli's womanist classroom engaged gender through queer films that portrayed gay and lesbian relationships. The films led to discussions of gender in relationships where the legitimacy of heteronormative behavior was interrogated. In addition to my conservative viewpoint, more liberal Christian views, polytheistic liberal views, secular homocentric views, and religious homocentric views were expressed. Layli participated in the discussion and didn't attempt to have the last word or even referee the talks. The conversations were intense and it seemed that no one had been won over to a competing side. Nevertheless, at the end of the semester, the class met together for dinner at a nearby casual Jamaican restaurant. The food took me back to my vegetarian lifestyle, which had lasted six years and ended during my first pregnancy. It reminded me that I had given up an idealistic diet for a practical one that fit my new family dynamic. I was again apprehensive that Layli would find my final paper offensive, as it espoused my conservative convictions, but I had been confident of the convictions it expressed and that it had been written well and respectfully. All of us had had to exercise tolerance on a daily basis just to exist and communicate within the classroom.

The lesson learned here is that fostering a respectful atmosphere will model for students the ways to respond to ideas and ways of living we don't agree with. If, as professors, we are quick to try to shut down dissident ideas that don't agree with our own political commonplaces, students will pick up on it and mimic the behavior. If, on the other hand, we prioritize tolerance among difference, students experience the value of coalition firsthand and will build upon it. If we enter the women's studies classroom focused on teaching approaches rather than ideologies, we can anticipate and engage resistance in constructive ways, in harmony with the foundational principles of the field. But if we see students as clean canvases upon which to paint our political ideologies, we will betray our disciplinary call to be compassionate, inclusive, and collaborative.

MEETING ELIZABETH FOX-GENOVESE

My Atlanta residence and good fortune provided me a personal encounter with a scholar-practitioner of women's studies who remains one of the most influential in my life and guides my understanding of the changing nature of the field. Dr. Elizabeth Fox-Genovese had begun her academic career as a Marxist writing about the relationships of Black and White women in the South. Her teaching and writing on motherhood and inter-action in her local Catholic community carved out a place for her as the keynote speaker of the Georgia Right to Life Conference (GRTL) in Octo-ber of 2005. When Dr. Fox-Genovese made her way to the podium, I had high expectations for what I'd hear because of her accomplishments as a humanities scholar, but I expected her to speak in the measured diction that most academics use in circles outside of their immediate collegiate alliances. Before her name appeared on the GRTL pre-conference web-site, I had never heard of her. Ironically, I was teaching ESL at Emory University at the time. Emory is the school where Fox-Genovese founded a women's studies program in 1986 and where she helped establish the first PhD in women's studies in the country in 1990. Her name had not been mentioned in the women's studies courses I took in graduate school, nor had she ever been brought up at the Women's Resource and Research Center at my undergraduate women's college when I met there with other interested students. After hearing her speak, I wondered why no one had ever mentioned her. A little research told me why. Ironically, Elizabeth Fox-Genovese is remembered in much of women's studies literature as an anti-feminist because of her criticism of elite feminism, which she believed had lost touch with the lives of average women. Her criticism of what she called feminist elites culminated in her book *Feminism Is Not the Story of My Life*. I ingested the book and for the first time read ideas about feminism that I wholeheartedly agreed with. For those ideas to have come from one so instrumental in the field was strong validation that my affinity for and criticism of the field could comingle. In her example, I also noted how the field could disdain one of its founders for her adoption of conser-vative ideas, which for me, underscores the lack of tolerance for broader interpretations of the women's movement and ideals. Fox-Genovese's approaches were unquestioningly inclusive and collaborative and in her scholarship, she remained committed to principles of social justice. For her, justice in the contemporary sense in the private and public spheres had often left children the most unprotected, vulnerable class of human beings. Fox-Genovese appealed to women to take up their cause by embracing traditional roles as caretakers of their children because no one else was filling the gap that had been left as women chose vocations outside of the home. In her support for traditional motherhood roles, she drew the ire of many of her former colleagues. Those who remember her life and work note that she had always been a "consistent moralist" who searched to find "the appropriate relationship between moral and civil law" (Paquette). She was drawn to Catholicism for the moral objectivity that she found in the religion. Religious convictions, especially in relation to sexuality and reproduction, often bring together conservatives and often drive a stake in the ground, preventing would-be feminists from pledging complete allegiance to the ideology. Many such persons refuse to reconcile the act of abortion with their moral convictions about human life. Elizabeth Fox-Genovese died in 2007, shortly after I heard her speak at that GRTL conference; however, her voice and work for women's studies continue to speak loudly about the ways that the field sometimes chases an ideal that alienates the most vulnerable, who many presume to speak for.

Lesson 3: The Feminist Scholar Should Remain Devoted to Her Faith.

At Spelman College—To Reject or Employ Feminist Pedagogies?

Spelman College has a special place in the hearts of its alumna. Having experienced an undergraduate curriculum and campus life experience designed for Black women and explicitly from a Black women's perspective, I see Spelman as the cornerstone of my affinity for women's studies. When I returned to Spelman as an English instructor, I was faced with a choice to focus on ideology or methodology in my classroom; I could have either steered my students to embrace my political affinity or to explore political rhetoric so that they could find their own place within systems of life and governance. It was 2008 and I knew most of my students would identify with the platform of the Democratic party and liberal social movement on campus that framed reproductive justice more rigidly than I did. I also knew the students had probably not interrogated their ideologies. Ironically, a majority of those same girls would not self-identify as feminists, for the reasons expressed by Natasha Crooms and Dimpal Jain in "Purple is to Lavender," where they argue for women of color to be introduced to alternatives to feminism that don't feel quite so uncomfortable to them.

Black women resisted participation in the women's movements for the reasons Elizabeth Fox-Genovese wrote about in *Feminism Is Not the Story of My Life*. The issues that leaders and theorists in the movement had expressed throughout the waves after suffrage have not been the issues most pressing to women of color. Women of color had never experienced the sheltered environment of the home that White women of the second wave sought to escape. Those concerns were the concerns of the middle class at a time when a majority of Black women had not reached that socioeconomic tier. Nor were Black women primarily concerned about stigmas related to gender or sexual preference, the issues that came after that. Black women had their very own stigmas to fight against and until recently, through theories of interlocking oppressions and intersectionality, they had no framework for articulating their competing simultaneous oppressions. They often considered color discrimination a much heavier burden than gender discrimination in the 90s and the early 2000s.

Black women and women of color have tended to be attracted to womanism for many reasons. Womanism expresses a more collective understanding of the upliftment of women. Womanism has intended to keep a woman connected to the family as opposed to articulating the individualistic rights of a woman. Elizabeth Fox-Genovese didn't call it "womanism," but her research uncovered that women of color tended to be very protective of their sons and the men in their lives. Therefore, they rejected some of the harsher connotations of men as oppressors that had come out of the third-wave thoughts of popular feminists.

Another notion that put mainstream feminists at odds with women of color was the notion that modesty was an "elite White concept." A lot of support for abstinence historically came from communities of color, such as traditional Black Christians and traditional Hispanic Catholics. The practice of sexual abstinence can be tied to socioeconomic (and thus racial) status in two very different ways. Remaining abstinent prevented the financial hardships that came with supporting an unplanned child, and low economic status meant the erasure of the culturally enforced gender separations in public and at home in relation to courtship. Traditional Black Christians and traditional Hispanic Catholics supported the concept of modesty in conduct, including sexuality, based on their religious texts and traditions. Even traditional Jewish women support modesty.

Wendy Shalit, author of *A Return to Modesty* and *Girls Gone Mild*, wrote to me in an email that "[t]he real rebels today are the good girls. I also have an entire chapter about why the most articulate voices in the personal dignity movement are young African-American women" (Shalit, 2006). The two of us connected when I found her companion website to the first book. We agreed that the most closed and undignified view of sexuality is the one that says, "They're going to do it anyway, so just give them condoms." Add to that whatever other methods of contraception, no matter their physical or emotional risks. This attitude continues to be the mantra of liberals within college student programming around issues of sex. I remember writing a grant for a nonprofit that I direct. At the non-profit, we use creative programming to reintroduce abstinence and modesty to young women in college. In selecting foundations for the grant, I targeted only those that said they supported "women's interests," including reproductive health. In one foundation's decision not to fund our proposal, the female board member had said that our goals were "unrealistic." I remember being so upset that I called the organization in order to personally relay my story of becoming abstinent in college—after becoming sexually active in college—precisely as a result of a Christian campus organization that had creatively articulated abstinence as a dignified option. My impassioned explanation did not change the board member's decision, but my commitment to abstinence stuck throughout my undergraduate and graduate college experience until I got married.

Wendy Shalit's ideas about modesty and women were cemented in college as well. She had watched her friends suffer emotionally and otherwise from treating sex casually. They demanded no commitment from their partners and no protection for themselves, and ended up emotionally scarred and likely harmed otherwise. Her ideas were expanded in her follow-up book, *Girls Gone Mild*, wherein she forwarded the notion that emotional repression results from casual sex and harms women. Here again, a personal encounter helped to form my ideas about feminism and women's studies, but it was my training in composition theory and pedagogy that offered me the tools to teach in ideologically polarized environments.

One of the greatest tools of empowerment that women's studies has adopted from composition theory is the focus on voicing. Theorists such as bell hooks have talked about the power of signifying aloud in the feminist classroom, but in composition classrooms, voicing often starts as writing.

In a presidential voting year, I informally themed one of my composition classes "Political Rhetoric." Likewise, I chose readings and assignments that related to the issues that were being discussed during the campaigns. Many of those issues were deemed "women's issues," and candidates advocated for policy changes that would affect abortion and marriage laws, economic assistance, and the stimulation of the economy. I embraced the political climate as an opportunity to present a chapter from Elizabeth Fox-Genovese's *Women and the Future of Family*, a chapter from Wendy Shalit's *Girls Gone Mild* called "Against Repression," parts of Barack Obama's *Dreams From My Father*, and a chapter from Arthur Brooks's *Who Really Cares*. The chapters I chose discussed abortion, marriage, emotion, career, and economic behavior, respectively. Interesting discussions followed those readings, and like Layli Maparyan had modeled, I attempted to participate without having the last word or refereeing. In that class, the students could choose to engage any of those topics in a final self-governance policy paper. Many of them felt safe enough to present papers that gave personal accounts of sexuality, family values and contraception, and finances through many different ideological lenses.

From my time teaching using feminist approaches at Spelman, I vividly remember a paper that chronicled a young woman retelling how exposure to literature helped her discover that she was a lesbian. In the same semester, another student had written about the ways abortions of African American babies could be considered genocide. I marveled at the range of their experiences and their sense of liberty to express their controversial ideas in writing. It made me remember my time in Layli's class and our end-of-semester Jamaican dinner. In addition to research papers, students in the composition class at Spelman delivered spoken word pieces that began as written drafts. After reviewing and analyzing examples of traditional and beat-style poetry, the students anonymously workshopped their poetry. Both the self-governance policy and the spoken word assignment are ways any feminist teacher can incorporate classroom strategies that employ the feminist writing approach of voicing. Feminist writing approaches are apolitical. It is we as practitioners who either infuse the approaches with our political ideologies or choose not to.

Another feminist approach that we can present to students is revisionist practice in historiography. Revisionist practices aim to reinsert women's voices into the pages of literary and rhetorical history. Jacqueline Royster reinserted Black women such as Maria Stewart and Sojourner Truth into the rhetorical canon based on their oratory in the mid-19th century. Her book *Traces of a Stream* demonstrates the ways that Black women commanded rhetoric in ways that uplifted their race and communicated their awareness of the injustices that had been committed upon them. Many Black, female orators and writers of the 19th century understood justice within a Christian framework that saw God as an omnipotent lawgiver, so it is plausible that they would have found themselves among the women today who renounce power frameworks that prohibit justice for all. However, they would likely see men and leaders as being used by malevolent spiritual powers rather than wielding oppressive power in and of themselves.

In the book, Royster defines an "afra-feminist" research approach. This approach encourages a move away from blind objectivism to an author-revealed, passionate attachment to research that makes transparent the hopes for research findings. Royster's research approach is one of the many we can use to direct students' methodologies. When we do so, we frame their feminist approach without endeavoring to divert or frame their ideologies.

The pedagogical takeaway to my recounting these approaches, or Lesson 4, is that the philosophical underpinnings of women's studies demand a pedagogical balancing: We would betray inclusion, collaboration, and compassion if we focus more on ideology than pedagogy. Instead, when we go into the classroom centralizing our approaches above our ideologies, we are less likely to come away as frauds—those who articulate inclusion only in theory, but not in practice. The first place to begin this balancing is in the material we cover when we cover women's movements in the classroom.

Conservative Activism

I often teach a class at a pregnancy care center near my home. The students are single women who are either pregnant, already mothers, or those who think they would benefit from the class. The class is divided into six sections based on the themes of relationships, education, finances, and career. Of all the teaching I do, I often enjoy teaching this class the most. One of the reasons I find the class so rewarding is because I believe the content and atmosphere can help influence women to make transitions that can supernaturally transform their lives away from destructive patterns toward generative ones, and not just in the sense of physical new birth, but also spiritual rebirth. The other characteristic that endears me to the class is that I don't have to veil the ideologies and life experiences that have drawn me to teach the class in the first place. The pregnancy center is unapologetically evangelistic in its approach, and the women are repeatedly made aware of the pro-life and evangelistic mission of the center and of the class. However, they are not obligated to declare any new spiritual or ideological convictions as a result of the class, nor does doing so result in any preferential treatment in terms of services rendered or products given. Some of the students may be driven to complete the class based on the modest practical benefits, which include access to baby supplies, clothes, furniture, diapers, etc. Other women who attend are required to go by government-ordered rehabilitation programs. When they do attend, the director of the center and the program director of the Life Support Class have structured the class in such a way that all women who seek the services of the center will confront the spiritual realities that they and I believe have played a role in their formation of habits that shape their sexual, financial, educational, and relational philosophies.

Many of the women who work in crisis pregnancy do so because they are intimately acquainted with the feelings of helplessness and desperation that accompany the experience of a crisis pregnancy. Some of the workers have the experience of having chosen abortion and are living regretfully with the decision. Some have lived unorganized sexual lives where they faced multiple unintended pregnancies. Some have experienced horribly abusive relationships that challenged everything they believed about love. Most of the staff has worked to overcome rigid self-identity and gendered concepts that sometimes pervade communities of faith. Out of it, they have formed new identities in line with their understanding of the grace of God, and they hope that the women they serve will find ways to reinvent themselves and find support in their decision to become mothers.

Some women who visit the center seem trapped in disorderly lives. Some women who enter for a free pregnancy test and find that they are not pregnant are so shocked by the pregnancy that could have been that they learn to completely abandon the risky behaviors that sent them to the center in the first place. Most often, that change in behavior must be preceded by a shift in ideology. At one of my most vulnerable times, a pregnancy care center was spiritually driven enough to ask me about my relationship with God when I thought all I needed was a pregnancy test. Their conversation with me was another experience that helped me realign my beliefs and actions and set myself on a path to an abundant life.

The work of pregnancy care in centers like these is fertile ground for the interrogation and exemplification of the merge of autonomy and community support systems in the shaping of girls' and women's lives. So I get fighting mad when so-called women's groups target these centers in search of technicalities that could lead to legal grounds to shut them down. The ideology that the rejection of abortion is evidence of the repression of choice has created this reality. Our inclusion of women's movements within religiously conservative communities can help otherwise well-meaning practitioners to re-envision this work as a model of public and private partnership that is necessary to advance social justice. These centers illuminate that women have the right to choose motherhood even in the middle of the most chaotic events in their lives, and others have the right to create NGOs to support that decision. This work is profoundly important work that can be highlighted within courses that discuss sexuality and issues related to reproductive choice.

Some feminist scholars have found ways to initiate cultural dialogues about girls and women, the state, and the individual in ways that have the potential to move beyond polarizing political battle lines. Letizia Guglielmo's edited collection *MTV and Teen Pregnancy* combines approaches from media studies, pop culture, and women's studies to illuminates ways that the media frame narratives through reality television that challenge or conform to fluid notions of motherhood and gender. The collection also illuminates ways that masculinity and teen fatherhood is framed through teen pregnancy media in comparison to the portrayal of teen motherhood and the framing of contemporary masculinity itself. Further, the collection offers a discussion of the framing of abortion in ways that move beyond pro-choice and pro-life political commonplaces. This approach could breathe new life into the classroom subtopic of abortion so those on the conservative side of the political fence feel less alienated.

When treating the theme of abortion, composition's writing and healing approach is currently underutilized. The approach has been the subject of widespread theoretical and therapeutic investigation, particularly in Anderson and MacCurdy's *Writing and Healing* (2000), and Lepore and Smyth's *The Writing Cure* (2001). Many subsequent studies by James Pennebaker and other researchers have shown that practitioners would have substantial content with which to make an informed decision before employing the strategy. The combination of narrative instruction and psychological movement that the strategy demands has been shown to benefit students academically and socially. Students who engage the approach have been shown to improve their academic writing ability and to be able to re-enter public social spheres after experiencing traumas. In contrast, students who do not employ the strategy enter public spheres at lower rates than those who write expressively using the writing and healing approach (Pennebaker 2012).

This approach can be used to impact the incidence of women discussing their abortion, a move that Caryn Murphy noted to be missing in media portrayals of teen motherhood ("Teen Momism on MTV" 2013). We can borrow the pedagogical tool of rhetorical analysis from composition studies to offer alternative methods to engage the subject of abortion. Rhetorical analyses of print and multimedia advertisements of abortion services and pregnancy care center services may lead to multidimensional discussions of both sides of the issue.

Conservative Christians and feminists are converging on the practice and interrogation of observational forms of birth control in their effort to do no environmental harm and betray no religious conviction. Fertility awareness unites both camps, particularly ecofeminists and cosmologically interested feminists, within the feminist community. Likewise, women's studies often engages environmentalism and cosmology as new directions. Classes at Marquette University and Spelman College offer students a chance to discover and practice the approach and engage with research about its efficacy, ideological foundations, and implications. Books that can serve as classroom texts and references to fertility awareness and that espouse ecofeminism and/or religious solidarity include *Love and Fertility* from Family of the Americas, *The Garden of Fertility* by Katie Singer, and *Birth Control for Christians* by Jenell Williams Paris.

So, how many of you identify as conservative? Those are the words I wanted to use to start my paper on the same subject at a recent National Women's Studies Association conference. I opted against it, but still kept the question in the talk for the same reason I pose it now. If we believe our field is free of ideological bias, then why aren't more women in the room, more women reading these words, conservative? If we truly want to move women's studies into a more inclusive space, then the make-up of the field should reflect that priority. While I know that being conservative doesn't necessarily mean that a person is also pro-life, an overwhelming majority of feminist practitioners still reject and work to end activism at pregnancy care centers, which are central to conservative women's activism for women and social justice.

As instructors, offering these approaches to dialog about and analyze controversial topics will help our students focus on the actions of voicing and interrogating. Our equal responsibility as part of the field is to welcome conservative viewpoints alongside others and to evaluate both fairly. When our field begins to reflect diversity by including conservative ideas and the people who champion them, we will embody the inclusion and collaboration we endeavor to teach.

NOTES

1 According to David Horowitz and Michael Bérubé, 75% of academics define themselves as liberal, 15% as conservative, and 11% vote Republican.

2 In May of 2014, students and professors at Rutgers University protested the selection of former Secretary of State Condoleezza Rice as that year's commencement speaker. Though the president of Rutgers stood by the selection, Rice turned down the invitation amid the protests, noting that she was "unwilling to detract" from the ceremony in any way (Anderson).

3 In April of 2014, Brendan Eich, CEO of Mozilla, resigned among protests about the discovery that he gave $1,000 to support Proposition 8, a ballot initiative in California to support traditional marriage (Wilde).

4 Head nigga in charge (HNIC) is popularly associated with Morgan Freeman's line in the 1998 movie *Lean On Me*, in which he uses the acronym.

WORKS CITED

Anderson, Kristen Solis. "Rutger's Silly Condoleeza Rice Protest." The Daily Beast. May 14 2014. Web. 9 July 2014.

Budziszewski, Jay. *How to Stay Christian in College*. Colorado Springs: Think, 2004.

Crooms, Natasha, and Dimpal Jain. "Purple Is to Lavender: Womanism, Resistance, and the Politics of Naming." *Negro Educational Review* (Spring 2011–Winter 2012): 67–88.

Horowitz, David, and Michael Bérubé. "Facing Off on Political Diversity." Diverse: Issues in Higher Education 23.18 (2006): 10–11. Academic Search Complete. Web. 3 July 2014.

Murphy, Caryn. "Teen Momism on MTV." Ed. Letizia Guglielmo. *MTV and Teen Motherhood: Critical Essays on 16 and Pregnant and Teen Mom*. Lanham: Scarecrow Press, 2013. 3–18.

Paquette, Robert L. "Introduction to 'Unbought Grace—Reading Elizabeth Fox-Genovese." National Association of Scholars. May 2012. Web. 6 July 2014.

Pennebaker, James. "Writing about Emotional Experiences as a Therapeutic Process." Psychological Science 8.3 (1997): 162–166. Academic Search Complete. Web. 9 September 2012.

Shalit, Wendy. Personal Email. 2006.

Some, Malidoma Patrice. *Of Water and the Spirit*. New York: Penguin Compass, 1994.

Wilde, Robert, "Truth Revolt Blocks Mozilla Firefox to Protest Anti-Christian Discrimination." Breitbart. April 4, 2014. Web. 9 July 2014.

For more reading on conservative Christians in the New Abolitionist movement see:

Bernstein, Elizabeth. "Militarized Humanitarianism Meets Carceral Feminism: The Politics of Sex, Rights, and Freedom in Contemporary Anti-Trafficking Campaigns." *Signs: Journal of Women in Culture and Society*. 36.1 (Autumn 2010): 45–71. 3 July 2014. Web.

Engle, Karen. "Calling in the Troops: The Uneasy relationship among Women's Rights, Human Rights, and Humanitarian Intervention." *Harvard Human Rights Journal* 20 (Spring 2007): 189–226. 3 July 2014. Web.

For a paper chronicling ideas about crisis pregnancy see:

Kelly, Kimberly. "In the Name of the Mother: Renegotiating Women's Authority in the Crisis Pregnancy Center Movement." Signs: Journal of Women in Culture and Society. 38.1 (Sep 2012): 203–229. 3 July 2014. Web.

Response: "It don't matter if you're black or white!"

Feminist Pedagogy, Isolation, and the Growth of the Discipline

Le'Brian A. Patrick

Racial segregation and discrimination have tended to trump gender segregation. Beyond those reasons, politics in higher education where women's studies is taught swings sharply left, alienating moderates and conservatives. If practitioners of women's studies can shift their classroom environment such that they focus on making their examples of women's movement more representative of the social, religious, and political activity of moderates and conservatives, and if we focus on approaches to movement, we have a chance of attracting diversity in the field and staying focused on the interests of all women rather than a few.

—Cantice Greene

I have constructed my response to Cantice Greene's "Negotiating Feminism When Color and Credo Trump Gender" in two sections. First, I attempt to address Greene's primary argument for a more inclusive classroom to help student growth in the field through an examination of her pedagogical imperatives. Second, as I continue my discussion of her pedagogical visions, I conclude this response with an evaluation of the troubles she has faced and offer suggestions for presentation that may help her find solace in her life, personally and academically.

I must confess that during my initial reading of Greene's work, I found myself wondering if we were in the same academic field at all, or worse, if, in her classroom, she was undoing one of the very things that feminist scholars have worked so hard to achieve: Equality both inside and outside of the classroom. I found myself thinking, "What/how was she teaching?" I admit I did not recall who she was, as our initial meeting had been a few months prior at a social event for incoming freshmen to the university. After coming across an image of her, I could not fathom an African American woman, who was both religiously and politically conservative, teaching in such a liberal field with ease. After reading her work, I learned, neither could she.

Greene argues that women's studies remains exclusionary and in order for it to grow as a discipline and in its popularity among college students, four pedagogical tools must be used in the classroom: (1) The classroom must be inclusive, (2) the classroom must value discussion and sometimes decentralize the teacher, (3) the feminist scholar must remain devoted to her faith, and (4) the feminist scholar must strive for a pedagogical balance, as we would betray inclusion, collaboration, and compassion if we focus more on ideology than pedagogy. I concur that these are important issues and that any feminist educator would benefit from understanding their impact and implementation in the classroom. In the following pages, I address her main observation about women's studies as well as each of these tools individually.

Arguably, the entire women's movement has fought for inclusion from its inception; however, academic backlash towards this transformative movement really took shape in the wake of the second wave of the movement, as feminist scholars began to take note of the shortcomings of the "White" women's movement. Feminists of color have fought, in the ways that have been afforded to them, for gender equality for centuries. Yet, despite their contributions, the feminists who've emerged as academic and household names in the United States tend to be White—Susan B. Anthony, Betty Friedan, and Gloria Steinem, for example. The reality is that Latina, Asian American, African American, and Native American women have deepened the struggle for women's rights by discussing how patriarchy intersects with race, class, gender, and sexuality. Whereas Black feminists such as Patricia Hill Collins, the writer Alice Walker, and activist Angela Davis are well known for their efforts to end racism and sexism, a number of notable feminists of color remain largely anonymous to the general public. However, to argue that women's studies has overlooked and is lacking the implementation of the findings of these and so many other feminist thinkers in the classroom is tragic. I do not mean to imply that I do not agree with Greene's pedagogical vision for the classroom; conversely, I believe it is a matter of semantics that has Greene at a tipping point for leaving the discipline.

First, she argues that the classroom must be inclusive and welcome conservative ideas alongside the dominant liberal ideologies that pervade feminist classrooms. I wholeheartedly agree with this sentiment. One of the principles of feminist pedagogy is concerned with cooperation and community building within the classroom (Scering, 1997). This is critical to the feminist environment because feminists value community and equality, so all members must feel included, respected, and equally valued for participation (Schniedwind, 1993; Webb, Allen, and Walker, 2002). Additionally, creating a caring community in the classroom is one of the most effective strategies for addressing students' basic needs in a way that makes them open to learning, feel hopeful about the future, and helps them reach their full potential for knowledge and understanding, order, and beauty (Bickhart, Jablon, and Dodge, 1991).

Second, Greene implores that the classroom must value discussion and at times decentralize the teacher. She couldn't be more accurate with such a statement. The primary goal of feminist pedagogy is empowerment, which highlights the democratic environment that is produced as power is shared in the classroom (Chapman, 1997). Chapman (1997) educates that the practice of freedom emerges through empowerment, which has been absent in the teacher-centered model that is generally used in classrooms.

Greene's third assertion that the "feminist scholar must remain devoted to 'her' faith" is a tough one for me to align myself with for a number of reasons. First, while feminist pedagogy challenges the notion that knowledge and teaching methods can be value-free, it is also built on a foundation of challenging traditional views and practices (Webb, Allen, & Walker, 2002). With such a strong pedagogical stance, the possibility of ideological shifts becomes difficult. Yes, it is true that "feminist pedagogy makes explicit that how we experience and understand things is rooted in our social position based on a variety of factors, including gender, race, ethnicity, class, and sexual preference" (Parry, 1996, 46). However, personal experience is a central component of learning, and with an implementation of feminist techniques in the classroom, there must be a place for teachers to learn from their students, as those students become educators through their experiences. Shrewsbury (1993) tells us that the feminist teacher becomes a role model of a leader. Being a leader that resists learning, especially learning from one's students' experiences, is in direct contrast to the principle of making the classroom collaborative that feminist pedagogy hopes and aims for.

The second reason that I am uneasy with her third assertion is her choice to use "her" in that statement. Whether intentional or not, it is built on the assumption that the feminist is, and can only be, female. bell hooks (2000) sharply carved out a place for the male feminist as she discussed the imperative need for men in the feminist struggle. To exclude males destroys the very fabric of inclusion and equality that the movement so tirelessly fights against. It is important to note for those in their infancy of the field that feminism is not against men; rather, it is against androcentric (male-centered), misogynistic (woman-hating), and sexist (gender-discriminating) ideology.

IT'S NOT WHAT YOU SAY, IT'S HOW YOU SAY IT!

Reflecting longer on Greene's point, I questioned whether it was a matter of semantics that has created the cloud of alienation that she feels in her life and that I felt after reading this last point. I am certainly hopeful that she does not exclude/isolate anyone; however, presentation could be the key to helping her in her classroom and also in her personal battle with this field and her beliefs. Her final point is important to go ahead and mention here. She explains that women's studies demands a pedagogical balancing, which is only possible if we do not betray inclusion, collaboration, and compassion by focusing on ideology more than we focus on pedagogy. This pedagogical vision supports my belief that it is a matter of semantics, because she clearly is against exclusion and welcomes collaboration (even from males).

I believe that semantics, or presentation, has been at the root of her struggles to have her personal and academic circles peacefully coexist. For example, she has juggled with the dilemma of deciding if it is more important to focus on ideology or methodology in her classroom. She mentions that her students had not begun to interrogate their ideologies. However, this chapter does not indicate how she introduced ways of interrogating ideologies. In fact, it honed in on her point that "the feminist scholar should remain devoted to her faith."

While she mentions that women's studies pushed her to further comprehend her faith and/or ideology, this chapter does not give an indication that she truly interrogated it. While she has gained more of a grasp on the totality of her religious teaching, she does not make mention of anything that was unsettling about it. Certainly, to question something implies that one is at odds with some part of what has been presented. After reading this, it appears that she has found ways to use her academic background to support her strong conservative beliefs. In other words, her academic training has been interrogated, but not her personal life. For instance, Greene presents Natasha Crooms and Dimpal Jain's (2011) argument that women of color have found comfort in identifying with womanism more so than feminism. I think that is great, but comfort is not at the base of intellectual and spiritual questioning.

Another issue that came to mind as I read is an appreciation of differences alongside an examination of similarities for unity. An exploration of difference is highly recommended by feminists, as we all experience life subjectively. However, this is just as important in understanding our similarities. Reading further and discovering that Greene and I come from the same religious background helped me empathize with her experience somewhat. For many women, including women of color, and men, the trouble they have with feminism is that they lack a full understanding of the term (Kourany, Sterba, and Tong, 1999). It evokes images of unattractive, angry women who want to abandon their families and hate men, but this is a gross misrepresentation. While they have controversial ideas about such topics, they are not as radical as the public may perceive them to be. Not only that, feminists come from all religious, educational, ethnic, racial, and class backgrounds, and vary in body size, age, and sexual orientation. Furthermore, they have also fought for all sorts of issues, such as slavery, suffrage, education, and healthcare, just to name a few. I will say that not all have fought for these issues equally, and not all feminists agree on what feminism looks like and how to achieve it. This has been the primary issue with the movement: A lack of unity. I believe that Greene's use of womanism here is a great example. Instead of trying to find similarities, there is a focus on separatism and difference. While it is true that womanism has intended to keep a woman connected to the family as opposed to articulating the individualistic rights of a woman, it is also true that it expresses a more collective understanding of the upliftment of women. This is also key to the term "feminism." A suggestion that I think Greene already uses is finding ways to express similarities between both her personal circles and academic circles as she speaks with each group. Again, the trouble I return to is how those similarities are expressed.

For example, her "making peace" with ideologies that place a husband as the head of the household is an area that has raised eyebrows in her feminist academic circles. Finding comfort in her religious upbringing helped her come to terms with this. It is my guess that her reasoning behind beliefs such as these are not adequately explained to and/or understood by her colleagues. She goes on to explain that she "welcomed the sabbatical from being HNIC," and that her husband was a representation of the God she worshiped. For her personal life, this may be a sufficient reason, but for others, an understanding of being tired and welcoming help, not a master, to take care of the household is paramount. However, she described this as a declaration of the "freedom of submission" and this is contradictory to her overall peace with having her husband be the head of the household.

As feminists or womanists, it is important to remember that these are her choices, whether we like them or not. We must remember that freedom of choice is one of the ultimate rights that feminists have fought for, even if that choice is to remain "connected" to family, or have a male as the head of the household.

Presentation and semantics have proven to be the largest issue for Greene, from my perspective. Even in this chapter, it appears that she has only used her academic background to solidify her religious and political beliefs, rather than interrogating all areas equally. Moreover, the discourse used to express her beliefs to friends and academic colleagues has been misleading and has not worked the same externally as it has internally to provide her with comfort. For this reason, she has questioned whether or not this is the field for her. This questioning is important because it appears that this "liberal field" of study is what is being questioned, not her personal ideology. I do believe her intentions within the classroom (primarily her first, second, and fourth assertions) are definitely necessary and supported by feminist pedagogy; however, her third argument, for a feminist scholar to remain devoted to her faith, is where her trouble stems from, both academically and personally. It is not a question of Black or White, or liberal or conservative; rather, we must appreciate our differences, understand our similarities, and respectfully and comprehensibly articulate them to each other to increase inclusion in our lives, in the classroom, and in the academic field that has grown out of women's studies.

WORKS CITED

Bickhart, T., J.R. Jablon, & D.T. Dodge. "Building a Classroom Community." *Building the Primary Classroom: A Complete Guide to Teaching and Learning.* Beltsville, MD: Gryphon House, Inc, 1999. 44–95.

Chapman, E. "Nurse Education: A Feminist Approach." *Nurse Education Today* 17 (1997): 209–214.

hooks, b. "Men: Comrades in Struggle" *Feminist Theory: From Margin to Center.* Cambridge, MA: South End Press, 2000. 68–83

Kourany, J., J. Sterba, & R. Tong. Eds. (1999). *Feminist Philosophies.* 2nd ed. Upper Saddle River, NJ: Prentice Hall.

Parry, S. "Feminist Pedagogy and Techniques for a Changing Classroom." *Women's Studies Quarterly* Nos. 3 & 4 (1996): 45–54.

Scering, G. (1997). "Themes of a Critical/Feminist Pedagogy: Teacher Education for Democracy." *Journal of Teacher Education* 48: 62–68.

Schniedewind, N. (1993). "Teaching Feminist Process in the 1990s." *Women's Studies Quarterly* 21.3/4: 17–30.

Shrewsbury, C. (1993). "What Is Feminist Pedagogy?" *Women's Studies Quarterly* 21.3/4: 8–16.

Webb, L., M. Allen, & K. Walker. (2002). "Feminist Pedagogy: Identifying Basic Principles." *Academic Exchange* 6: 67–72.

5 The Metaphysics of Social Justice

Coalitional Activism at the Intersections of Sexism, Racism, and Heterosexism

Jennifer McWeeny

From 2007 to 2012, I taught nine sections of an upper-level undergraduate course called Philosophy of Love and Sex: Ethics, Intimate Violence, and Activism at John Carroll University, a Jesuit institution committed to pluralistic education that seeks and recognizes diverse perspectives. I first developed this course in the aftermath of a series of four sexual assaults that were reported on John Carroll's campus during the fall semester of 2004.[1] As these tragic events unfolded, students and faculty members expressed concerns that the university's institutional structure was not as supportive of the assault survivors as it could have been.[2] Moreover, several noted that the university's response to the reported assaults did not appear to be informed by recent scholarship on the causes and prevention of sexual violence. Absent any program or department like women's studies, gender studies, or ethnic studies, the university seemed to likewise lack the capacity to counter intimate violence with *scholarly* tools, that is, with rigorous education that empowers a community from within. Instead, the university administered a series of prohibitions that aimed to shape the campus culture from without. For example, in a campus-wide letter announcing that "several" incidents of sexual assault had occurred, administrators primarily focused on the suspicion that "date-rape" drugs were being used and on the task of raising awareness about the possibility of assault so that potential victims could "protect themselves and others" (Rombalski and Crahen, 2004). In a follow-up memo to this letter, women were given specific recommendations such as "choose the buddy system," "pour your own drink," and "choose to communicate your desires clearly," with the parenthetical caveat that "the survivor of sexual assault is not to blame" (Harshbarger, 2004). As a professor who both specializes in feminist theory and had taught in a women's and gender studies department before arriving at John Carroll University in September of 2004, I was troubled that the structure of my new university seemed to be affirming "rape culture" through an embrace of traditional sex roles and suggestions that rape victims should adjust their own behavior to minimize incidences of rape.[3] Many students were also critical of these aspects of the institutional response to sexual assault and organized collectively to demand that the institution and the John Carroll community reconsider their structural attitudes about sex and gender.[4]

My motivations to develop the course The Philosophy of Love and Sex: Ethics, Intimate Violence, and Activism involved the need to provide students with an *academic* space where they could explore this local crisis. I wanted to give students access to cutting-edge resources from fields like feminist theory, critical race theory, queer theory, and de-colonial theory so that they could craft informed conceptions of sex and sexual differences and cultivate ideas of healthy and non-violent sexual relationships. I also hoped students would gain a sense of self-empowerment in regard to their own intimate histories and futures, as well as in relation to the structures and practices animating their local communities. To balance the course's focus on violence and oppression, I devoted considerable amounts of class time to the theory and practice of activism—of generating hope and resistance individually and collectively. I also required that all students design and execute a collaborative "activism project" that would make a difference in their community, both in terms of preventing violence and opening the campus culture to multiple kinds of diversity.

The course's integration of radical social theory with a traditional Catholic milieu proved fecund, pedagogically speaking, as it provided students with opportunities to explore complex relationships between theory and practice in concrete ways. Specifically, The Philosophy of Love and Sex offered students an educational space where they could examine philosophical tension that is present in the university's Catholic Jesuit identity and that was exposed during the community response to the sexual assaults of fall 2004. Namely, there is an opposition between doctrinal Catholic attitudes toward sexual differences and sexuality, on the one hand, and the Catholic mission of serving others—of cultivating, respecting, and offering institutional protections to *all* kinds of diverse or marginalized populations, on the other. One of the student activists who helped organize the response to the sexual assaults of 2004, Dana Dombrowski, makes this opposition especially clear: "[T]here is never an excuse for rape . . . The issue at hand has been disguised as a warning for women—be very aware; someone could be using the 'date-rape' drug. However . . . it is primarily a crisis concerning the attitude that males hold in regard to female sexuality . . . In order to progressively conceive of the 'greater good,' begin by cultivating a new attitude amid our male colleagues."[5]

It is precisely such dissonances between a community's metaphysics and its possibilities for cultivating social justice that generate the need for scholarly analysis of the issues. An examination of the relationship between metaphysics and social justice thus served as a foundational question that grounded and motivated other inquiries in The Philosophy of Love and Sex. But it was the way this tension took root in the lives of the students themselves that led them to pose the question to their community loudly so the collective task of articulating a metaphysics of social justice could no longer be ignored. Although teaching frequently involves moments of pedagogical reversibility where the "teacher" learns from her "students," I experienced this reversibility in a most profound way the third time that I taught the course in the spring of 2010. Just three weeks into the semester, a group of John Carroll students staged a campus protest at a high-profile men's basketball game to ask that the university change its EEO policy to include sexual orientation. What soon came to be called "The LGBTQ Protest" [6] not only gave me considerable insight into the theory and practice of activism and showed me new ways to participate in the teacher-student relationship, but also provided the John Carroll community as a whole with opportunities to think more deeply about these tensions between belief and action, theory and practice, and metaphysics and justice. In what follows, I raise and answer some scholarly questions that emerge from a consideration of John Carroll's LGBTQ protest and its role as a meeting point for traditional values and progressive politics. In so doing, I address a variety of subjects relevant to critical social theories, including the intersections of oppressions like sexism, heterosexism, and racism; the importance of coalition to political movement; and the pedagogical potentials of academically engaged activism.

I. THE LGBTQ PROTEST AND SURROUNDING EVENTS

In October of 2008, the faculty of John Carroll University made a formal recommendation to the university president and board of directors that the university's EEO policy be amended to include sexual orientation alongside "race, age, color, sex, religion, ethnic or national origin, disability, [and] Vietnam veteran status or special disabled veteran status" (Non-discrimination/Equal Employment Opportunity Policy, 2009–2011). The motion to make this recommendation carried by a wide measure in both the Faculty Council and the general faculty meetings and was subsequently sent out as a written ballot to the whole faculty. The resolution passed with considerable support: ninety-five faculty members voted in favor of the resolution, eight voted against it, and seven abstained. Shortly after the vote was taken, Faculty Council officers presented the faculty's formal recommendation to the University President, Rev. Robert L. Niehoff, S.J.

The faculty resolution to recommend the inclusion of sexual orientation in the university's non-discrimination policies is a concise document that cites three primary reasons in support of its aims (John Carroll University Faculty Council, 2008). First, the document references relevant aspects of the university's mission, including its commitment to creating "an inclusive community where differing points of view and experiences are valued" and its "appreciation that our personal and collective choices can build a more just world" ("Vision, Mission, Core Values," 2009–2011). Not protecting lesbian, gay, bisexual, and queer individuals under the university's EEO policy undermines the inclusive community and experiential diversity that the university's Jesuit mission seeks to cultivate. Second, the resolution affirms that the faculty of John Carroll University believes that individuals should not be discriminated against in the workplace on the basis of sexual orientation. Third, it mentions a study conducted by a John Carroll student that showed that seventy-nine percent of the twenty-nine Jesuit colleges and universities in the United States do include sexual orientation in their EEO policies (Coats, 2008).[7]

This faculty resolution occurred at the same time that diversity was becoming a central issue at many levels of the university. The discussion at faculty meetings made clear that many faculty members were concerned about the overall campus climate for LGBTQ individuals and persons from other traditionally marginalized groups, such as women and people of color. Concurrently, the Faculty of Color Association and the Women's Faculty Caucus began to take a more prominent role in consulting with the university's administration on issues of diversity. In 2008, the Faculty Council developed and implemented a standing committee to deal solely with matters of "gender and diversity." Several faculty members were also members of President Niehoff's newly formed "Institutional Task Force on Diversity," which was convened for the purpose of making recommendations about how the university can "best coordinate [our] commitment to diversity, inclusion, and multiculturalism" (Institutional Task Force on Diversity, 2008, 1). Of the many recommendations included in the Task Force's final report of October 2009 was amending the university's EEO policy to include sexual orientation.

Although individual faculty members had been expressing concerns in regard to the campus climate for members of marginalized groups for years, the movement for a more inclusive campus gained considerable momentum in the five years leading up to the protest for several reasons, not the least of which is the community activism surrounding the sexual assaults of 2004. In addition, President Niehoff began to issue statements about the importance of diversity in conjunction with his 2005 inauguration. A large portion of his inauguration speech discussed a "racial incident" that had just occurred on campus where a student had shouted racial slurs and threatened violence toward an African American custodian who was walking outside of the student's dormitory (Niehoff, 2005). President Niehoff apologized to the victim of this attack, Nelson Robinson, and inspired the university community with his call, "We must be the change we want to see in the world." In light of these statements, faculty and students began to notice places where diversity was simultaneously encouraged by the administration and essentially unsupported within the foundational structures of the institution. This tension between word and deed was heightened by the absence of academic programs in women's studies, ethnic studies, and related fields; the absence of a Women's Center, LGBTQ Center, or Diversity Center; and the lack of protection and recognition for LGBTQ individuals in university policies and practices. It seemed to many that faculty members were being asked to welcome and foster diversity without being given the resources and institutional backing to do so.

On February 2, 2010—more than one year after John Carroll University's faculty had submitted its recommendation that the university's EEO policy be changed—President Niehoff issued a letter to all faculty, staff, administrators, and students stating that he could not approve the faculty's resolution and that he would not expand the university's EEO policy (Niehoff, "Letter to Schick"; "Letter to John Carroll"). In his communication, President Niehoff quoted the *Catechism of the Catholic Church* as saying that GLBT individuals must be "accepted with respect, compassion, and sensitivity" and that "every sign of unjust discrimination in their regard should be avoided" (Niehoff, "Community"). Rather than expand the 6+ university's "legally mandated" EEO policy to include sexual orientation, President Niehoff suggested that the university community instead adopt a "Community Standards Statement," which would detail the university's favorable attitude toward GLBT individuals. In other words, President Niehoff believed that a Community Standards Statement would essentially perform the same work as amending the university's EEO policy. The President circulated a draft of this statement to the entire campus community with his February 2, 2010 letter and asked faculty, in particular, to "promulgate" the statement so that it could be adopted by semester's end (Niehoff, "Letter to John Carroll").

The text of President Niehoff's "Community Standards Statement Draft" addresses three primary topics: 1. The Catholic Church's stance against discrimination of "more vulnerable and marginalized members" of the community, 2. the Catholic Church's moral teaching on sexual activity, and 3. the reasons why amending the university's non-discrimination policy is an "unwise and inappropriate" action. In regard to this last topic, the statement cites as its rationale the imprecise legal definition of the terms involved, the difficulty of codifying societal attitudes, and the concern that "John Carroll University must always and will always avoid any attempts by external civil judicial bodies to determine how it may or may not conduct itself according to its special religious identity" (Niehoff, "Community").

While faculty members discussed how best to respond to President Niehoff's decision and whether to pursue official channels (as was done with the initial resolution) or to enact a more powerful challenge, several John Carroll University students took action immediately. The setting they chose for their protest was a "Jesuit Spotlight" basketball game where a prestigious faith-based student service award, the St. Edmund Campion Award, would be presented at half time. Due to the ceremony and theme, it was rumored that many of the university's high-ranking administrators, members of the board of directors, and Jesuits would be in attendance. On the night of February 3, 2010, a courageous group of John Carroll University students and alumni held rainbow flags and marched onto the university's basketball court following the award ceremony. They sat down in the middle of the court and sang together until they were physically escorted out, one by one, by campus security. This first stage of the LGBTQ protest lasted less than nine minutes in total, but its impact on John Carroll University's community will resound for decades to come.

On that February night, there were many more students involved in the protest than those who sat and sang on the court. Several students were positioned in the audience with flyers that they handed out as the protesters took to the court, which explained the reasons behind the demonstration. Still other students were prepared to offer support after the protest was over, not knowing what the punishment would be for the demonstrators and what kinds of logistical assistance they would need.

The protesters and their allies came from a variety of social locations and demographics, and so theirs was a coalitional politics that used diversity as a resource for their activism. The activists included practicing Catholics and non-Catholics as well as those who identify as LGBTQ and others who identify as heterosexual. A number of the activists were leaders in the African American Student Alliance and the Latin American Student Alliance, and others were residents of the Living Simply environmental justice community. When I asked the activists if these intersectional coalitions were intentional organizing strategies, they responded that students from all of these marginalized groups were already friends with each other. The formation of such personal and political coalitions between members of seemingly distinct oppressed groups prior to and during the LGBTQ protest likely reflects a felt awareness of the ways that sexism, homophobia, racism, and speciesism are often interwoven in the fabric of John Carroll's Catholic institutional culture, which is in turn tied to a metaphysical view of identity categories that many felt may be at odds with cultivating social justice.

News of the protest spread quickly, thanks to the many advances of this technological age. One individual filmed the entire protest, which is now readily viewable on YouTube and had garnered 28,000 views by the time that this chapter was written, 10,000 of which occurred during the first week following the protest.[8] The *Cleveland Plain Dealer* wrote an article on the protest, a segment about the protest aired on the local news, links to the protest were being distributed on LGBTQ listservs across the country, and Perez Hilton posted the news on his celebrity gossip website.[9] President Niehoff flew back from a funeral he was attending in Jamaica on short notice to address the situation and held an emergency meeting with the campus community on the morning of Sunday, February 7, 2010. At that meeting, students expressed well-crafted arguments about the need for the inclusion and recognition of LGBTQ individuals in the university's policies and practices. Students also made it clear to all present at that meeting that they would not stop demanding justice until the university changed its EEO policy.[10]

In the weeks that followed, the students formed an unofficial student organization called the "Concerned Collective," which, among many other activities, staged a round-the-clock hunger fast in the Student Center Atrium and organized its members to remain standing at evening mass each Sunday until the EEO policy was changed. Such actions eventually led to the students being allowed to speak at the March 10, 2010 meeting of the university's board of directors and present their case. However, during the month between the protest and the board of directors meeting, the student activists weathered much hostility from other students in person and online, including the formation of a Facebook group designed to counter the work of the LGBTQ activists and allies called "Bringing Back JCU." Many of the students also received formal warnings from administrators that stated that the conduct process would be initiated if their protests interfered with classes, activities, and the overall functioning of the university.

Despite these hardships, the Concerned Collective prevailed at the board of directors meeting. The board supported the student's views, and the university's EEO policy was scheduled to be changed in September of 2010. Ultimately, however, the policy change was never implemented. The university community and the student activists believed that the change had occurred due to the fact that a policy labeled "Equal Employment Opportunity Policy" that was inclusive of the phrase "sexual orientation" was posted on the university's website on August 5, 2010.[11] A story even ran in the *Cleveland Plain Dealer* reporting that the policy had been changed (Farkas and Gillispie, 2011). But the online policy document of August 5, 2010 was then incrementally changed so that by October of 2010, it no longer referenced employment. Moreover, by this time, it was called the "Non-Discrimination Policy" rather than "Equal Employment Opportunity Policy." Because only the latter would be legally binding, many questioned whether the policy change had occurred as directed. The university administration would not lend clarity to the matter and so an ad hoc faculty governance committee consisting of seven members was formed and charged with determining whether the policy had indeed been changed. After a year-long investigation, the committee concluded in their final report of May 2012 that the university's EEO policy had never actually been changed to include sexual orientation, despite website postings that suggested otherwise (John Carroll University Faculty Council Ad Hoc Committee, 2012). The university administration did not confirm the faculty committee's findings until after the protesters had graduated in May 2012. Thus, the majority of the student protesters left John Carroll University believing that their activism had effected structural change at the level of the university's EEO policy, even though this was not the case.

II. THE INTERSECTIONS OF SEXISM AND HETEROSEXISM

One of the great benefits of teaching courses on diversity and oppression at a Jesuit Catholic institution is that the students are by and large already committed to the aims of social justice and to the belief that they are in part responsible for ensuring equity and justice in their communities. For example, during the 2009–2010 academic year when the LGBTQ protest took place, John Carroll students performed 38,788 hours of community service, which is significant considering that total university enrollment, including graduate students, is roughly 3,700. The majority of these students take seriously the task that Jesuit priest Pedro Arrupe has termed becoming "men and women for others" (Arrupe, 1973).[12] This attitude can in turn provide a ready entry into the perspectives and struggles of oppressed/resistant individuals and marginalized groups

Although cultivating social justice is an essential part of the university's mission and curriculum, there are multiple ways to interpret this core value, some of which are more effective than others. Specifically, it makes a world of difference, both in the overall campus climate and the impact of social justice initiatives, whether the university's mission is informed by an "additive" analysis of oppression or an "intersectional" analysis. One of the main reasons that the LGBTQ protest occurred is because the institution was operating with an additive metaphysics of identity, and its students—the protesters and their allies—were operating with an intersectional view.

The concept of "intersectionality" represents what is probably the most significant advance in feminist theory in the last three decades. Kimberlé Williams Crenshaw was one of the first theorists to use the term in her account of rape and domestic violence, specifically as these abuses pertain to black women, whose experiences have been repeatedly marginalized by those accounts that take racism and sexism to be distinct oppressions (Crenshaw, 1989, 1991).[13] Whereas an intersectional approach to oppression makes visible the unique kinds of discrimination that a person located at the crossroads of two or more oppression experiences, an additive analysis tends to see each oppression (and social identity) as separate from the others. For example, according to the additive view, a student who is a black woman is potentially subject to at least *two* kinds of oppression due to her identity: sexism and racism. In this analysis, it is theoretically possible to eliminate sexism on campus, but still have racism, and vice versa. It is also theoretically possible for a person to be sexist but not be racist, and to be racist but not be sexist. Alternatively, an intersectional analysis suggests that the characters of racism and sexism change in fundamental ways when they crisscross in the lives of women of color. Intersectional theory maintains that not only is a black woman likely to experience sexism differently than a white woman, but racism and sexism are intertwined oppressions. In other words, the eradication of one oppression necessarily depends on the eradication of the other.

Given the above descriptions, it is logically consistent for a person who holds an additive analysis of oppression to believe in the social justice mission of the university in some areas and at the same time believe that because John Carroll is a Catholic university it need not include sexual orientation in its EEO policy. Such a person could also believe that not including sexual orientation in the university's EEO policy in no way affects the university's stance on racism, ageism, sexism, religious discrimination, ableism, and those "other" oppressions listed in its current policy. However, a person who operates according to an intersectional analysis of oppression could not logically hold all of these beliefs at the same time. Indeed, this person would find the social justice orientation of the university mission and the drive to fight against certain "model" oppressions like racism and sexism thoroughly incompatible with the exclusion of sexual orientation from the university's EEO policy. After all, there are LGBTQ individuals who are women, people of color, veterans, people of diverse faiths, and people of different abilities. More important, as the coalition that was the Concerned Collective demonstrated, the metaphysical system that abets one oppression, like sexism, is the very same system that supports other oppressions, such as racism and heterosexism.

Suzanne Pharr locates the intersections of sexism and heterosexism in the common tools of domination that propel them, such as economic exploitation, threats of violence, and normalizing disciplinary techniques like stereotyping, blaming, isolating, and assimilating (1997, 5).[14] Although I agree that seemingly distinct oppressions often share a reliance on such techniques, I ultimately think that such an analysis allows for too much contingency in regard to the connections between oppressions. Just because two oppressions work according to the same technologies of domination does not mean that having the beliefs or attitudes necessary for one entails having the beliefs and attitudes necessary for the other, or that one is an integral component of the other. I think that the circumstances of the LGBTQ protest make the mutual entailment of sexism and heterosexism especially discernible and therefore provide us with important tools to extend our ideas about the mechanisms of intersectionality and the mutual entailment of oppressions.

As Michel Foucault indicates in *The History of Sexuality*, Catholic teaching and practice often codifies in explicit ways the relationships between productive power, social norms, and sex that are operative but less perceptible in wider society (1978).[15] I believe that the Catholic context of the LGBTQ protest gave heightened visibility to the way that normative power was/is functioning to control the university population and that this is partly why so many individuals on both sides of the debate had such strong reactions to the issue. In what was, for the protesters and their allies the most incendiary paragraph of President Niehoff's "Community Standards Statement Draft," he writes,

> Not only does the University call upon each and every one of its members to respect and honor all other members as brothers and sisters in one Lord God, it also draws to the attention of all its members the traditional Catholic moral teaching that properly locates sexual activity within the relationship of a man and a woman united for life through marriage as husband and wife. Our religious identity therefore impels us to recognize the norm of chastity for everyone, whether homosexual or heterosexual, just as that same identity likewise impels us to recognize the norm of universal love and respect. (Niehoff, 2010)

Reading this passage, we cannot help but notice the affirmation of traditional gender roles throughout. In the same document that states that "transgender students, faculty, staff, and administrators are welcome members of the University community, as the children of God they are," President Niehoff calls upon the campus community to respect its members *as brothers and sisters*. The proclamation thus disappears transgender individuals at the same time that it speaks for their inclusion. Moreover, the gender roles that this passage affirms are explicitly heteronormative, for a woman is identified with her ability to become a "wife"—one who desires to be united to a man for life through the sacrament of marriage. This narrow interpretation of sexual difference not only excludes lesbian, gay, bisexual, and transgender individuals from having a sex (is a lesbian a woman or a man, according to this view?) and therefore from participating in "proper sexual activity," but also excludes any individual who is "queer," in the literal sense of the term as "straying from the norm," as is the case with unmarried individuals, asexuals, tomboys, and others.

If, along with thinkers such as Monique Wittig (1992) and Judith Butler (1990), we take seriously the idea that a person's language, concepts, and structures of thinking help to constitute her reality, her behaviors, and her planes of possibility—and as an educational institution we *must*, for dismissing such an idea undermines our reasons for being—then we are compelled to strive to think, speak, and model liberatory words and concepts in all of our activities. We are obliged not only to be cognizant of the literal meanings of what we say, but also of the *performative* meanings of our speech and of the discriminatory categories of thought with which our speech tallies. Although the "Community Standards Statement Draft" was explicitly intended as a document of inclusion, it also performed exclusion as a result of its conceptual structure and underlying metaphysical commitments, which embrace and naturalize traditional sex roles and the primacy of heterosexual unions that are sanctioned by church *and* state.

The performative hierarchies and exclusions present in the language of the first sentence of President Niehoff's words quoted above are further entrenched by its second sentence, which enacts a curious deconstruction of its predecessor. According to the first sentence, the proper location of sexual activity is within heterosexual marriage and yet, by way of the second sentence, we are told that there is a "norm" of chastity for *everyone*. Unless President Niehoff is equating chastity with heterosexual marriage, there are at least two community standards operative in the passage: One for heterosexual, married individuals who are permitted to transgress the norm, and one for everyone else, who are not permitted any transgressions. If this interpretation is correct, then the tone of the passage is potentially captured by the famous Orwellian phrase, "All animals are equal, but some are more equal than others" (Orwell, 2003). Even if chastity is expected in marriage outside of "procreative" activities, that chastity and its transgressions are not surveyed and disciplined in the same way as they are in regard to non-heteronormative members of the community. A case in point is "the distinctions between sexual orientation and sexual conduct essential to Catholic teaching" that President Niehoff cited as a justification for not amending the university's EEO policy (2010a). A charitable reading of this idea is that homosexual orientations are welcomed and accepted, but actually engaging in homosexual sexual activity is not. The change in the EEO policy that the faculty had requested mentions "sexual orientation" rather than "sexual conduct" and rightfully so, for it would be absurd (not to mention illegal and likely immoral) to examine a faculty member's actual sexual practices to see whether that individual should be protected under the university's EEO policy. However, President Niehoff's deployment of the distinction between sexual *orientation* and sexual *conduct* indicates that LGBTQ individuals occupy a different moral category than heterosexual individuals in regard to the "norm" of chastity. From a purely logical perspective, the mention of sexual conduct in this context would make sense only if it were fueled by a belief that either 1. LGBTQ individuals are less likely to comply with the "norm" of chastity than heterosexual individuals, and that protecting them in the EEO policy would therefore be tantamount to sanctioning violations of Catholic teaching or 2. when LGBTQ individuals violate the "norm of chastity for *everyone*," it is of much greater concern than when heterosexual individuals do so and that therefore it is more important for institutional structures to regulate the activities of those individuals through its official sanctions and exclusions. In the absence of a conceptual structure that entails the differential treatment of those with heterosexual and non-heterosexual orientations vis-à-vis the norm of chastity, we would be hard-pressed to find a reason why sexual conduct would be relevant to a discussion about changing the university's EEO policy.

The use of the word "norm" in the passage speaks to this point, for it does not appear that "norm" is being used in a descriptive sense to say that it is "normal" for people (and college students, in particular) to either be chaste or to confine sex within heterosexual marriage. Rather, the term is used here to indicate that chastity is a "norm" in the Foucauldian sense: a standard of behavior by which people measure themselves and others and toward which the community and the institution aspires.[16] My concern is that when the "norm" of chastity is spoken about in conjunction with the pronouncement that "the proper location of sexual activity" is heterosexual marriage, the norm will most likely become operational in the community only as a means to police and discipline the behavior of those individuals who cannot be seen as part of a vision of heterosexual marriage. Read thus, the language of the "Community Standards Statement Draft" at best sends a mixed message about who is included in all of the protections of the community, and at worst performatively sanctions discriminatory behavior against non-heteronormative community members.

We can see from this brief analysis of the ideas animating President Niehoff's "Community Standards Statement Draft" that sexism and heterosexism are related, not simply because they both work according to norms backed by institutional power, but because the metaphysical views about sexual difference required by one are the same views that enable the other. This kind of metaphysical exposure is the power of an intersectional analysis and its importance in resisting multiple, intertwined oppressions. Inherent in President Niehoff's proclamation that the "proper location" of sexual activity is between husband and wife is not only an affirmation of the primacy of heterosexuality, but also a vision of the "proper woman" and the "proper man." The concepts of "woman" and "man" that are proliferated in heteronormative culture always already involve a heterosexual orientation, as well as images of race, age, and ability. Indeed, in the academic world of the twenty-first century, the assumed attribute of hetero-desire is perhaps the most efficient way to demarcate the stereotypical categories of "woman" and "man." Not only does a heterosexist orientation necessarily entail believing, however consciously or implicitly, in some version of hard and fast sexual difference, but it also entails the belief that these "hard and fast" differential ontological groups warrant differential treatment *and* differential regulation.

According to this intersectional interpretation, it is easy to see why an institution that would address sexual assault on campus by suggesting restrictions on women's behavior would also choose to exclude sexual orientation from its EEO policy. These are not separate issues, but symptoms of the same underlying metaphysical structure. If one believes that women are essentially different kinds of beings than men, especially in regard to men's purportedly uncontrollable desire to transgress "the norm of chastity for everyone," then it would make sense that one would also believe that regulating women's behavior is the most efficient way to prevent sexual assault on campus. Bound up with this kind of institutional response to sexual violence and its embrace of normative and naturalized sex categories is also the assumption that sexual violence is always *hetero*sexual violence, thus disappearing students who are survivors of same-sex violence or family violence or priest violence, or who are harassed and threatened due to their sexual orientations. In like manner, responding to concerns that LGBTQ members are excluded from the community by offering community standards that affirm (that is, offer special protection to) the social locations of "husband" and "wife" and their college-aged precursors encourages the disproportionate surveillance of the sexual conduct, however broadly defined, of LGBTQ individuals and "un-wifely" women over that of others. In both cases, the intentions to protect women and LGBTQ individuals and include them centrally in the activities and visions of the university are co-opted by a metaphysics of sexual difference that performs the differential treatment and regulation of these groups. I also suspect that the same phenomenon of dissonance between institutional proclamations of racial inclusion, on the one hand, and institutional concepts and practices girded by ideas that race, like sex, constitutes a "natural" or *metaphysical* difference, on the other, helped lay the groundwork and create the opening for "the racial incident" on campus that targeted African American custodian Nelson Robinson.[17]

III. COALITION AND DISAGREEMENT WITHIN THE CONCERNED COLLECTIVE

In addition to addressing the problem of how best to understand the intersections of oppressions, the LGBTQ protest made manifest the usefulness and necessity of forming political coalitions amid pronounced differences in social, political, and religious identities. Although this coalitional strategy proved tremendously effective, it was not without its difficulties along the way.

The Concerned Collective was very nearly fragmented at times over the question of which tactics to use to meet their goals, as well as that of whether to have movement leaders or a coalitional collective without hierarchy. The students held no illusions that changing the university's EEO policy would in itself fix all of the problems with the exclusion, marginalization, and intolerance of underrepresented groups in the campus culture. As a result, their organizing involved many debates about whether to ask for additional structural changes alongside their one demand that the policy be amended. In the end, the Concerned Collective settled on fighting only for the policy change because such an amendment would serve a symbolic function in addition to providing actual legal protection for LGTBQ persons. This singular focus was strategic, because it both made clear to the administration what was desired and struck at the very core of the university's metaphysics, which underlay its policy decisions. If the metaphysical belief in heterosexual difference could be shaken, then, according to an intersectional analysis of oppressions, the conceptual ground of other purportedly natural metaphysical differences might also give way.

Another site of discussion within the Concerned Collective involved disagreement about whether to employ reformist activist tactics that worked within the formalized guidelines of the institution or radical tactics that sought to express ideas that would not be condoned or facilitated by those guidelines. In the end, the group chose to deploy both kinds of tactics strategically in complementary ways. For example, a subgroup of students who would present arguments in favor of amending the university's policies to the board of directors formed within the Collective. Their calls for the board of directors to act in accord with the university's Jesuit Catholic mission represent reformist activist tactics at their best. As these students were preparing their arguments, other students were demonstrating, fasting, and raising awareness at what they came to call "Camp Hope"—a well-trafficked area in the atrium of the Student Center that they made sure was occupied by student activists twenty-four hours a day. This was no simple task, given the series of new prohibitions that the administration levied on this space during this time, including a restriction against bringing furniture into that area, which meant that those individuals on a hunger strike could not sit down, and an injunction that the area be vacated from 3:00 a.m. until 5:30 a.m. for cleaning. The Concerned Collective had additional radical strategies organized and ready to be implemented should the board of directors decide against amending the university's policies. This combination of reformist and radical tactics was highly effective in achieving the Concerned Collective's goals, and did so in a very short time.[18] In recognizing multiple ways of proceeding, it also encouraged individual members of the Collective to participate in the styles of activism that respectively suited them best. The group did not turn away those who wanted to be involved and did not demand that everyone employ the same strategies to achieve their common goal. This coalitional inclusiveness fueled the efficacy of their activism.

IV. THE PEDAGOGICAL POTENTIALS OF ACTIVISM

The student protesters and the Concerned Collective not only exposed the John Carroll community to several "teaching moments," but also taught us vital lessons about the meaning of the university's mission, the theory and practice of activism, and the importance of responding to injustice in ways that are jointly reflective *and* courageous. In addition to recognizing what these students have done for our university community, I would also like to offer some pedagogical remarks about what participating in activism can do for the students themselves, especially if that activism is integrated with the university's curriculum.

First, offering opportunities for activism in one's courses and supporting community activism outside of the university's official program of study encourages students to take responsibility for their own learning by identifying what issues are important to them and designing and executing methods for addressing those issues. Activist experiences therefore foster creativity in students and provide them with opportunities to be engaged participants in their own learning.

Second, activist projects invite students to have first-hand experiences organizing, communicating, and cultivating relationships with other people, many of whom may have different ways of looking at the world. Such practical, experiential learning helps to prepare students for work in a variety of different careers and for life in general.

Finally, activist experiences frequently empower students to trust their own beliefs more than they ever have before and inspire them to follow their greatest hopes and dreams. I suspect that the impact of their actions on John Carroll's community will result in students who are less likely to doubt their ability to make a difference and less likely to question the importance of their contributions to the world. What the LGBTQ protest taught its participants is an invaluable lesson: that they can make a difference if they work together and refuse to give up. Although John Carroll's EEO policy was never actually amended to include sexual orientation, the campus community did change for the better due to the actions of the Concerned Collective. And many of the coalitions that were forged as a result of their activism—between radical feminists and gay men, students of color and white students, Latin American and African American students, environmentalists and consumers, reformists and radicals, Catholics and atheists, teachers and students—are still ongoing to this day.

Approximately two months prior to the protest in December of 2009, more than one LGBTQ student told faculty members that they had experienced harassment and threats of violence by other students in their dormitories in regard to their sexual orientation. Just as with the sexual assault incidents of 2004, there was concern that the institutional structure was not as supportive as it could be of victims of homophobic and heterosexist harassment and violence. A group of concerned faculty members organized and decided that one way that the faculty could effect positive changes in the campus climate was to develop and team-teach the course Introduction to Queer Studies, which would provide students with a scholarly setting where LGBTQ voices and perspectives could be acknowledged and engaged. Like The Philosophy of Love and Sex course, Queer Studies occupies the border of theory and practice and provides a space where current theoretical scholarship can be put into conversation with concrete local realities that effect personal lives and the very constitution of a community.

Although many members of John Carroll's community believe that including sexual orientation in the university's EEO policy is the right thing to do, it is important that we strive to articulate *why* it is the right thing to do as a community. It is also important that we continue to discuss justifications for the protesters' actions, especially in light of new information that the policy was never actually amended. This chapter offers one interpretation of why it is right for any institution that seeks to undermine oppression to include sexual orientation in its EEO policy. Moreover, this chapter considers why the activist strategies employed by the Concerned Collective were largely successful. Both explanations hinge on recognizing an intersectional metaphysics whereby the identity categories necessary to maintain one oppression, such as heterosexism, are also entailed by those necessary to sustain other oppressions, such as sexism and racism. If an intersectional analysis is on track, then it is no wonder that the everyday experiences of students who belong to seemingly disparate marginalized groups on a Catholic campus—LGBTQ students, feminists, women, people of color, and their allies—intertwined in such a way during the LGBTQ protest so as to form the basis for a radical, powerful, and lasting coalition. Only through having these conversations as a community and integrating theory and practice, thought and performance, scholarship and policy, and metaphysics and politics will we be able to envision and enact the kind of inclusive campus toward which the activism of the Concerned Collective points us. And only by encouraging the continuous reversibility of teacher and student—by encouraging students to self-direct and self-motivate the learning of their academic community—will we be able to engage these conversations to their fullest potential and to reach ours, both as individuals and as an educational community.

The actions of the Concerned Collective reveal that social justice must be tied to metaphysical beliefs that support and proliferate that vision. Their cause was not simply to change an institutional policy; they aimed to change the institution's very structures of thought. These students knew that in order to effect change, they would need a political practice that was informed by theory and a theoretical orientation relevant to practical ends. The Concerned Collective thus articulated and performed a metaphysics of social justice and, in so doing, embodied education at its finest—theirs was a practical, liberatory, and coalitional pedagogy that showed us all a way to a more just world.

NOTES

I would first and foremost like to thank the courageous students and alumni who organized and participated in the LGBTQ protest for igniting dialogue and change in John Carroll's community. Conversations with the students in my spring 2010 Philosophy of Love and Sex course and students in the first Queer Studies course taught at John Carroll during the spring of 2011 also helped me to formulate many of the ideas presented here. In addition, I am sincerely grateful to those students and faculty members who participated in discussions with me about this chapter at various stages in its evolution. They include Alix Audi, Chris Axelrod, Sephora Fadiga, Peter Hayden, Kevin Henderson, Kristen Kolenz, Barrie Landrock, Courtney Miller, Anastasia Mitchell, Marissa Patsey, Mindy Peden, Natalie Terry, Andy Trares, and Bridie Wyrock. Andy Trares, in particular, clarified many of the details of the events for me. Finally, students Brian Bayer and Nick Wojtasik helped me to find the articles on the sexual assaults of 2004 from the *Carroll News* archives.

1 For relevant news stories on these events, see (Galbincea, 2004), (Tinsley, 2004), (Hoener, 2004), (Brett, 2004), (Schwan, 2005), ("John Carroll Informs Students"), ("JCU Students Come Together to Stop Sexual Assaults"), and ("John Carroll University, OH: Rape/Sexual Assault).

2 For example, one news article reports that "some [students] suggested that victims should be allowed to report attacks to someone who wouldn't intimidate them" ("JCU Students Come Together to Stop Sexual Assaults"). Another quotes student Nathan Szabo as saying, "Something needs to be changed and it can't be solved by an e-mail and a simple meeting" (Tinsley, 2004).

3 For scholarly discussions of the concept "rape culture," see (Buchwald et al., 1993). As a result of the community response to the events of 2004, John Carroll's institutional support structures for survivors of intimate violence have improved considerably in the past ten years. For example, in 2008 Student Affairs won a competitive grant from the United States Department of Justice Program to Reduce Domestic Violence, Dating Violence, Sexual Assault and Stalking. This grant helped John Carroll University to create and staff a Violence Prevention and Action Center, which runs a 24-hour violence hotline and organizes a variety of educational activities for students.

4 See (Dombroski, 2004), as well as the sources cited in note 1.

5 See (Dombroski, 2004).

6 LGBTQ is a commonly used acronym that stands for "lesbian, gay, bisexual, transgender and/or transsexual, and queer and/or questioning."

7 Jeremy Bryan Coats was a graduate student and research assistant in the English Department who was asked to compile this information for the University's Institutional Task Force on Diversity. This study subsequently became a subject

of controversy as the events that I detail below began to unfold because the study mentions Xavier University on the list of Jesuit universities that include sexual orientation in their employment policies. Whereas Xavier University does address sexual orientation in its *Student Handbook 2010–2011* (p. 6), it does not include sexual orientation in its EEO policy. Thus, the question as to whether this confusion was made in the case of any of the other Jesuit schools was raised by John Carroll's president and administrators. The confusion is largely a result of different universities labeling their EEO policies differently. In 2008, John Carroll University was also referring to its EEO policy as its "non-discrimination policy," but by fall of 2011 it had two separate policies, one for each label, with the former referring to employment and the latter pertaining to an internal institutional guideline.

8   "John Carroll University GLBT Protest" at http://www.youtube.com/watch?v=Nc3er geeZok.
9   See (Oboken, 2010), (Hilton, 2010), and (Gaffney, 2010).
10 Senior Andy Trares is quoted saying as much in (Oboken, 2010).
11 The amended policy was posted on August 5, 2010 at http://www.jcu.edu/fas/docs/hrpolicies/EO_Policy.pdf. A copy of the posted policy can be found in the final report of John Carroll University Ad Hoc Committee on the Equal Employment Opportunity Policy (2012).
12 Note that this famous Jesuit phrase affirms a binary metaphysics of sexual difference.
13 For other relevant analyses of the concept of intersectionality, see (Davis, 2008), (Garry, 2011), (Lugones, 2007, 2010), and (McAll, 2005).
14 See also (Adams, 1990), who offers a similar analysis of the relationship between oppressions, especially in chapter two.
15 See especially Foucault's discussion of the sacrament of confession (1978, pp. 18–20). For an account of the differences between productive power and restrictive power, see Foucault's analysis of lepers and plague victims in *Abnormal: Lectures at the Collège de France 1974–1975* (2003, pp. 31–54). I am grateful to Dr. Dianna Taylor for pointing me to this last reference by teaching about it in John Carroll's first Queer Studies course, which was offered in the spring of 2011.
16 See, for example, (Foucalt, 2003, pp. 162–63). Again, I am grateful to Dr. Dianna Taylor for pointing me in the direction of this reference in her January 20, 2010 lecture to the team-taught "Queer Studies" course at John Carroll University.
17 For descriptions of an alternative metaphysics that can support social justice by rejecting sexual and racial essentialisms while nonetheless acknowledging bodily and social differences, see McWeeny (2013, 2014).
18 For an account of how a similar mixture of tactics functioned successfully in the anti-rape movement, see (Bevaqua, 2001).

WORKS CITED

Adams, Carol J. *The Sexual Politics of Meat: A Feminist-Vegetarian Critical Theory.* New York: Continuum, 1990. Print.
Arrupe, Pedro. "Address to the Tenth International Congress of Jesuit Alumni of Europe." Valencia, Spain. 31 July 1973. Speech.
Bevaqua, Maria. "Anti-rape Coalitions: Radical, Liberal, Black, and White Feminists Challenging Boundaries." *Forging Radical Alliances across Difference: Coalition Politics for the New Millennium.* Ed. Jill M. Bystydzienski and Steven P. Schacht. Lanham, Maryland: Rowman & Littlefield, 2001. 163–176. Print.

Brett, Regina. "Assault Allegations Change John Carroll Image." *Cleveland Plain Dealer* 10 (Dec 2004): n. pag. Print.

Buchwald, Emilie, Pamela R. Fletcher, and Martha Roth, Ed. *Transforming a Rape Culture*. Minneapolis, MN: Milkweed, 1993. Print.

Butler, Judith. *Gender Trouble: Feminism and the Subversion of Identity*. New York: Routledge, 1990. Print.

Coats, Jeremy Bryan. "Study of Non-Discrimination Policies: Jesuit and NOCHE Four-year Colleges and Universities." 28 June 2008. Print.

Crenshaw, Kimberlé Williams. "Demarginalizing the Intersection of Race and Sex: A Black Feminist Critique of Antidiscrimination Doctrine, Feminist Theory and Antiracist Politics." *University of Chicago Legal Forum* 140 (1989): 139–167.

Crenshaw, Kimberlé Williams. "Mapping the Margins: Intersectionality, Identity Politics, and Violence against Women of Color." *Stanford Law Review* 43.6 (1991): 1241–1299.

Davis, Kathy. "Intersectionality as Buzzword: A Sociology of Science Perspective on What Makes a Feminist Theory Successful." *Feminist Theory* 9 (2008): 67–85.

Dombroski, Dana M. "JCU Students Take a Stand against Sexual Violence." *Cleveland Indy Media Center*. 6 Dec 2004. Web. 7 July 2015.

Farkas, Karen, and Mark Gillispie. "Students Got JCU to Change the Institution's Bias Policy." *Cleveland Plain Dealer*. Jan 24 2011. Print.

Foucault, Michel. *Abnormal: Lectures at the Collège de France 1974–1975*. New York: Picador, 2003. Print.

Gaffney, Emily. "Mixed Feelings about LGBT Methods." *Carroll News*. 18 Feb 2010. Print.

Galbincea, Barb. "JCU Investigates Assault Reports: Women Haven't Filed Complaints or Charges." *Cleveland Plain Dealer*. 4 Dec 2004: n. pag. Print.

Garry, Ann. "Intersectionality, Metaphors, and the Multiplicity of Gender." *Hypatia* 26.4 (2011): 826–850.

Harshbarger, John. "What Can the John Carroll Community Do to Prevent Sexual Assault?" Memo to All John Carroll University Students, Faculty, Staff, and Administrators. 1 Dec 2004. E-mail.

Hilton, Perez. *Perez Hilton*. N.p., nd. Web. 8 Feb 2010.

Hoener, Greg. "Four Sexual Assaults Reported." *Carroll News* 9 Dec 2004: n. pag. Print.

Institutional Task Force on Diversity. "Final Report." Oct 2009. Print.

John Carroll University Faculty Council. "Resolution for Non-Discrimination of Persons Based on Sexual Orientation in the Workplace." 8 Oct 2008. Print.

John Carroll University Faculty Council Ad Hoc Committee on the Equal Employment Opportunity Statement. "Final Report." 2 May 2012. Print.

Lugones, María. "Heterosexualism and the Colonial/Modern Gender System." *Hypatia* 22.1 (2007): 186–209. Print.

Lugones, María. "Toward a Decolonial Feminism." *Hypatia* 25.4 (2010): 742–759.

McAll, Leslie. "The Complexity of Intersectionality." *Signs* 30.3 (2005): 1771–1800. Print.

McWeeny, Jennifer. "Feminist Ontology for the Twenty-first Century." *Hypatia* 15 November 2013. Hypatiaphilosophy.org. Web. 7 July 2015.

McWeeny, Jennifer. "Topographies of Flesh: Women, Nonhuman Animals, and the Embodiment of Connection and Difference." *Hypatia* 29.2 (2014): 269–286. Print.

Niehoff, Robert L. Community Standards Statement Draft. 2 February 2010. E-mail Enclosure.

Niehoff, Robert L. "Inauguration Address." Jcu.edu/president. John Carroll University. 11 Oct 2005. Web. 13 Oct 2015.

Niehoff, Robert L. "Letter to Dr. Paul Shick, Chair of the Faculty Council." 27 January 2010. Print.

Niehoff, Robert L. "Letter to John Carroll University Students, Faculty, Staff, and Administrators." 2 Feb 2010. E-mail.

Non-Discrimination/Equal Employment Opportunity Policy. "John Carroll University's Faculty Handbook." p. 18. Also in John Carroll University's Undergraduate Bulletin 2009–2011, p. 2. Print.

Oboken, Janet. "Discord Grows at JCU over Anti-Bias Policy that Excludes Gays." *Cleveland Plain Dealer*, 6 Feb 2010: n. pag. Print.

Orwell, George. *Animal Farm*. New York: Plume, 2003. Print.

Pharr, Suzanne. *Homophobia: A Weapon of Sexism*. Berkeley, California: Chardon Press, 1997. Print.

Rombalski, Patrick, and Sherri Crahen. "Memo to All John Carroll University Students, Faculty, Staff, and Administrators." 1 Dec 2004. E-mail.

Schwan, Lisa. "Sexual Assault Suspect Expelled." *Carroll News*. 27 Jan 2005: n. pag. Print.

Tinsley, Jesse. "JCU Students Plan Demonstration over Sexual Assaults." *Cleveland Plain Dealer*. 7 Dec 2004: n. pag. Print.

"Vision, Mission, Core Values and Strategic Initiatives Statement." John Carroll University Undergraduate Bulletin, 2009–2011: 7. Print.

Wittig, Monique. "The Straight Mind." *The Straight Mind and Other Essays*. Boston: Beacon Press, 1992: 21–32. Print.

WORKS CONSULTED

Foucault, Michel. *The History of Sexuality, Vol. 1*. Trans. Robert Hurley. New York: Vintage Books, 1978. Print.

"JCU Students Come Together to Stop Sexual Assaults." WKYC.com. 7 Dec 2004. Web. 7 Dec 2004

"John Carroll Informs Students of Three Sexual Assaults." WKYC.com. 2 Dec 2004. Web. 3 Dec 2004.

"John Carroll University, OH: Rape/Sexual Assault." Campus Incident Reports. *Campus Watch* 12.1: 6. Print.

Response: Prevailing Values amidst Seasonal Activism

Latona F. Disher

John Carroll University ranked number seven on the *US News & World Report*'s list of best colleges in 2014 as a regional university in the Midwest. Named after the first Catholic bishop in America, this private, Jesuit institution found itself in a firestorm of cultural controversy a mere decade ago amidst the campus response to four sexual assaults. It was common opinion that the John Carroll administration did not adequately demonstrate care and support to the victims of the sexual assaults. Yet, the institutional structure's attempt at decreasing vulnerabilities to date rape was interpreted as insensitive and devoid of the growing sentiment of the day. According to Dr. Jennifer McWeeny (2011), an academic scholar of causes and preventions to sexual violence extracted from feminist theory, critical race theory, and queer theory, the best solution was to inject the academic culture with the forced acceptance of ideologies that were inferred to be rejected upon enrollment. McWeeny's (2011) assumptions that feminist theory was the cure-all for the situation at hand then, and that feminist theory would be later used to change the campus culture and prevent intimate violence are not the cultural shingles that the John Carroll campus is proudly waiving today. Instead, they tout in the *US News & World Report* safety and security services such as 24-hour foot and vehicle patrols, late-night transport/escort services, 24-hour emergency telephones, lighted pathways/sidewalks, and controlled residence hall access. These safety and security features are among the reasons that John Carroll University has had its largest freshman class in a decade for two consecutive years.

When parents assist their emerging adult child with the selection of a college to attend, security and safety features and crime statistics are key factors that are researched next to one's major. Teaching moments like those described by McWeeny (2011) in her writings point to the theory and practice of activism and how one responds to injustice with reflection and courage. Yet, what injustice was truly committed here? A softball response by the university administration that encouraged students to "choose the buddy system," "pour your own drink," and "communicate your desires clearly". This on its face is good advice. Could the university have said more? Sure, they could. Based on the current safety and security features and programs, they have done much more. Still, this is hardly an affirmation of rape culture. What I believe the university was doing here was encouraging each individual to increase his/her personal responsibility to decrease one's vulnerability to instances of sexual assault, pure and simple. Yet still, a decade later, the law in California is calling for written consent to sex on campus in order to change the game so that the "justice is in" and not stacked against survivors. So by stating that "yes means yes," this will upset the rape culture and teach males not to rape? Really? Pimping women out is the solution?

Further still, as Dr. McWeeny continued to look for issues of offense on campus at John Carroll some six years following the sexual assaults, students were encouraged to search for the same offenses and label it activism. Through this activism, students took on this learning of activism and tossed it back at the university in the form of an uprising at a popular, well-attended, campus-wide event because the non-discrimination policy did not include sexual orientation, an alternative practice that runs counter to the natural cycle of life, even though there was no action taken by the university to discriminate against this segment of the campus community. Still, these lifestyle choices are not in alignment with the core values (Christian) of the university. For example, a few of the university's core values are listed below and include a commitment to learning in order to create:

- An environment of inquiry that embraces Jesuit Catholic education as a search for truth where faith and reason complement each other in learning in pursuit of our educational mission, the university welcomes the perspective and participation in our mission of faculty, staff, students, and alumni of all faiths and of no faith.
- A rigorous approach to scholarship that instills in our graduates the knowledge, eloquence, sensitivity, and commitment to embrace and to live humane values.
- A campus committed to the intellectual, spiritual, emotional, and physical development of each student.
- An inclusive community where differing points of view and experiences are valued as opportunities for mutual learning. ("University")

These few values cited here do not exclude or shun the practice of alternative sexual lifestyles. If anything, they leave room for it. These values give this lifestyle a place to live. So why an uprising and total disruption of campus operations? And why does the school of thought on sexual orientation and the LGBTQ lifestyle discount the diversity of others? There is a demand for the acceptance of their own lifestyle, but a distain for the lifestyles of others, which thus shows them to be lacking in diversity.

John Carroll University, however, is an affirmative action, equal opportunity institution of higher education. The university is committed to diversity in the workplace and strongly encourages applications from women and minorities when employment opportunities arise. This information can be found on the John Carroll website and speaks to the position that the university holds concerning its faculty. Therefore, I am unclear about why faculty of the university would promote through their writings and coursework an activist uprising and disrupt the peaceful operations of an educational institution of higher learning. It is ironic how some groups self-represent as the voice of injustice, inequality, and tolerance. These constructs (i.e., injustice, inequality, and tolerance) would be best treated as diversity concepts and productively used to educate the students of John Carroll from a position from which they could all be engaged in diversity matters.

The topic of diversity matters remains on the education and management agenda in organizational and leadership development. This agenda and/ or diversity initiative is promoted vigorously within university and corporate organizational cultures. For an organization, the impact of a corporate diversity strategy is significant to its overall success. However, what is even more essential is a personal diversity strategy for students and leaders that has a significant impact on the university or corporate strategy.

Diversity matters in an organizational environment are often thought of in terms of demographics; yet, the topic extends beyond race, gender, and age. It can be addressed with regard to informational differences (i.e., education, experience, skills, etc.) and values or goals. Whether diversity is demographic, informational, and/or values-driven, the existence of diversity within a college campus or a workforce can create enhanced performance, as it is related to extraordinary results (Neale, Northcraft, and Jehn, 1999). In that light, the personal diversity aptitude of a student or a leader would enhance the leadership efforts of that student leader, thus having influence on followers and, ultimately, the organization at large. It is my opinion that this consideration was lost in the John Carroll example.

According to Maxwell (2002), leaders who celebrate diversity accomplish more. This works best when the leader builds a team spirit that goes beyond the commemoration of diverse differences and instead produces the celebration of unique differences. Team or student groups that celebrate versus commemorate diversity minimize conflict and increase cooperation, which generates efficacy and effectiveness among the community (Neale, Northcraft, and Jehn, 1999). McWeeny's perspective, a perspective taught to the activist students at John Carroll University, somehow missed out on this manner of diversity matters. Their activism, instead of unifying the campus, generated conflict and disruption.

In the next portion of this response, I will outline a personal diversity strategy that readers can use to examine their own behaviors. Applying such considerations introspectively and comparing them to the example of the protesting students at John Carroll will provide an alternative lens from which to view activism and or self-governance in relation to diversity issues.

In self-examination, consider whether you have a personal grasp on diversity matters. With your reply in mind, consider a set of leadership guidelines that can cause you to gain proficiency with, direct efforts to, and excel in matters of diversity. With or without your own personal philosophy, Table 5.1 presents a template of leadership principles that may be used as an introspective gauge to measure where you are in your personal leadership with diversity. The principles are cited and defined in Table 5.1. Following the table, three concepts are represented for self-analysis to measure your behaviors and practices in comparison to the definitions and in relation to the impact that these diversity matters have on your organizational system and your immediate team or group.

The guidelines in Table 5.1 provide a starting point for self-analysis. By further addressing the aforementioned diversity guidelines, perhaps the objectives and summary below will delve further into the matter of diversity. Review the features of each diversity principle and assess yourself according to the rating tool provided for each one.

Master Diversity: This point speaks to the intrinsic personal experiences that bring about a healthy perspective on the issue. In order to master diversity, you will need to have an honest assessment of the circumstances that impact your ability and/or inability to be objective with individuals that are different from and/or share aspects of your own diversity. Here is where you measure and correct, if necessary, the biases, prejudices, and or favoritisms that surround your leadership. Rate yourself in mastering diversity according to the following:

- Outstanding (exceeds in mastering diversity)
- Satisfactory (meets mastering diversity expectations)
- Marginal (meets most mastering diversity expectations)
- Unsatisfactory (does not meet mastering diversity expectations)

Manage Diversity: In today's university and corporate environment, students and leaders must be willing to identify and administer both small- and large-scale individual and organizational diversity. This involves the oversight of strategies for promoting diversity within the organization.

Table 5.1 Diversity Leadership Guidelines

Leadership Guideline	Definition
Master Diversity	To acquire and develop a sum of behaviors, public and private, that model an appreciation of individual differences
Manage Diversity	The implementation and incorporation of a diversity strategy to improve diversity representation
Maximize Diversity	The constant assessment, communication, benchmarking, and future planning with regard to diversity matters

Managing diversity also comprises practices such as the distribution of literature to other students and employees and the sponsoring of diversity training sessions. Other efforts include active advocacy for work/life situations (i.e., telecommuting, flextime, child care referrals, and tuition waivers/reimbursement) and the inclusion of diversity goals in performance reviews (CLC, 1999). Rate yourself in managing diversity according to the following:

- Outstanding (exceeds in managing diversity)
- Satisfactory (meets managing diversity expectations)
- Marginal (meets most managing diversity expectations)
- Unsatisfactory (does not meet managing diversity expectations)

Maximize Diversity: It takes courage to lead with excellence. A wise leader seeks a future of excellence for the whole organization, and compassion for each individual member (MacMillan, 2001). As for the leader that maximizes diversity, the focus is on how he/she approaches the matter. This focus typically includes a long-term strategy that yields constant results. Maximizing diversity encompasses mastering and managing diversity; it further includes creating departments and/or positions that concentrate exclusively upon diversity matters, ensuring that diverse candidates are trained for advancement, and promoting available positions within organizations while maintaining a minority focus (CLC, 1999). Furthermore, maximizing diversity incorporates ongoing qualitative and quantitative diversity audits based on current diversity demographics and patterns in the industry with the goal of exceeding the trends. As a leader in your department and in the development of women's studies curricula, rate yourself in maximizing diversity according to the following:

- Outstanding (exceeds in maximizing diversity)
- Satisfactory (meets maximizing diversity expectations)
- Marginal (meets most maximizing diversity expectations)
- Unsatisfactory (does not meet maximizing diversity expectations)

For leaders, there is an enormous responsibility with regard to diversity and leadership. Leaders should exemplify what is required of those that the lead. Followers often emulate leaders (Hackman and Johnson, 2000); therefore, the most effective processes and strategies regarding diversity will be spread throughout an organization whose leaders are personally set on adhering to research-driven diversity practices. In closing, mastering, managing, and maximizing diversity are qualities that are supported by research on organizational leadership development (CLC, 1999, 2001). The issues of unique differences and diversity have their origins in literature with eternal relevance: Scripture. A passage from the New Testament references informational distinctions among members of an organization and emphasizes how their diversity matters to the overall core values, mission, and strategy. First Corinthians 12: 14–31 (Buzzell, 1998) denotes the following:

> *[14]Now the body is not made up of one part but of many. [15]If the foot should say, 'Because I am not a hand, I do not belong to the body,' it would not for that reason cease to be part of the body. [16]And if the ear should say, 'Because I am not an eye, I do not belong to the body,' it would not for that reason cease to be part of the body. [17]If the whole body were an eye, where would the sense of hearing be? If the whole body were an ear, where would the sense of smell be? [18]But in fact God has arranged the parts in the body, every one of them, just as he wanted them to be. [19]If they were all one part, where would the body be? [20]As it is, there are many parts, but one body. [21]The eye cannot say to the hand, 'I don't need you!' And the head cannot say to the feet, 'I don't need you!' [22]On the contrary, those parts of the body that seem to be weaker are indispensable, [23]and the parts that we think are less honorable we treat with special honor. And the parts that are unpresentable are treated with special modesty, [24]while our presentable parts need no special treatment. But God has combined the members of the body and has given greater honor to the parts that lacked it, [25]so that there should be no division in the body, but that its parts should have equal concern for each other. [26]If one part suffers, every part suffers with it; if one part is honored, every part rejoices with it. [27]Now you are the body of Christ, and each one of you is a part of it. [28]And in the church God has appointed first of all apostles, second prophets, third teachers, then workers of miracles, also those having gifts of healing, those able to help others, those with gifts of administration, and those speaking in different kinds of tongues. [29]Are all apostles? Are all prophets? Are all teachers? Do all work miracles? [30]Do all have gifts of healing? Do all speak in tongues? Do all interpret? [31]But eagerly desire the greater gifts. And now I will show you the most excellent way.*

As scholars, educators, and leaders of organizations, we must consider the more excellent way as it relates to celebrating our differences and factoring diversity into personal leadership, and this is what ultimately happened at John Carroll University. Hence, it is ranked seventh of the 134 best Midwest colleges on a prestigious list of colleges and universities in the United States.

WORKS CITED

Buzzell, S. *The Leadership Bible.* Grand Rapids, MI: Zondervan, 1998.
Corporate Executive Board. *Management Accountability Methods and Measures for Diversity: Fact Brief.* Washington, DC: Corporate Leadership Council, 1999.

Daft, R.L. *Organization Theory and Design.* Cincinnati, OH: South-Western College Publishing, 2001.

Hackman, M.Z., and Johnson, C.E. *Leadership: A Communication Perspective.* 3rd ed. Prospect Heights, IL: Waveland Press, 2000.

Macmillan, Pat. *The Performance Factor: Unlocking the Secrets of Teamwork.* Nashville: Broadman and Holman Publishers, 2001.

Neale, M.A., G.B. Northcraft, and K.A. Jehn. "Exploring Pandora's Box: The Impact of Diversity and Conflict on Work Group Performance." *Performance Improvement Quarterly* 12.1 (1999): 740–763

Pfeffer, J. *The Human Equation: Building Profits by Putting People First.* Boston: Harvard Business School Press, 1998.

Stott, J. *Galatians: Experiencing the Grace of Christ.* Downers Grove, IL: InterVarsity Press, 1998.

"University Mission and Identity." John Carroll University, n.d. Web. 5 Nov. 2015

WORKS CONSULTED

Bass, B. M. (1990). *Bass & Stodgill's Handbook of Leadership.* 3rd Edition. New York: The Free Press, 1990. Print.

Corporate Executive Board (2001). *Diversity Advisory Council: Key findings.* Washington, DC: Corporate Leadership Council.

Daft, R. L. (2001). *Organization Theory and Design.* Cincinnati, OH: South-Western College Publishing.

Kuhatschek, J. (2000). *Galatians: Why God Accepts Us.* Downers Grove, IL: InterVarsity Press.

Yukl, G. (2002). *Leadership in Organizations.* 5th Edition. Upper Saddle River, NJ: Prentice Hall.

6 Women's Learning Circles in Conservative Churches

Monica Carol Evans

INTENTION/PURPOSE

My Home Point of View

My first memories of church are in charismatic Pentecostal house churches and storefront Holiness churches. Churches, for my childhood self, were places of thrumming gospel music, ecstatic congregational dance, the whoop and shout of preachers, and joyful speaking in tongues. My mother is my family's spiritual compass and she feels much more at home in the spontaneity of "Holy Ghost-filled" singing and preaching. She knows God is in attendance when the service gets "high."

My spiritual formation was not just in the mystical arts of the church. As young as eight years old, I remember many altar calls where I tearfully prayed that God would forgive my sins and save me from hell. The small churches in which I was brought up tended to take a more literal approach to Biblical interpretation, following the letter rather than the spirit of the text. Constant spiritual preparation coupled with literal biblical interpretation created a world that rejected all things "worldly." Pentecostal belief and frequent preaching on Jesus' second coming, eternal condemnation in hell, and the need to always be repented and spiritually prepared for the rapture were staples of Sunday services, Tuesday prayer meetings, and Thursday evening Bible study. The conservative beliefs of these churches created a world that policed and suppressed femaleness and sensuality that was not for the glory or benefit of the masculine. It was a world of explicit, in-your-face sexism and strict gender roles.

As a young woman in these churches, I was taught that bodies, especially female bodies, needed to be completely covered at all times. The dress code for women and girls required long sleeves, long dresses, and skirts. Women and girls were not allowed to wear pants, as those were men's apparel (Deuteronomy 22:5 KJV). Women and girls were not allowed to wear makeup or jewelry, as "adornment" was forbidden. Women were not allowed to cut their hair, as a woman's hair was "her glory," but it needed to be piled on her head in a bun (1 Corinthians 11:6 KJV). A woman's strict adherence to these rules meant that she was an asset to her family and church community. Women who deviated from these rules were likely to be a source of God's contempt, or at least a source of temptation for men.

There was so much wrong with the messages that I was taught about being a woman. I learned the dangers of interacting with men and boys, the temptations of my body, and the need for plain and modest appearance. These messages about the dangers of women and humanity's innate sinfulness provided a metaphor for the church's doctrines about the relationship between God and humanity, the relationships between men and women, relationships between women, relationships in families, and individual and communal relationships in the world.

I was given implicit and explicit messages about "a woman's place." I learned that all relationships between people and with God are hierarchal, and as a young woman of color, I would always be near the bottom of the ladder. Only men were allowed to take leadership roles in church, only men were preachers, only men were allowed to teach Sunday school to middle and high school students. On the other hand, all congregational meals were prepared by the women of the church, and all child care was provided by the women of the church. I learned that young women should not be smarter than young men, that young women should aspire to marriage and should plan for a life as a housewife and mother. Above all, even at the turn of the 21st century, girls and women were taught to be obedient and quiet.

As a funny, rebellious, and outspoken child, I often found myself in trouble at church for failing to fall in line. There was no place for the questions I asked the pastor, and Sunday school teachers who wondered how weak my faith was, that I could not just take their word for everything. There was no place to exercise my intellect. Why must I "show off" by consistently winning every game of Bible trivia? I wasn't allowed to experience the free rambunctiousness of childhood or stretch into my spiritual curiosity. Why couldn't I learn to be quiet and still? Unfortunately for me, I was a ringleader of unruly shenanigans among the church youth. I was known to collapse into giggles at the least provocation and provoke all the other young people into "inappropriate" behavior. Of course, this was a sore spot for the adults, especially the pastor, who didn't understand why my mother just let me be.

After a particularly "funny" church service where I must have been in rare form, I found myself cornered by the pastor. He backed me into a corner, scolding me for my willful behavior during the service. He asked me to explain what I could have possibly found funny about spending eternity in hell. I could barely keep a straight face as I turned the scolding into a joke. As I worked my way out of the corner, he called me back and warned me that there would be repercussions if I didn't learn my place. This warning has reverberated in my mind for over 20 years.

What Happens to Young Women in Conservative Churches Who Do Not Learn Their Place?

When I graduated from high school and left home for college, I said good-bye to Pentecostal churches. In fact, it would be nearly ten years before I would regularly attend any organized religious services. However, I didn't say goodbye to my spirituality, and over the course of many years, I found, cultivated, and incorporated life-giving rituals and practices into my life that accurately expressed my spirituality. At the same time, I also dealt with many nagging questions about God, the Bible, and the Church and I really wanted answers from a reputable, objective source. I found myself on a spiritual quest that eventually led me to a seminary. I am so thankful for my seminary experience, and I see it as a privilege that many other women are not able to undertake.

What If Women Had Safe Learning Spaces of Their Own for Spiritual Contemplation?

There are few places in conservative churches where women are free to ask and answer spiritual questions. The overwhelming suppression women and girls face in some churches limits their lives and outcomes and does not allow them to develop and utilize their best and greatest spiritual gifts or contribute to the wholeness of the religious community. Instead of suppression, church should be a place where women feel uplifted, encouraged, and empowered to live lives that are pleasing to God and to themselves.

Conservative church women need spaces where they are free to discern how God manifests in their own lives. Women's spiritual spaces should include a curriculum in women's studies to help women gain awareness about the ways that sexism shows up in their lives. This curriculum should consist of a facilitated group discovery process that develops women personally and allows them to practice authentic leadership and exercise their spiritual gifts. Women's learning circles in conservative churches are meant to help women recover and trust their own voices, let them practice taking spiritual authority to define what is holy, and have a space to exercise their voices and listen for the voice of God in their own experiences.

It is not my intention to make women and girls feel uncomfortable in their faith communities. Nor is it my intention that women get up en masse from conservative congregations in search of more affirming congregations. I seek only to bring awareness and empowerment, and to help women create new spaces and new ways to be involved in their communal church life. My deepest desire is for women to transform themselves and each other, so that regardless of the congregations where they choose to worship, they are able to do so as whole, authentic, full members of those communities, and are no longer satisfied with secondary status.

Learning circles will empower women to discover and create forms of spiritual experience that are life-affirming and grounded in women's lives. They provide a safe space for women to critically engage with their church's sermons so that they are able to distinguish sermons that are useful for their lives from those that are misogynistic or damaging to women's psyches. Women will learn to listen to themselves as well as to their preachers, so they are not forced to accept the interpretations of others. Women's own voices and experiences will be added to conservative biblical interpretation and have the potential to change socio-religious culture. Learning circles can provide a mechanism for women to organically transform their churches so that all members become full participants in congregational life by giving women a spiritual voice.

MY SPIRITUAL COMMITMENTS

As a theologian and spiritual director, I enter with particular theological, sociological, and communal commitments. My first commitment is that of the womanist; that is, I am committed to the health and well-being of the members of my primary communities. My commitment to the wholeness of women, people of color, and LGBTQ people comes from my own under-standing of the intersectional nature of the oppressions faced by these communities, and the ways that power and privilege function in our society, especially in our churches. I am committed to empowering and working towards liberation with/for people facing intersectional oppression. The church as an institution has historically been a site of solace and justice for people of color, but it has also been a primary site of oppression for women and the LGBTQ communities. My hope is to transform churches to become sites of justice and love for all people.

Intersectionality and Womanism: Working Definitions

Intersectionality is a concept coined by Kimberlee Crenshaw to define the ways in which "single axis discrimination frameworks" minimize the experiences of Black women in cases of race and sex discrimination (Crenshaw, 40). Crenshaw's work highlights the unique situation faced by Black women in terms of gender and racial discrimination. She asserts that Black women's reality differs from Black men and White women in situations where White women "but for" their gender and Black men "but for" their race would not be discriminated against. Discriminatory actions against Black women who face both race and gender discrimination have no place for rectification, because Black women are not a protected class.

Intersectionality affects the lives of all people who belong to two or more marginalized groups and demands that people facing multiple streams of discrimination—Black women, some LGBTQ people, people in poverty,

differently abled people—require an "and" rather than an "or" to identify the complex ways that they are oppressed in our society. My commitment to intersectionality means that I analyze oppression from the place of
"and" rather than "or." I consider the ways that gender, race, and sexuality
work together to oppress and demean rather than considering each form of
oppression separately.

Womanist Theology, Theory, and Praxis

Most importantly, I am committed to womanist spirituality and I believe
that any curriculum of women's studies in conservative churches should be
informed by womanist principles. The facilitator should develop journal
and discussion questions that consider womanist theory and the reality of
women's lives. The learning circle should spend considerable time walking
through Alice Walker's definition of womanist, which can be found in her
collection of essays, *In Search of Our Mother's Gardens.*

*Where do the members of the learning circle see themselves in Walker's
definition?*

Womanist

1. From womanish. (Opp. of "girlish," i.e. frivolous, irresponsible, not
   serious.) A black feminist or feminist of color. From the black folk
   expression of mothers to female children, "you acting womanish," i.e.,
   like a woman. Usually referring to outrageous, audacious, courageous
   or willful behavior. Wanting to know more and in greater depth than
   is considered "good" for one. Interested in grown up doings. Acting
   grown up. Being grown up. Interchangeable with another black folk
   expression: "You trying to be grown." Responsible. In charge. Serious.
2. Also: A woman who loves other women, sexually and/or nonsexually.
   Appreciates and prefers women's culture, women's emotional flexibil-
   ity (values tears as natural counterbalance of laughter), and women's
   strength. Sometimes loves individual men, sexually and/or nonsexually. Committed to survival and wholeness of entire people, male and
   female. Not a separatist, except periodically, for health. Traditionally
   a Universalist, as in: "Mama, why are we brown, pink, and yellow,
   and our cousins are white, beige and black?" Ans. "Well, you know
   the colored race is just like a flower garden, with every color flower
   represented." Traditionally capable, as in: "Mama, I'm walking to
   Canada and I'm taking you and a bunch of other slaves with me."
   Reply: "It wouldn't be the first time."
3. Loves music. Loves dance. Loves the moon. Loves the Spirit. Loves
   love and food and roundness. Loves struggle. Loves the Folk. Loves
   herself. *Regardless.*
4. Womanist is to feminist as purple is to lavender (Walker).

Womanism is a theological perspective, a praxis, and as a liberationist stance. Layli Phillips in *The Womanist Reader* defines womanism as "a social change perspective rooted in Black women's and other women of color's every day experiences and everyday methods of problem-solving in everyday spaces, extending to the problem of ending all forms of oppression for all people, healing humanity's relationship with the environment, and reengaging a closer relationship with the spiritual world" (Phillips, XXIV). Womanism starts with the experiences of Black women, the queens of intersectionality, but the activism of womanism does not end there. Womanism is also concerned with the liberation of whole communities, because when those who are intersectionally oppressed become free, those who are free "but for" are also freed.

In *The Womanist Reader*, Phillips defines womanist methods for social transformation, suggesting that the ways that Black women are already working in community are the starting point for liberation. She writes that through "relationship building and dialogue, communication between the material and the spiritual worlds (prayer, contemplation, communing with nature), hospitality, mutual aid and self-help, and motherhood," womanists contribute to the healing and reconciliation of relationships in the community and between people and nature (Layli Phillips, xxx). In this way, the formation and success of women's learning circles are an act of womanist activism that hold the possibility of transforming the sexist cultures of conservative churches.

As a theological perspective, womanism acknowledges that all theology is particular, and that the particular lived experiences and cultures of Black women and women of color are theologically important and insightful. Women's personal and collective experiences speak to the ways that women experience and perceive God in their lives. The womanist relates to God from the stance of a multiply oppressed person living in a world, in communities, and in bodies that desperately need healing, reconciliation, and liberation from powerful oppressive forces. The womanist considers her own life and the lives of her primary communities and uses these experiences, along with other factors, to create her theological perspective.[1] James Cone, a Black, male theologian writing about the importance of social location and experience to Biblical interpretation writes, "[I]f it can be shown that God as witnessed in the scriptures is not the liberator of the oppressed, then Black Theology would have to either drop the 'Christian' designation of choose another starting point" (Cone).

Likewise, Margaret Farley, a White, female theologian, asserts that there are some convictions so basic to a person's understanding that a contradictory witness cannot be believed without doing violence to one's self (Farley). Womanism stands alongside these witnesses to assert that, with the Bible, experience might be the most important way that God reveals God's self to humanity. When traditional Biblical interpretation and one's own experience are not aligned, a critical spiritual break occurs, and one struggles to determine who is to be believed, the church or themselves. The critically engaged womanist understands that she sometimes serves in religious communities and belongs to a faith tradition that is complicit in her and her communities' oppression. She works to transform these places, working to find and support appropriate, uplifting ways to create change and find a way forward with God. Womanist learning circles are one place where church women can become critically engaged in biblical interpretation, and can be in religious dialogue with other women working to come up with their own spiritual conclusions.

Women's learning circles serve as learning environments that hold space for women's spiritual and personal freedom. In *Mining the Motherlode*, Stacy Floyd-Thomas suggests an interesting thematic framework for Walker's womanist definition. She suggests the following themes: Radical subjectivity, traditional communalism, redemptive self-love, and critical engagement. Floyd-Thomas's womanist framework can serve as a thoughtful way for women to consider spirituality and sexism in their lives and churches, while also discovering ways to move towards wholeness in their own lives.

Radical subjectivity suggests that the womanist "claims her agency and has a subjective view of the work in which she is a responsible, serious and in-charge woman" (Floyd-Thomas, 8). This means that the womanist is one who does not take someone's word for granted. She does her own research and draws her own conclusions. The womanist is not comfortable or satisfied with the superficial or the status quo, but is interested in knowing the "why" of things, and forging her own path forward. The womanist isn't one that sits back waiting for the world to be made better, but she works toward the liberation of her entire community.

Traditional communalism refers to Black women's abilities to "take into account the various gifts, identities, and concerns of black people in order to strengthen the community as a whole" (Floyd-Thomas, 9). Traditional communalism acknowledges that the womanist stands in a long line of women activists working for justice for her community. While the womanist's work begins with women and girls in community, she does not neglect the well-being of men and boys. The womanist is able to see the uniqueness of community members and the collective of the culture as a banquet of goodness. The womanist strives to incorporate those gifts into the creation of a better reality for all people.

Redemptive self-love "reimages the perceptions of black women's bodies, ways, and loves as beautiful and precious" (Floyd-Thomas). This tenet allows the womanist to see herself in the mirror and love what she sees reflecting back at her, regardless of what negative or misguided messages she receives about herself. It also allows her to be in the presence of other women and affirm what she sees in them. She is able to consider women's lives, experiences, and distinct culture as something to be cherished, preserved, and celebrated. The womanist also understands that the veil between the material world and the spiritual world is thin, and that love through nature, experience, and culture are access points to the divine.

Floyd-Thomas asserts that the womanist *critically engages* with the broader world in which she lives, because she has "borne the brunt of social injustice through the history of the modern world" (Floyd-Thomas). Black women, based on their race, gender, class, and sexuality, have found themselves near the bottom of every American institutional hierarchy because they deviate so starkly from the historical American ideal of the straight, White, landowning male. Because of the interlocking systems of oppression that are always at play in society, the womanist understands her life and her work, not as an individual action, but as political activism on behalf of justice and liberation for the communities to which she belongs.

Which of these themes speaks loudest to you? Which theme is most challenging for you? Why?

RECOVERING WOMEN'S VOICE IN THE LIGHT OF PATRIARCHY

In *Counseling Women*, Christine Neuger asserts that what women need when they come for pastoral counseling is a space to hear and record their own voices and the voices of other women as they share their experiences and truths because "women's stories, experiences and ways of making meaning have been left out of the public discourse, leaving women with little of themselves in the culture" (Neuger 8). Neuger suggest that women seeking pastoral care require "reconstructive approaches" that help women fill in the blanks of what men's construction of reality has left out of their lives.

VOICELESS AND INFERIOR WOMEN

One of Neuger's reconstructive approaches is bringing women "to voice." Neuger's definition of voice is having the ability to "find language and models that validate one's own experience and communicate a sense of entitlement to that experience as authentic and important" (73). Likewise, being voiceless is "feeling powerless to speak and sensing that there is no one who speaks for us" (73). This is why it is important for women not only to tell their stories, but also to listen and acknowledge the stories of other women in the learning circles. Creating a volume of stories has a cumulative effect of validating the voices and the truth of women's experiences, and it lets women know that they are heard and corroborated.

The research of Carol Gilligan suggests that in adolescence, girls learn what it means to be a good woman. A good woman is one who is selfless in her caring for others. Compulsive caring and connection are so driven into young girls that they learn to orient their own identity as secondary and are left feeling silent and lost in their relationships. Becoming a good woman in patriarchal society involves learning to sit, stand, and talk in the appropriate ways and to make these ways appear natural even when they are not. In *The Birth of Pleasure*, Gilligan quotes an interview with a young girl: "[I]f I were to say what I was feeling and thinking, no one would want to be with me, my voice would be too loud . . . but you have to have relationships" (Gilligan, 10). And so girls learn to mute their own voices so that they can maintain and develop relationships with people that they perceive would not want to listen to their true selves. Girls learn to hide their own voices in order to be thought of as "nice girls." If they refuse to be silent, they take the risk of becoming alienated socially, politically, and religiously.

Sue Monk Kidd, in her memoir *The Dance of the Dissident Daughter*, recalls the incident that radically made her aware of patriarchy in the world. She visits her teenage daughter at work in a drugstore—on her knees, innocently stocking shelves. Sue Monk Kidd overhears a couple of men further down the aisle staring at her daughter, whispering and laughing together, "[T]hat's how I like to see a woman, on her knees" (Kidd, 8). Seeing her young daughter in a vulnerable position and hearing the men speak in such a demeaning manner pushed Monk Kidd on her spiritual journey against patriarchy.

Whereas the men in Monk Kidd's story were speaking with a sexual innuendo, the metaphor of the woman on her knees before a man is one that plays out in American culture all too often. Patriarchal society in America, with its interlocking hierarchal systems of race, class, and sexual oppression, work to keep women and other minorities subjugated in all our socio-religio-political institutions, including our churches. I have been the young woman on my knees, figuratively and literally subjugated by patriarchal oppression and male dominance in conservative churches. The gender roles and rules for women that I lived through in churches are among the ways that I was kept on my knees, forced to submit to the spiritual will and biblical interpretation of men who were not capable of understanding the experiences and spiritual needs of women and girls. This is most often the place that women are instructed to know, on their knees in service to men.

Describe times in your life where you found yourself without a voice. What strategies did you use to regain your voice?

AMERICAN RELIGIOUS PATRIARCHY: A DECONSTRUCTION

Patriarchy is the dominant language in American culture. The male and the masculine are the universal default experiences that permeates all levels of language. The male experience is the normative experience because so much of our cultural, religious, and political histories, including sacred texts, are written for male audiences from the perspectives of men. Women's stories are largely invisible in the corporate human discourse. In situations where women's or a feminine experience surfaces in history, myth, and in our cultural narratives, it is quickly stifled, downplayed, diminished, or simply erased.

Language is largely how we communicate—language creates and reflects reality. Unfortunately, the lack of easily accessible language to positively describe women in secular and spiritual arenas is an obstacle to women's wholeness. Because our cultural language does not carry the experience or the perspective of women of color, the culture often does not operate in women's best interests. Patriarchy is set up to protect the interests of the dominant group (men), so even when it is not actively trying to keep women subjugated, it does nothing to lift them up.

It is in this context of male-oriented, universal, cultural language that women and girls learn about themselves and their culture, and what they learn is that they don't matter except in the ways that they relate to and serve male interests. They learn that women's personal journeys, goals, and quests are secondary, and should not interfere with the well-being of the other members of the family unit. When a girl grows up, it is taken for granted that she will attach herself to a man, and her needs will not be primary. It is not taken for granted that she will lead an important life on her own terms, or that she will have access to power the way that men do. She is not meant to lead her own life, but is "meant" to be secondary to her male partner.

God-Language

This same male-dominated language that has proliferated in American culture also runs deeply in the Judeo-Christian language about God. God is nearly always referred to using male language: Him, King, Father, Husband, Warrior, and Prince. Jesus, God's incarnation, is the Son of God. In biblical language, God is often associated with political and familial power and authority, control, war, anger, vengeance, violence, and maleness. These associations create a normative effect on what it means to be male, and what it means to be God and female are excluded.

Language about God is important, because the ways that God is named and imagined affect how we understand ourselves, how we understand our purpose in the world, and how we order our social and familial relationships and our culture. When God is imaged as a male and all God-language is male-centric, this gives us a framework for how we are to relate to God—and how we are to see ourselves (or not) in the image of God. Women often cannot imagine themselves in the image of God. Further, when we look at Biblical women, what we see are women who are virtuous, subject to men, extensions of men, helpmates to men. We only know of these women because of their relationship to a man. When it comes to women who lead their own lives—their stories are few and far between.

Stories that help us make meaning—cultural and religious histories and mythologies, whether oral and written—have the power to reach us long after the time of the original happening. These stories recall to us a hint of the universality of human experiences, thoughts, and feelings. The way stories are told and retold and remembered does not happen within a vacuum. They are updated and revised to fit changing contexts. The language used to tell stories also must shift so that future generations of listeners are able to understand the underlying core message. These stories are still the same, but they should be told within the cultural framework of the time. Sometimes stories do not shift; they remain stuck because of the language that we use to tell them.

This is what has happened with biblical stories. They have not been able to shift and grow with our changing cultural contexts because the old patriarchal language is still being used—a new language cannot be developed because the old language endures. Those listening, especially women and girls, to the stories are unable to receive new revelations from God because they are often unable to move past the limits placed upon them by the patriarchal language in the stories.

Write the story of an unknown biblical woman. How would a woman's experience make a difference in the telling of a biblical narrative?

THE WORK OF THE LEARNING CIRCLE: AWARENESS, FEELINGS, SPACE

Our lives are made of stories that make meaning out of the things that happen to us. Each of us creates the narrative of our lives out of the language and frameworks available to us. This means that for women, especially Black women, our narratives are created using cultural tropes that are not easily relatable to our experiences. Women are bombarded with messages, language, cultural myths and stereotypes, and images that teach us that we are inferior to men. Male universal language and White supremacist media messages cause women to feel like invisible members of society. Many women use these negative tropes to build their personal narratives. This means that they are internalizing these messages and passing on the messages that society tells us about women to other woman and girls. When there is not an available cultural language for our experiences of selfhood, it is difficult to build said experience into our personal narrative, which leaves us with personal narratives filled with weak self-esteem and few female role models.

Many women internalize shame, guilt, and self-loathing in association with the ways that they deviate from the dominant cultural stories that highlight the worth of the White male ideal. Sue Monk Kidd acknowledges this phenomenon when she recalls confronting feelings of shame and guilt in her own life. Writing in her journal about her life as a woman, a thought rose within her: "[Y]ou're going to have to forgive yourself for not being born male. You're going to have to learn to love your real female life." Sobbing, she wrote in her journal, "I'd lost the voice of my native soul, the innate mother tongue. I had learned to speak the father tongue, the dominant cultural language" (Kidd, 25). What Monk Kidd acknowledges is that she became complicit in her own oppression by believing that she was worth less as a woman than she would have been as a man.

There are ways to help women recover and relearn their mother tongue. Women first need to be brought to awareness of the ways that patriarchy and racism exist and affect their lives. Women need to be taken through a process of anger, grief, and healing as they acknowledge their "feminine wound" and learn to create a new female life (Kidd, 28). Women need to build relationships with other women based on authenticity, so that they can learn to trust and respect the experiences and knowledge of women rather than relying on patriarchal cultural lies.

Monk Kidd suggests that the first part of female awakening is "deep sleep" (Kidd, 25). In deep sleep, a woman is unaware of the ways that patriarchy has affected her life's choices, her relationships, and the organization of her life. She has so internalized female oppression that her standing in life feels right and true. Her life is often tightly wound around the men in her life, be they her father, husband, son. She rarely has close female friends. The woman in deep sleep resembles the mother in Ntozake Shange's *Sassafras, Cypress and Indigo* who, after hearing about the close friendships that her daughter Cypress was developing with women, admonished her that women can't be trusted around one's man. For this woman, the male is the center of her life, and "close women friends are always more trouble than they are pleasure . . . seems like we can't be true to anyone who isn't family" (Shange, 139).

A woman in deep sleep can be brought to awareness when she experiences something new, a trauma or some other experience that causes such strong cognitive dissonance in her patriarchal worldview that this new experience cannot be conveniently tucked into her patriarchal personal narrative. It may be the ending or beginning of a romantic, business, or therapeutic relationship, a growing awareness of sexism or racism in the lives of her daughters, an aha while reading a book or watching a documentary, or through an epiphany in a religious ceremony where the gap between herself and the male image of God becomes too great. Many women hear a still small voice within themselves, or a shout and sudden anger where their authentic voice suddenly pushes herself to the surface. A woman can also be brought to awareness in relationship with other women in a facilitated learning circle, where the women are able to deconstruct patriarchy, speak about their experiences, and unravel the ways that patriarchy and White supremacy are guiding influences in their narratives.

When a woman comes out of deep sleep, there is usually regret, grief, anger, disappointment, and sadness to meet her on the other side. She has to mourn the life that she must leave behind because it is nearly impossible for an awakened woman to contently go back to a patriarchal life. She must work through her new feelings. *How could she have lived unaware under such oppression?* She also must think about she will live her new life. *How will her relationships shift? How will she re-order her life?*

The relationship building that takes place in women's learning circles creates a safe container where she can discuss her feelings and practice new behaviors. Growing relationships among women that are built on awareness of patriarchy and mutual respect allow women to voice their experiences of sexism and intersectional oppression. These relationships help women feel validated and become spaces where women can learn to make choices for themselves that reject male privilege. Learning circles become spaces where women can speak their own experiences, hear the stories of other women, allow women to see the world as it really is, and help them see that women's issues with patriarchy and racism are not pathological or a problem with the women themselves—but are a symptom of patriarchal systems that have kept them subjugated and unable to live up to their full potential.

Creating New Narratives

Neuger suggests a form of pastoral care called feminist narrative theory. She asserts that many of the "ailments" that cause women to seek mental health counseling with pastoral and secular counselors are symptoms of women struggling through a process of feminine awakening.

Narrative theory is a set of beliefs about the strength and resilience of people who have the possibility of "re-authoring their lives in ways that make them more able to live full responses to their vocation" (Neuger, 55). Narrative theory assumes that our interpretation of reality is reality, and this reality is constructed using the sensory data that we have at our disposal. We all take in information about ourselves, others, and the world, and then we synthesize the information to make decisions, create relationships, analyze our possibilities, and take action. The personality is not a static entity: The more experiences one has, the deeper the levels of analysis, and the more multifaceted the personality becomes.

Personal narratives are self-developed using the language and frameworks that are available. The stories we make our own are informed by our relationships with families, with our culture, with our peers, and our bodies. When personal narratives are built in a way that they do not give access to the acknowledgement or expression of a person's experience, then that person is likely to experience cognitive dissonance, which leads to relational issues, as the meaning of experiences has to be distorted in order to fit the narrative and women learn not to trust their experiences. Women and other non-dominant groups have learned to interpret their own stories and experiences, needs, and goals through the lenses of the dominant culture. Often, they lose access to their own truths and their honest strengths. Women need strong role models to provide them with alternatives to the modes of the dominant culture of seeing their experiences.

Women's learning circles become the bastion for women's culture and experience. The learning circle provides a clean slate for women to clear their cognitive dissonance. In the learning circle, women learn to remove the mask of patriarchy and feel comfortable voicing, acknowledging, and trusting their and other women's stories and begin to see them as valid and valuable in their own right.

The Awakened Woman

Women's learning circles that help conservative church women deconstruct patriarchy and help them understand hierarchal systems of oppression and the ways that scripture has been used and interpreted against women will cause women to awaken. Women who have woken out of "deep sleep" will not be able to stay silent in their churches. However, female awakening and learning circles should not destroy the important parts of women's lives, but should help them integrate their new worldview. Women's learning circles become safe spaces for women who are awake. In these spaces, women learn to experiment with ways to reconcile their new state with the important familial and church relationships that will have necessarily shifted during this time of growth. Even as women wake up in conservative churches, they will not wish to leave. They will have to learn how to be awake while remaining in conservative churches. This is not impossible, as women will have the communities and support that they have established in their learning circles.

Human beings are fundamentally communal, and our choices are shaped by our being with others. Plaskow shares that in spite of the patriarchy of current Jewish faith communities, she is unable to leave, saying about her faith community, "[A]s patriarchal as it is, it is a place of belonging, a place of upbringing, community, and identity" (Plaskow, 19). For Plaskow, leaving Judaism would mean "sundering her being." She also acknowledges that, in our society, there are no non-patriarchal spaces to go create a new feminist religion, and that she prefers to use her energy and creativity to transform Judaism.

What are the biggest challenges facing conservative church women as they re-order their lives when they wake up?

What are some reasons that an awakened woman may remain in her conservative church?

VISION OF WOMANIST LIBERATION

> "Ah wanted to preach a great sermon about colored women sittin' on high, but they wasn't no pulpit for me . . . So whilst Ah was tendin' you of nights Ah said Ah'd save de text for you. Ah been waitin' a long

time, Janie, but nothin' Ah been through ain't too much if you just take a stand on high ground lak Ah dreamed" (Hurston, 19).

In Zora Neale Hurston's *Their Eyes Were Watching God*, Nanny, grand-mother to the main protagonist Janie, tells Janie her deep hope for Janie's life. For me, this is the most beautiful part of Nanny's speech, because it is my womanist hope for women. I am working for the day where Black women are able to sit on high—extolling their value, their brilliance, and their goodness. Claiming spiritual authority for themselves. I believe this is the dream of all our womanist foremothers, that we access and exercise all our gifts becoming fully expressed. In order for Janie (and all of us) to preach this sermon, we must have an authentic voice and have access to the pulpit.

When I reimagine my childhood spiritual home, I wonder how my life would be different if my spiritual gifts and natural exuberance had be nur-tured rather than stifled. Who might I have become if I had been invited to stand behind the pulpit and see that as my rightful place? What if learning my place had meant the ability and the means to experiment—that I was free to discover my place rather than be pushed into a corner? My vision for women is a world where women are empowered to live into their full power as creative spiritual beings and have the authority to create and name the world according to their experiences and perspectives.

NOTE

1   Other factors include Biblical interpretation, experience, reason, and tradition.

WORKS CITED

Crenshaw, Kimberlee. "*Demarginalizing the Intersection of Race and Sex: A Black Feminist Critique of Antidiscrimination Doctrine, Feminist Theory, and Antira-cist Politics.*" *University of Chicago Legal Forum* 140 (1989): 139–167.
Floyd-Thomas, Stacy. *Mining the Motherlode: Methods in Womanist Ethics.* Cleve-land: The Pilgrim Press, 2006.
Gilligan, Carol. *The Birth of Pleasure.* New York: Alfred A. Knopf, 2002.
Hull, Gloria T., Patricia Bell Scott, Barbara Smith, eds. *All the Women Are White, All the Blacks Are Men But Some of Us Are Brave: Black Women's Studies.* New York: The Feminist Press, 1982.
Hurston, Zora Neale. *Their Eyes Were Watching God.* New York: HarperCollins Publishers, 2009 (Kindle Edition).
Kidd, Sue Monk. *The Dance of the Dissident Daughter: A Woman's Journey from Christian Tradition to the Sacred Feminine.* New York: HarperOne, 1996.
Neuger, Christine Cozad. *Counseling Women: A Narrative Pastoral Approach.* Min-neapolis: Fortress Press, 2001.
Phillips, Layli, ed. *The Womanist Reader.* New York: Routledge, 2006.

Plaskow, Judith. *Standing Again at Sinai: Judaism from a Feminist Perspective*. San Francisco: HarperSan Francisco, 1990.

Shange, Ntozake. *Sassafrass, Cypress, and Indigo*. New York, St. Martin's Griffin, 1982.

Walker, Alice. *In Search of Our Mother's Gardens: Womanist Prose*. New York: Harcourt, 1983.

WORKS CONSULTED

hooks, bell. *Ain't I a Woman: Black Women and Feminism*. Boston: South End Press, 1981.

hooks, bell. *Sisters of the Yam: Black Women and Self-Recovery*. Boston: South End Press 1993.

Response: The Gospel of Gender
Ethically Teaching Social Liberalism in Conservative Contexts

Veronica N. Gravely

When introducing material that will potentially be viewed as threatening to the receiver, it is necessary to take the utmost precaution so that the receiver does not shut down at the beginning of the conversation. In the previous discourse, the language seems to attack the church and scripture before getting around to introducing the solution (consciousness-raising groups) to remedy the problem (oppression of women via patriarchal constructs). Whereas I agree that consciousness-raising groups and storytelling are important and necessary for validating the lives of women in conservative circles, I take issue with the language used to introduce the material of discussion. I will elaborate on why I support the praxis structure (consciousness-raising groups) while critiquing the handling of scripture, gender bashing, and feigned high principles in the verbiage used to introduce and lay the framework for the author's point of departure for doing theology.

There is a distinct difference between care and enabling. Care is "the provision of what is necessary for the health, welfare, maintenance, and protection of someone or something" ("care"). Enabling is "to give power, means, competence, or ability to; authorize; to make possible or easy" ("enabling"). I certainly agree that care for women needs to be emphasized, enlightened, and outlined; however, we must be careful not to enable our fellow sisters in the faith in finding strength in tearing down others, especially when those whom they are attacking are proponents of the same body of faith.

I get it; I really do get it. I am a woman. I am Black. I am a Christian. I am American. I am also a daughter, sister, wife, mother, friend, theologian, engineer, and minister; however, these are all parts of a whole. I am a spirit being housed in a Black, female body in America. My primary identification is as a Christian. My membership in the Christian family is paramount to any other societal or cultural labels. By shifting the vantage point from a microscopic view to a macroscopic one, I am not suggesting that we begin to accept lies as truth or take the injustices thrust upon us as the way it is supposed to be indefinitely. I am not saying that there is only one locus of operandi from which to do theology. What I am suggesting is that there is a way to "fight" that is biblical. Womanist theologian Rosetta Ross posits in her discourse on John H. Yoder's pacifist teachings that:

> In the meantime, as Cannon argues, it is necessary to take account of Black women's (and others') subordinated realities to develop ethical methods that discern how subordinated persons exercise moral agency in the face of subordination while also presenting models that emulate Jesus' efforts to bring change to the world. 'In order to work toward an inclusive ethic,' Cannon states, 'the womanist struggles to restructure the categories so that the presuppositions more readily include the ethical realities of black women.' (Ross 5707)

Here, Ross refers to Katie Cannon, fellow womanist and liberation theologian and ethicist. I would like to place emphasis on the ethical responsibility here. Yes, the conversation that has begun in this chapter is necessary, but there is a more beneficial way for the discourse to be initiated for the best interest of women, the Church, and most importantly, the integrity of the Gospel.

Christian ethicist, theologian, and professor of the history of Black theological thought, Riggins Earl, Jr. makes the case that "[c]ommunication is ethically fundamental to Black scholars' ways of being and relating to each other in the world. The institutionalization of Black theology is ethically basic to Black scholars' self-esteem as makers of the world. Finally, hermeneutical method is ethically crucial to the way in which scholars make value judgments about the experiences of oppressed people" (57). The consciousness-raising groups would provide a vehicle for a very necessary dialogue to take place and for women (not only in conservative circles, but in all church settings) to discover their own voices and to tell their own faith stories in light of scripture. These groups would provide the communication that Dr. Earl says is ethically fundamental to making value judgments about the lives of oppressed people. With that in mind, I would like to propose that the author model what she would like to see, namely hermeneutical integrity and uplifting language.

Religious ethical mediator and womanist theologian Marcia Riggs posits, "Because we name and know ourselves through socially constructed lenses, we frequently see one another out of focus. We attribute meaning that, in effect, often annihilates our embodied differences and leads us to label one another in ways that judge, dismiss, objectify, and silence . . . the harm we do is sometimes psychological/emotional; other times, physical; and frequently manipulative/coercive or exploitative. The harm we do, in any form, is always violence" (249). We must be careful in finding our voices not to attempt to mute others. Let us allow "church hurt" to stop with us. Female awakening is fine; gender bashing is not. To perpetuate the "us and them" paradigm is to fan the flames of division within the body of Christ. The question then becomes to what are we subscribing—an Old Testament doctrine or a New Testament freedom? Throughout the author's presuppositions, there are opportunities for reconciliation.

The author's common ground with Christian women in conservative environments is the fact that she is a woman and she is a Christian who is guided by God's living and written Word. It is detrimental to her purpose to attempt to liberate other women by attacking one of the cornerstones of their faith. To attack (the inerrancy of) scripture is to close the doors to dialogue in the one main/major area of commonality. It would feel less threatening, and encourage vulnerability as conservative sisters begin to share out of their own faith stories, if the groups sought to highlight women's strength in the truth of the Word rather than forcefully attempt to get them to see how scripture has been misconstrued by church leaders who happen to be of the opposite gender. Women don't need to be told how they should think or feel; that would make the author's value judgments of their experiences no better than the "patriarchal Christianity" that she is seeking to expose. Rather, we may see more women be more receptive and responsive to the call to write their own faith stories in light of scripture by simply upholding the integrity of scripture.

For example, on maleness and God, rather than asserting that women metaphorically de-throne men from the creation story, you could highlight the truth of the creation story. God is a spirit—meaning God is neither male nor female. God is not either or, like the author is proposing with regards to Black women (being both Black and women, not just Black or just female), God is an "and"; God is male and female and more. We (humans) are but complementary parts of a whole image. Men are no more lone creators than women are. The scientific explanation of reproduction illustrates my point. Instead of pitting the two creation stories against one another, show how they are complements of a whole. The second creation story does not show that Adam created woman any more than women who become pregnant and birth a child "create" that child. Their bodies are but vessels that are used as a part of the creative process. Even when these two physical aspects of egg and sperm are present, life does not always occur each time. Life takes more than science, and language is not able to fully capture the true essence of God, which is why in Exodus, God reveals himself to Moses as "I Am" (New Revised Standard Version, Exod 3.14). The goal in the consciousness-raising groups is not simply to replace maleness with femaleness, but to replace oppression with freedom, and freedom comes by way of the truth. The truth will make you free (John 8.32). We must be ever conscious of what is at stake in our attempts to free people, namely the integrity of the Holy Text that we call the Bible. We must be mindful of how we are perceived in our zealousness. As theologians, we are to handle the scriptures with care, not wield them wildly, with passion and no clear focus. The author as a womanist is held to the same standard of handling scripture with reverence as the male purveyors of "patriarchal Christianity" that she is critiquing. We are trained and expected to perform responsible biblical exegesis (to draw out the meaning)—to do hermeneutics (to interpret and explain) with fear and trembling, not with contempt.

Storytelling is powerful. It can convey my life or your life in a way that is particular only to our individual selves. Yet, storytelling can be simultaneously daunting, because you don't know how your story will be received. I can recall driving to work once and passing a billboard for a local children's hospital that said, "Bring your child to a place that knows her." It made me smile. In that one moment, I felt as if I as a female was seen as normative in the world. It was assumed for once that a child could be a female and that a feminine pronoun could be used as inclusive of both genders. What it did not make me do was want to see all male references for inclusiveness done away with. In my opinion, we do not need to use extremes to make our point(s) valid. Truth will always stand out—it doesn't need help.

By initiating the groups that are proposed, many trials and triumphs can be shared, validated, expounded upon, and addressed with Biblical legitimacy. The goal of the groups as has been outlined—"to empower women to move beyond old ways of thinking about God's image and God's acts in the world . . . so that they are able to claim their power as women, their power to create, their power to name the world and the holy, and the power to speak their truths"—will organically come to pass by way of community to promote women's health and wholeness. I have discovered via facilitating a small support group of women in my home church that when women are allowed to tell the stories of their faith journeys without forcing them to recognize or identify with a victim status, they eventually are able to point out ways that they have experienced disservice and deception and to take ownership for their own decision-making in light of their present situations. They are able to come to a place of peace, but not complacency; this place provides a firm foundation upon which to build a new life—a new way of being—going forward. Women journey on with a profound new awareness of self, a sober assessment of the reality of their faith, and empowerment to live their lives with a new sense of ownership that they had not previously embodied. Their perspective is changed from what people did to them to what they will allow to be done and what they will actively choose to do. This paradigm shift will lend itself to a way of living that is fearlessly sincere.

When a majority group is met with an unwavering sincerity, they themselves are deemed defenseless. How do you annihilate an opposition that is not fighting, but rather being—simply existing authentically? You do not. The majority group (or the group in power) begins to realize that they are not what they once thought they were. They are exposed for their true selves as well and are forced to construct a new value system, because the one that formerly existed has collapsed under the minority group's refusal to acknowledge it. There can be no value system where both those on the profitable end and those on the short end do not agree to the values assigned in the system. Deception cannot be rendered effective if the oppressed do not acknowledge the strong's use of it or attempt to use it themselves. As such, I would like to offer that the effectiveness of the consciousness-raising groups will validate women in such a way that they will begin to live their lives fully and unapologetically; resultantly, the inconsistencies and unbiblical structures found in many individual churches will begin to crumble in light of the truth—that "there is no longer male and female," for all of us are one in Christ Jesus (Gal. 3.28).

As a firm believer in the cause of Christ outlined in Isaiah 61, I am keenly aware as a Christian woman in America who is Black that "freedom for the captives and release from darkness for the prisoners" (New International Version, Isa. 61.1) may not come the way that the captives and prisoners want it to come. I am also certain that my freedom should not come by putting another in chains. I am driven by discovering truth above all else. The truth makes you choose. There will be no fence straddling in the kingdom of God. Christ intended for us all to be free, not just certain subsets of people.

WORKS CITED

"Care." *Oxford Dictionaries*. 2015 Oxforddictionaries.com.Web. 28 June 2015.

Earl, Riggins R., Jr. "Black Theology and the Year 2000: Three Basic Ethical Challenges." *Black Theology a Documentary History Vol II*. Maryknoll, NY: Orbis Books, October 2003, 57.

"Enabling." *Dictionary.com, Unabridged*. 2015 Dictionary.com. Web. 28 June 2015.

Harold W. Attridge. *The Harper Collins Study Bible: Fully Revised and Updated New Revised Standard Version Including Apocryphal/Deuterocanonical Books With Concordance*. Gen. ed.New York, NY: Harper Collins, 2006.

New International Version. Biblica 2011. Biblegateway.com. Web. 28 June 2015.

Riggs, Marcia. "Living as Religious Ethical Mediators: A Vocation for People of Faith in the Twenty-first Century." *Womanist Theological Ethics: A Reader*. Eds. Katie Geneva Cannon, Emilie M. Townes, and Angela D. Sims. Louisville, KY: Westminster John Knox Press, 2011, 249.

Ross, Rosetta E. "Yoder on Pacifism." *Beyond the Pale: Reading Theology from the Margins*. Eds. Miguel A. De La Torre and Stacy M. Floyd-Thomas. Louisville, KY: Westminster John Knox Press, 2011, Kindle edition, location 5707.

7 Practicing Conversation

Feminist Research on Conservative Women[1]

Lihi Ben Shitrit

Over the past ten years, my research has focused on Jewish and Muslim women who are leading activists in what some have called "fundamentalist movements." Although I avoid using the term "fundamentalist"—which has become largely a pejorative, and is rarely a word activists use to describe themselves—I refer to it in this chapter, as it conjures up the images and stereotypes I wish to question and complicate. Also, because some of the literature I engage utilizes the term, I uncomfortably use it throughout the chapter. What I want to do here is to offer an account of the challenges confronting a self-critical, liberal, feminist researcher when choosing to study women in what I call "socially conservative religious-political movements," glossed as "fundamentalists" in much of the older literature and popular imagination (Sivan and Almond, 2001; Kramer, 2003; Marty and Appleby, 2004; Feige, 2009) The challenges lie both in the research process, which entails finding paths to conversations with women whose life-worlds and religious-political visions are so different from mine, as well as in the fair representation of their worlds and commitments in the research product.

In what follows, I first briefly introduce the Jewish and Muslim movements that I study, their family resemblances that are most conspicuous in the type of gender politics they advocate, which they term conservative, and the challenge women's activism in them poses to liberal feminism. Next, I review some of the literature on the representation of "fundamentalists," which has been critical of the production of this category in secular liberal discourse, and describe how this literature helped me navigate the research process. However, I also argue that the critique of secularism and political liberalism has been limited in that it has remained highly Western-centric, even when studying non-Western movements. In its effort to question the binary categories of religious and secular, liberal and fundamentalist, and critique "Western" secular liberalism, this literature has often either erased differences that are deeply important to its research subjects, the so-called "fundamentalists," or, on the other extreme, constructed irreconcilable differences of its own, which again, do not always reflect the priorities and self-presentation of the research subjects.

THE MOVEMENTS

In my book *Righteous Transgressions: Women's Activism on the Israeli and Palestinian Religious Right*, I study the work of women activists in four groups that have formed in the seventies and eighties of the 20th century: First, the Orthodox strands of the Jewish settler movement in the West Bank that seek to entrench Jewish control over the occupied Palestinian territories through the construction of civilian settlements—a project they see as hastening religious redemption and the coming of the messiah. Second, the ultra-Orthodox Shas movement, which is committed to spreading piety among the Jewish population of Israel and enhancing the religious character of both citizens and the states. Third, the Islamic Movement in Israel, an off-shoot of the Egyptian Muslim Brothers that strives to strengthen orthodox piety among Muslim citizens of the state of Israel. And finally, the Palestinian Islamic Resistance Movement Hamas, which is committed simultaneously to Islamizing Palestinian society and fighting against the Israeli occupation.

Labeling these groups "socially conservative religious-political movements" rather than fundamentalist movements, I adopt Nikki Keddie's definition for the type of new religious politics such groups advocate. This includes: a. "[A]n appeal to a reinterpreted, homogenized religious tradition, seen as solving problems exacerbated by various forms of secular, communal, or foreign power," b. a political agenda, an engagement with formal or informal politics in an attempt to influence policy and c. conservative social views. "For most groups this includes patriarchal views regarding gender, family relations and social mores" (Keddie, 1998, 697)

The "movement" part of the term also requires explanation. Unlike a political party, a movement is a much more amorphous and often also more heterogeneous phenomenon. I use a truncated version of Snow et al.'s account of social movements, which defines them as "collectivities acting with some degree of organization and continuity . . . for the purpose of challenging or defending extant authority, whether it is institutionally or culturally based, in the group, organization, society, culture, or world order of which they are a part" (Snow et al., 2008, 11) Although the four movements I study and many other religious-political movements in the Middle East are affiliated with political parties, I extend my research to the wider movement aspect of their activities. This is because most of them also exert significant influence through informal channels and their political action cannot be reduced to participation in elections. In addition, women's activism is often not fully captured if attention is paid only to party politics. Activists and especially women activists work in diverse political spheres, both formal and informal, and the agendas their movements promote go far beyond the bounds of party politics.

Below, I outline some of the key shared features of the movements' gender ideology that is amply present in their literature and teachings. Of course, the gender ideology, discourses, and practices of the movements are not static and unchanging. However, four principal commitments have remained intact for all four groups over the last thirty years. First, for the four movements, religion as the main source of legislation remains an articulated commitment, though one whose contours are often vague. To what extent and in what areas religious law should be paramount is a subject of contention within the movements and in their interaction with secular political actors. Yet for all four, the one area where compromise cannot be accommodated is in the field of family law. The movements insist on the primacy of halachic (Jewish law) or sharia law in matters of marriage and divorce, which are both grounded in traditions of religious jurisprudence that are inherently disadvantageous to women. Now, it is crucial to note that given the movements' emergence in the 1970s and 1980s, they are not the ones responsible for cementing the hegemony of religious law in the legislation of family law; the religious court system currently in use in Israel and Palestine has been entrenched by the Ottoman, British, and then the nationalist governments that succeeded them (Ghandour, 1990; Sezgin, 2013). Yet the movements have now become the most vocal supporters of this system and opponents of secular reform efforts. Though they are open to measures mitigating some of the burdens such a system places on individuals, and particularly on women, they oppose efforts to make civil options available for marriage and divorce or to establish full equality between men and women (and LGBTQ persons) in matters of family law.

Second, for all four movements, heterosexual sexual difference and the role-complementarity that is derived from that difference is a fundamental commitment. A sexual division of labor, in which women's most important duty is motherhood and caregiving, whereas men dominate public religious and political leadership, occupies a central place in the movements' teachings and is promoted as an expression of an ideal, pious, moral order. However, it would be wrong to conclude that role-complementarity confines women to their homes. All four movements value and encourage women's secular education and women's employment to support their families. Women's education and professional attainment is viewed positively, as the movements see these as avenues that make them better mothers, wives, and homemakers. New forms of women-oriented religious study and women's public engagement in mostly sex-segregated activism are also important facets of role-complementarity in the movements.

Third, the regulation of the interaction between the sexes is paramount in the movements' teachings, rhetoric, and practices. Female modesty and sex segregation where possible are emphasized as the fundamental tools to regulate public interaction between the sexes, and they make up the building blocks of a pious, moral society. Degrees of stringency and mildness in practice vary within each movement. However, on the level of official discourse, the movements construct observance of feminine modesty through dress, comportment, and interaction with the opposite sex as an ideal to continually aspire toward. Finally, the four movements largely view feminism, both in its transnational and local manifestations, as a highly problematic foreign (Western) influence that threatens to undermine the proper, authentic, and moral social and religious order. They perceive feminist discourses as blurring sexual difference and gender role-complementarity, which imperils the morality and character of communities.

For a feminist scholar like myself, women's active participation in such movements is surprising given the movements' gender ideology. To me, women's support for progressive feminist movements or women's movements in the Middle East seems like the more commonsensical choice, even considering the historically problematic association between feminism and colonialism in the region. British and French colonialists in the 19th and early 20th centuries and the United States in the 21st century have repeatedly justified intervention in or occupation of Middle Eastern and Muslim lands with the language of "liberating" Muslim women from the oppression they were subjected to due to the purported "backwardness" of their culture and religious traditions (Ahmed, 1992; Abu-Lughod, 2013). This rhetoric has done much to make the word "feminism" itself suspect. But nevertheless, given the very real challenges Middle Eastern women encounter today, both local and Western feminists believe that the best recipe for change is an explicit struggle for gender equality and women's rights. Yet feminism has not enjoyed the kind of support from women in the region that the socially conservative religious-political movements of the kind that I study in Israel and Palestine have received. This puzzle has motivated me to make the study of women's activism in these movements the center of my research.

REPRESENTING "FUNDAMENTALISTS"

When coming to study and write about the women activists whose life projects involve the transformation of the public sphere via the promotion of a religiously conservative gender ideology, the question of representation and the possibility of conversation preoccupied me. In this endeavor, I turned to other scholars who have reflected on the difficulties that such an engagement entails. I want to first discuss some of the hazards of representation, before turning to the more difficult task of conversation.

In her much-cited article from 1991, Susan Harding powerfully critiqued academic and popular representations of "fundamentalists," referring in her case to Protestant Christian fundamentalists. She explained that while the subjects included in this category put forward a particular self-representation, they are not the sole authors of their image. They are "also constituted by modern discursive practices, and apparatus of thought that presents itself in the form of popular 'stereotypes,' media 'images,' and academic 'knowledge.' Singly and together, modern voices represent fundamentalists and their beliefs as an historical object, a cultural 'other,' apart from, even antithetical to, 'modernity,' which emerges as the positive term in an escalating string of oppositions between supernatural belief and unbelief, literal and critical, backward and progressive, bigoted and tolerant. Through polarities such as these between 'us' and 'them,' the modern subject is secured" Harding (1991: 374).

Joyce Dalsheim applies Harding's critique to the discourse on Jewish fundamentalism in Israel, particularly to the way secular, liberal, left-wing Israelis construct religious settlers as their complete, archaic, anachronistic, and irrational "others" (Dalsheim, 2011). Dalsheim argues that at the root of this othering lies the anxiety of secular Israelis about the underlying commonalities that exist between them and the settlers, in that both belong to a hegemonic Jewish identity that marginalizes and colonizes Palestinians and their lands. By othering religious settlers, according to Dalsheim, mainstream Israeli discourse obfuscates its own implication in settler colonialism.

Echoing Harding's observation when examining writings about the Middle East, Roxanne Euben has argued that Islamic fundamentalism in both scholarship and media coverage has been equated with "irrationality." She points to the description of Islamic fundamentalism as a fearful, almost panicky, reaction to modernity and as "the persistence of the archaic and particularistic" (Euben, 1999, 15). But she also describes another widespread representation of fundamentalism in the Middle East—its account as an epiphenomenon. Most common among scholars of the Middle East, she writes, is the attempt to provide materialist explanations to the surfacing of fundamentalism. In this account, fundamentalism is not an irrational but rather a rational response to prevailing socioeconomic and political conditions, such as the persistence of despotism, the failure of alternative ideologies like nationalism and socialism, growing economic inequalities, the frustration of the poor or the educated but unemployed youth, etc. Whereas such descriptions endow fundamentalism with rationalist capacities, as employing appropriate means toward a specified end, they empty the phenomenon of any unique ideological content. They also imply a certain false consciousness among adherents of fundamentalist movements, who displace their legitimate anger at economic and political injustices onto a religious language that masks or distracts from these more earthly concerns.

Focusing on representation and gender, Saba Mahmood has pointed out that Western feminists in particular tend to explain away women who advocate a socially conservative gender agenda grounded in orthodox Islamic teachings and practices as either suffering from the kind of false consciousness Euben describes, or as completely oppressed and devoid of agency (Mahmood, 2005). Mahmood's account goes beyond the critique of orientalist othering that Western liberal feminists perpetrate for the purpose of their own identity construction as "liberated." She questions the very assumption that the desire for freedom and the valuing of autonomy is a universal attribute of the human subject. Pious Muslim women (and this could be applied to pious women of Jewish, Christian, and other religious backgrounds) are exercising their agency not only when resisting conservative norms, as Western feminist would have it, but also when working on themselves through embodied practice to better comply with the conservative norms that constitute them. The obsession with resistance that Western feminists suffer from, according to Mahmood, leads them to privilege moments of women's resistance and devalue women's compliance with norms that uphold women's docility, modesty, and submission. While Mahmood studies Egyptian women who are not political activists, her insight is important when studying so-called "fundamentalist" religious-political activists too.

These important contributions by scholars of Christian, Jewish, and Islamic socially conservative activism was helpful in alerting me to be vigilant when writing about my research interlocutors. It was crucial not to add to the reductive and problematic tropes about "fundamentalists" that have become a sort of cliché in some of the academic and popular discourse. Yet, I felt that the preoccupation with the critique of a secular, liberal West, while indispensible, entails some problems of its own. To begin with, the West, the secular, and the liberal remained the center, the real subject of analysis, for which the lives and commitments of "fundamentalist" activists served as a backdrop for critique. Rather than making these lives and their projects as their actors understand and construct them the center of analysis, much of the focus was on exposing and denouncing secular misconstructions, instead of expounding on religious "fundamentalists" self-construction. These critiques taught us more about the West than about its "other," and presented it as the all-powerful and sole designer of its own image and the image of the "other."

To avoid Western-centrism, my approach was to ground my writing in the words, self-descriptions, and analyses of the women activists I studied. I highlighted their, rather than my own, critiques of secular liberalism, feminism, and the West, and asked them explicitly to articulate in our conversations the meanings behind their choices and actions. What I found in their articulations was significantly different from secular liberalism on the question of formal political and legal arrangements, in particular their rejection of the secular separation or "twin toleration" between religion and state. Yet I also found some underlying shared commitments with liberalism to notions of freedom and autonomy.

In my 2013 article in the *Journal of Middle East Women's Studies* (JMEWS), I interrogated some of the motivations for women's participation in socially conservative religious-political movements, using as case studies the Islamic Movement in Israel and the ultra-Orthodox Shas (Ben Shitrit, 2013). Drawing on my ethnographic work and interviews with activists, I argued that these movements in fact offer women powerful liberatory narratives. I found that women activists' interpretations of agency in piety practices were highly invested in the idea of the autonomous individual. The validity of practices, according to activists, rested on the choice and consciousness of the individual and on the rejection of submission to social norms. Furthermore, I contended that when we take into account the various class and cultural contexts of Middle Eastern women's piety practices and activism, we find that for many women, religious movements offer real liberation from oppressive socioeconomic realities and limiting cultural norms. In what follows, I reproduce my main arguments in that article.

In her groundbreaking book *The Politics of Piety*, Mahmood artfully articulates the argument for de-coupling the understanding of agency from the concepts of "freedom" and "autonomous will." She argues that feminist notions of freedom, conceived as self-realization, rely on the liberal requirement that "in order for an individual to be free, her actions must be the consequence of her 'own free will' rather than of custom, tradition, or social coercion" (Mahmood, 2005, 11). Drawing on poststructuralist insight, Mahmood argues that such a separation between an autonomous individual and external forces like custom, tradition, and social coercion is impossible. Following Michel Foucault, Mahmood convincingly claims that these external forces are constitutive of the individual; they give rise to a subject that does not exist prior to them or transcend them. Agency, therefore, should not be understood as the individual's ability to act for self-realization in opposition to and against the weight of external customs, traditions, or norms. Rather, agency could also be understood as the work individuals perform on themselves to better comply with the external norms that constitute them. Emancipatory desire, she writes, is not a universal attribute of the individual, but rather a manifestation of a patently Western, liberal tradition that privileges individual autonomy.

Consider the following discussion of freedom by one of the most respected Islamic Movement women's leaders in the Bedouin Negev Desert of the Israeli south, whose lessons attract Bedouin women of all ages and educational backgrounds.[2] Her popularity and outreach in the Negev make her one of the most influential feminine voices within the movement in the region.

> There are some who think that woman's freedom is that she is able to go out of the house whenever she likes, at any hour and with anyone she likes, and come back at any hour, eat whatever I want, drink whatever I want, do whatever I want. But according to Islam this is not freedom. Freedom is not to go out with a boy today and then pay a high price for it later. When her reputation will be harmed no one will respect her; the boys will treat her like a football, play with her. It is not freedom to wear what I want and display my body in front of young men. It is the opposite. I think that woman's freedom is freedom from thoughts that could ruin her. Most importantly, the religion does not forbid education, and does not forbid a woman from going out if she is with a chaperon (*mahram*)—the husband, or brother, or father, or uncle, or a group of women that go out together. Her freedom is that her religion does not

prevent her from doing anything, but everything has to be done within limits (*hudud*), with some restrictions (*quyud*). . . . Today people think that freedom is behaving in whatever way I want. No, the religion gives us boundaries and restrictions. It doesn't tell us not to stay out late, but it tells us where it is appropriate to do so, in what places.

For this *da'iya* (Islamic preacher), "doing whatever I want"—being free from external obstacles to pursuing my own desires—is not freedom at all. Acting autonomously without regard for social implications (reputation, for instance), for the presence of others (the company or absence of a chaperone), and for context (in what context can one go out, in what context can one stay out late) is injurious to the individual, rather than emancipatory. She argues that freedom is achieved when a woman is able to follow the correct path with the guidance of Islam. The boundaries, limitations, and conditions that Islam presents enable women to achieve their self-interest. However, disregard for and shirking of Islamic boundaries, limitations, and conditions lead not to freedom, but to harmful consequences for the individual.

Another, younger Bedouin da'iya in her twenties offers another illustrative discussion of freedom, which she shares with her peers in the Movement's activities she oversees and in her work with high school girls.

Freedom is to give woman the key, and teach her how to use this key. . . . I give this allegory about Islam: Islam gives woman a key and tells her, there are two gates. This key opens both. It can open the first gate which will lead you to heaven, to happiness, to satisfaction, and conviction. The second gate, if you open it, a lion will leap at you. We give her this information but let her choose for herself; she is rational and intelligent, and she has to choose what is better for her life. The key is in her hand, and she is the one to decide. We don't give her the key and say open whichever gate you'd like without telling her what lies behind each gate.

Here, we see that the idea of the autonomous self is not at all alien to activists in contemporary religious-political movements, and neither is the commitment to an emancipatory discourse. Activists' discourse, largely shaped by the outlook of key women leaders, falls within the framework of traditions espousing "positive freedom."

To elaborate, let us consider again the concepts of negative and positive freedom. The tradition of negative freedom addresses the question, "What is the area within which the subject—a person or group of persons—is or should be left to do or be what he is able to do or be, without interference by other persons?" (Berlin, 1959, 155). Negative freedom rests on the absence of external obstacles, interference from others that comes in the way of self-realization. Positive freedom, on the other hand, answers the question, "What, or who, is the source of control or interference that can determine someone to do, or be, this rather than that?" (Berlin, 1959, 155). This second concept of freedom is also concerned with internal interference with a person's ability to realize herself, to act in accordance with her true will and in her own self-interest. Positive freedom often speaks to an internal conflict between different pulls on the individual, for example, between reason and instinct, unthinking habit, desire, unreflective influence, "brainwashing," or emotions.

The older activist rejects the notion of negative freedom: "Do[ing] whatever I want" regardless of external considerations is unacceptable. However, she distinguishes between a "desire" to "do whatever I want" and self-interest—not being harmed by the consequences of such actions. Similarly, in the younger activist's account, negative freedom, the complete absence of interference by others, conflicts with self-interest. Withholding guidance from an individual inhibits rather than enables her to pursue her self-interest. She describes the individual as an "intelligent" and "rational" agent that should act in her own best interests. However, her ignorance can come in the way of her realizing this best interest. It could make her open the door that would lead to the lion. Islam, according to the prevalent discourse among women leaders in the Islamic Movement, helps guide the individual to the right path that is in accordance with her true self-interest. It helps the individual overcome other harmful aspects within her, like unthinking ignorance or misguided desire. The Islamic narrative here espouses self-realization through correct guidance. In other words, this guidance helps the individual to uncover her true interest, which is obfuscated by desire, ignorance, and a focus on negative freedom. More generally, Islam is the framework through which one can achieve autonomy from harmful internal and external influences. Islam here performs the same role that reason, knowledge, education, or true consciousness (as opposed to false consciousness) play in other accounts of positive freedom.

In Mahmood's account, the agency of the women in the piety movement she studies is formed by the "customs and traditions" (in their words) they inhabit and not prior to and autonomously from them. Agency is not located in one's ability to achieve autonomy from what might be considered oppressive customs and traditions or to subvert them, but rather, in inhabiting them. The women activists in the Islamic Movement in Israel, however, do insist on the individual's resistance to unexamined customs and traditions.

But unlike approaches that equate customs and traditions, as well as social norms that subordinate women, with Islam, the Movement's activists make an unequivocal distinction between the two. The women associate customs, traditions, norms, and social coercion with the internal and external elements that prevent the individual from achieving true self-realization. This is clear in older da'iya's discussion of 'ada (custom) and 'ibada (worship):

> There is 'ada and there is 'ibada. For example, some women wear Islamic dress as 'ibada. I know that Islam says that a woman, when she leaves her house, must be *muhajaba* (veiled) and wear the *jilbab* (long coat). . . . Now, there are some women that wear this as 'ibada, as it is

mentioned in the Qur'an. Some other women don't wear it as an 'ibada, they wear it as 'ada. They wear it because most of the women in their family wear the hijab outside the home. Or because they are used to wearing certain clothes that their families think restrict women. . . . If we want to enter heaven we must think of everything we do as 'ibada, this should be our intention. If I work for others it counts as 'ibada, for example if I clean and cook for my husband and help him, I profit from it as if it is 'ibada [it counts as if I have performed 'ibada]. I receive my reward because these are things I was not required to do or forced to do, but I still chose to do them.

In her teachings, the da'iya draws a sharp distinction between 'ada and 'ibada. The act performed is identical in the eyes of an outside observer—donning the hijab. What makes one worthier than the other and what determines whether one would receive recompense from God, however, is the intention behind performing the act. The act of wearing the hijab, because it is an established tradition, a social norm, or because of coercion (because one's family uses it to restrict female members), does not have the same status as wearing it out of real conviction in its religious meaning. What validates an act as an 'ibada thus is the conscious decision of the individual to perform it independently of customs, traditions, or coercion. She goes even further to stress choice as the integral component of 'ibada. The recompense from God is not given for simply performing the act, but for choosing freely to do so.

By privileging intention, choice, and consciousness, the correct Islamic practice as activists understand it makes a sharp distinction between customs, norms, or blind imitation of others and autonomous, intentional action. Again, it is the independent intention of the conscious agent who understands Islam that validates the act as worship. The criterion for classifying an act as 'ada or 'ibada is not so different from the liberal classification of an act as free or coerced. The consent and intention of the agent are at the heart of both.

Focusing only on Muslim women's articulations of piety also risks essentializing the preoccupation with modesty and other patriarchal piety practices, seeing them as unique to Islam rather than as a wider tendency that finds expression in patriarchal religious movements in different faiths. My work with Jewish ultra-Orthodox women activists in Shas reveals almost identical articulations. Shas activists in the field of teshuva, like the Islamic Movement women, distinguish between 'ada and 'ibada—between doing something simply because it is required or for outward appearance, and doing it out of real internal conviction. A well-known rabbanit (wife of a rabbi) who teaches religious classes across Israel as part of Shas's outreach to women, uses the following story to elaborate this point:

We don't impose religion. Some girls come to my lessons with revealing clothes. In Passover I arranged a group lesson in Herzliya. They are very wealthy. I said, 'You are so wealthy, you have everything, so you don't need to wear clothes?!' They laughed but they understood that the way they were dressed bothered me a little. Slowly, I never asked explicitly, they began to dress a little more modestly and behave a little more modestly. After two years together they decided that each one of them will take upon herself something. They bought eight headscarves, eight long dresses, and wore them. It was a beautiful sight. They all waited for me to say something. . . . After the lesson started I said, 'Something is different.' I said, 'I understand that you want to be a good example for your daughters.' They said, 'No, we wanted to make you happy.' I said, 'You respect me, and I respect you. I don't even notice how you dress because I see what is inside you which is more important.'

The important thing is a person's soul, not his outward appearance. A woman can wear a head cover and hurt other people. For me she is not only not religious or Jewish, she is not a woman. They saw that I didn't get too excited about their head covers so they took them off. I told them, I don't need hypocritical head covering. When it will come it should come from the inside. . . . Someone told me yesterday that she is modest, but she was dressed immodestly. I told her, it is good that you think that you are modest. I think you are not modest in your appearance, but the fact that you feel modest and that you feel connected to the notion of modesty is already a great thing.

The extent to which Islam carries within it an emancipatory narrative for the women activists in the Islamic Movement is explicitly present when cultural customs and norms conflict with what the women activists understand to be true Islam. This conflict is most apparent among the Bedouin activists in the Negev. Another young da'iya, who leads the Islamic Movement's student group at her university, describes an instant of such conflict:

As I started to learn [about Islam], I felt that my understanding developed further. I understood what my obligations were and what my rights were, how to do everything within the accepted framework, what is forbidden and what is allowed. I feel that our society tries to suppress me and tell me that everything is forbidden, but I know that they impose rules on me that are not from Islam. These are traditions and customs that are oppressive. They have their own history but Islam is not their origin; Islam does not even say one sentence to their effect. They always try to confine the woman, keep her at home. But I have respect for the girl that goes out to study, to advance our society.

Other Bedouin activists take the distinction between 'ada and 'ibada a step farther. Their knowledge of Islam and their membership in the Islamic Movement gives them authority, in their eyes and in the eyes of others, to resist certain customs and traditions that they view as oppressive to women, as un-Islamic and therefore un-authoritative. Bedouin activists described to me resisting forced or early marriages, insisting on their right to attend university, when their families tried to forbid them from doing so, and gaining expanded freedoms from their families and communities by leveraging their religious learning against what they labeled un-Islamic, oppressive practices.

The women leaders' interpretations of piety practices in these two patriarchal movements reveal that a commitment to emancipatory desire, narrative, and action are not simply Western feminist impositions. The teachings of the women that shape the discourse of the Islamic Movement and of Shas, as it circulates among women in religious classes, lectures, and other activities, emphasize the conscious choice and consent of the individual as the most important criterion for judging the adoption of a piety practice. It is what distinguishes genuine worship from unthinking submission to external social, cultural, and even religious pressures. Furthermore, through their involvement with the Islamic Movement, Bedouin women in the Israeli south have been able to expand their educational and marriage opportunities, as well as the freedoms their traditional families grant them. Shas women, who generally share a history of poverty, have also succeeded in expanding possibilities for higher education, professional training, and employment as a result of their activism.

In conclusion, my JMEWS's paper that I reproduced here sought to counter a tendency toward what I saw as a sort of cultural relativism and romanticization of difference that exists in the scholarly literature and that runs the risk of essentializing certain patriarchal practices as "authentic" expressions of local, non-Western ethics. At the same time, I did not want to argue that liberatory narratives are the true "authentic" expressions of local traditions, nor did I trace the origin or lineage of emancipatory discourses. My aim was instead to highlight the fact that these narratives are as present among women activists in non-Western patriarchal religious movements as they are on Western and non-Western liberal feminist agendas.

SPEAKING WITH "FUNDAMENTALISTS"

Activists in Shas and the Islamic Movement proved easier research subjects for me than those in the two other movements I studied—the Jewish settlers and the Palestinian Hamas. Whereas the former two focused much of their political work on the promotion of piety, the latter were also engaged in the fortification of a religious-political hegemony that seeks to deny the equal rights of others (their religious-political rivals) to political self-determination. The Jewish settler strands I worked with denied the right of Muslim Palestinians to sovereignty in any part of historic Palestine, or Greater Israel, as they call it. Prominent Hamas activists, in a mirror image of the settlers, denied the right of Jewish Israelis to national self-determination on any part of the same territory.

Moreover, in their official ideologies (if not so much in every aspect of their practice), all four movements I studied would not allow equal freedom for secular citizens who disagree with their particular religious interpretations. To give some concrete examples: The movements, through the further fortification of halacha and sharia in the legal codes of their states, would severely limit the legal right of a Jewish or Muslim woman to marry outside of her faith in her country (or enter a same-sex marriage), they would deny her the right to convert to another religion in the way she deems fit, and they would deny her the right to complete equality in matters of marriage and divorce. My challenge when working with interlocutors who advocate such politics was to overcome my own secular liberal bias that seeks to exclude from the democratic public sphere those who reject equality, pluralism, and freedom of and from religion, and to be able to really hear and see my interlocutors' worlds through conversations and other forms of engagement.

Critiques of secular political liberalism have focused on its various contradictions and exclusions. But as Harding pointed out over two decades ago, these critiques "are now routine theoretical moves in studies of culture except for one thing: they are not routinely applied to specifically religious cultural 'others' such as [fundamentalists]. It seems that anti-orientalizing tools of cultural criticism are better suited for some 'others' and not other 'others'—specifically, for cultural 'others' constituted by discourses of race/sex/class/ethnicity/colonialism but not religion . . . " (Harding, 1991, 375). Her observations were followed by greater focus on the exclusion of certain religious-political subjects, hailing from other traditions such as Islam, Judaism, Hinduism, and so on, who have also been termed "fundamentalists."

Even accounts that reject the portrayal of fundamentalism as irrational have often deemed fundamentalist worldviews and subjects, after Rawls, "unreasonable." In *Political Liberalism*, Rawls offers a method by which a pluralist society, whose population is divided by reasonable (religious, philosophical, and other) comprehensive doctrines, may exist as a "stable and just society of free and equal citizens" (Rawls, 1993, 4). Rawls puts forth the idea of public reason—a method that does not rely on a single (religious, ideological, etc.) comprehensive doctrine, but rather rests on democratic principles that make up the public political culture of society and that are derived from an overlapping consensus of existing, reasonable comprehensive doctrines present in a polity. Rawls distinguishes between reasonable and unreasonable comprehensive doctrines, with fundamentalism falling under the latter category:

> When political liberalism speaks of a reasonable overlapping consensus of comprehensive doctrines, it means that all of these doctrines, both religious and nonreligious, support a political conception of justice underwriting a constitutional democratic society whose principles, ideals, and standards satisfy the criterion of reciprocity. Thus, all

reasonable doctrines affirm such a society with its corresponding political institutions: equal basic rights and liberties for all citizens, including liberty of conscience and the freedom of religion. On the other hand, comprehensive doctrines that cannot support such a democratic society are not reasonable. Their principles and ideals do not satisfy the criterion of reciprocity, and in various ways they fail to establish the equal basic liberties. As example, consider the many fundamentalist religious doctrines, the doctrine of divine rights of monarchs and the various forms of aristocracy. (Rawls, 1997, 801)

Rawls further states that "[u]nreasonable doctrines are a threat to democratic institutions, since it is impossible for them to abide by a constitutional regime except as a *modus vivendi*" (Rawls, 1997, 806). Critics of Rawls correctly point that he in fact defines "reasonable persons" only as those accepting the fundamentals of liberalism. Rawls's account is thus not at all neutral to different conceptions of the good, they argue, but is rather predicated on liberal values, whereby those who do not accept them are called "unreasonable." According to critics, what Rawls and other liberal thinkers do is attempt to transcend or erase plurality by relegating it to the private sphere and creating one hegemonic and exclusionary acceptable public discourse (Mouffe, 2006).

Critics like Talal Asad (2003) and Mahmood (2006), on the other hand, have seen the problem as one not of exclusion, but rather one of domination. They have stressed that whereas secular liberalism purports to be neutral toward religion and to simply separate religion and state so that neither dominates the other, what it does in practice is to violently shape a particular religious subjectivity compatible with a secular liberal framework. This places unequal burden on certain religious citizens whose form of religiosity does not fit the demands of secular political liberalism (like pluralism, tolerance, and reciprocity, which entails the acceptance that other citizens of other religions, atheists, or those holding vastly different conceptions of the good have an equal right to freedom of and from religion). As Mahmood puts it, "The political solution that secularism proffers, lies not so much in tolerating difference and diversity but in remaking certain kinds of religious subjectivities (even if this requires the use of violence) so as to render them compliant with liberal political rule. Critics who want to make secularism's claim to tolerance more robust must deal with this normative impetus internal to secularism, an impetus that reorganizes subjectivities in accord with a modality of political rule that is itself retrospectively called 'a religiously neutral political ethic'" (Mahmood, 2006, 328).

What, then, should be a less domineering and a more honest secular liberal approach to "fundamentalists" who profess intolerant worldviews that reject reciprocity, basic individual freedoms, and equal rights? This is the difficulty at the heart of the secular liberal, pluralist democratic project—how to include rather than exclude those who reject pluralism, how to resist the impetus to change the "fundamentalist" interlocutor so that she fits the requirements of liberalism—and it is insurmountable.

In my research, I chose to address this challenge through a different practice of conversation. When I engage with activists in religious-political movements who would be considered "fundamentalists," who would reject notions of the freedom and equality of all citizens or the idea that they should not impose their religious doctrines on others, I enter a strange kind of conversation. (It is crucial to note, though, that not all activists fall under this category. In my work, I have met many who accept the reality of pluralism and find methods by which worldviews that are in conflict with their own could be accommodated. But having accepted reciprocity, equality, and pluralism, these interlocutors are no longer "unreasonable" by Rawls's definition. Another important note is that in the context of Israel and Palestine, which are not established liberal democracies, religious-political movements are not the sole representatives of "unreasonable" doctrines. Mainstream Zionism and Fatah-style Palestinian nationalism hardly meet the criteria of liberal democratic pluralism.)

This conversation would take Habermas's (2006) notion of translation[3] but detach it from its reciprocal requirement. Whereas I am committed to listen to and translate "fundamentalist" arguments into notions I can understand, my interlocutor has no such commitment toward me. Because I believe her (the other's) point of view should have as much place in the public sphere as mine, I am required to try to understand her, but she, who thinks my view is blasphemous, is not required to make space for mine.

Instead of placing an unfair secular liberal burden on the religious "fundamentalist," forcing her to believe one thing but to shape her public sphere articulation of her belief in a way that adheres to the requirements of secular liberalism (which stipulate that she cannot deny me freedom of and from religion, even if she believes she has a moral and legal duty to do so), I should take on myself this burden. I should be responsible for the effort to hear what she says—for example, about the exclusive divine endowment that is the Holy Land of Israel/Palestine, which God permits only Jews, or alternatively, only Muslims, to rule—and translate it into a language I can understand. Moreover, in order to speak back my view, I should translate my positions from a secular liberal language to one grounded in religious justifications that my interlocutor could potentially accept. In this case, I could not deny the divine endowment of the land, but perhaps find resources in my interlocutor's scripture, interpretations, and practices, that question, for example, the ethnic and nationalist exclusivity of this endowment.

In my disagreement with her over the equal rights that should be granted to me as a woman—for example, to marry outside of my faith or to marry a person of my own sex, to have full equality in marriage and divorce, etc.—I would have to argue not that the denial of these rights interferes with my freedom of and from religion, but rather find, as Orthodox Jewish feminists and Islamic feminists do—religious justifications for such rights I demand for myself. In my book, I called this type of one-sided engagement "acting as if." Acting as if I am not completely opposed to my interlocutors' denial of the religious freedom of all members of society, in particular of the secular citizen. Acting as if I can be open to my interlocutor's position, and acting as if I could accept the authority of her religious outlook over my own life. In this way, I reverse the unequal burdens of inauthenticity that secular liberalism imposes on the non-liberal religious subject. Instead of demanding that she acts inauthentically to what she believes, I take it upon myself, in order to allow her true freedom of religion, which includes her ethical and moral commitment to articulate her positions in the public sphere and to try to enforce them on secular subjects through engagement in politics.

Some examples of this "acting as if" that I undertook during the research process for my book included acts that were easier, and ones that were harder. For example, I observed the rules of modesty that I do not adhere to, such as wearing the hijab or long skirts and long sleeve shirts, when I was in the orthodox Muslim and Jewish communities I worked with respectively. I did this even though that form of dress is inauthentic to me, and although I would never demand a conservative religious interlocutor to adopt my "immodest" form of dress when she visits my home or community. It included, for instance, visiting West Bank Jewish settlements even though politically I object to the distribution of privilege they entail, where Jewish Israelis have complete freedom of movement and access, whereas Muslim and Christian Palestinians are denied such freedoms. It included sitting in lectures at mosques, synagogues, and community centers where religious teachers often espoused racist, anti-Semitic, or Islamophobic messages, teaching them to small and large audiences as the word of God. It meant continuing to listen to the shaykh who taught that Jews have been a devious criminal people since the time of the Prophet Muhammad. It meant listening to the rabbi who explained that the very existence of Arabs is the product of evil inclination (*yetzer hara'*) and evil thoughts. It included sitting in lectures, in both communities, that taught that the secular woman (me) is garbage because she throws herself in the streets, whereas the religious woman is a jewel because she is safely kept in modesty and the home. And rather than objecting to, arguing with, and silencing the voices I heard, and instead of explaining them away as "false-consciousness," as a manifestation of other economic and political grievances, I tried to open myself up to what my interlocutors said these language and teachings meant to them.

NOTES

1   This chapter includes excerpts from my book: Ben Shitrit, Lihi. 2015. *Righteous Transgressions: Women's Activism on the Israeli and Palestinian Religious Right*. Princeton University Press, and my article: Ben Shitrit, Lihi. 2013. "Women, freedom, and agency in religious political movements: Reflections from women activists in Shas and the Islamic movement in Israel." *Journal of Middle East Women's Studies* 9(3): 81–107.

2 The Bedouin community is a historically pastoral, historically nomadic, Muslim Palestinian community of about 200,000 people residing in the Negev Desert in the south of Israel.
3 Habermas (2006) suggests that religious arguments and secular ones can be articulated in the public sphere followed by cooperative and mutual translation, in which secular citizens can translate religious arguments into secular ones in order to understand their values and contributions and vice versa. For this to happen, both religious and secular citizens have to undergo a "change in mentality," where each realizes the fact of pluralism; that their own doctrine is one among many equally legitimate positions. Yet, Habermas places conditions on participation in the democratic public sphere that significantly resemble Rawls's division between reasonable and unreasonable doctrines. Both these critics require what Rawls terms reciprocity: Acknowledging that one's comprehensive doctrine is one among many and, because all participants are free an equal citizens, our own comprehensive doctrine (whether religious or secular) cannot be imposed on others. Rules of engagement that all can accept must be put forward and abided by. In his alternatives to Rawls, Habermas still excludes "unreasonable" comprehensive doctrines from participation, as those do not accept the terms of reciprocity. Fundamentalists who believe that their religious truth must be privileged and imposed on others are left out, unless they relinquish what for them is a fundamental principle.

WORKS CITED

Abu-Lughod, Lila. *Do Muslim Women Need Saving?*. Cambridge, MA: Harvard University Press, 2013.

Ahmed, Leila. *Women and Gender in Islam: Historical Roots of a Modern Debate*. New Haven, CT: Yale University Press, 1992.

Asad, Talal. *Formations of the Secular: Christianity, Islam, Modernity*. Redwood City, CA: Stanford University Press, 2003.

Ben Shitrit, Lihi. "Women, Freedom, and Agency in Religious Political Movements: Reflections from Women Activists in Shas and the Islamic Movement in Israel." *Journal of Middle East Women's Studies* 9.3 (2013): 81–107.

Berlin, Isaiah. *Two Concepts Liberty: An Inaugural Lecture Delivered before the University of Oxford on 31 October 1958*. Oxford: Clarendon Press, 1959.

Dalsheim, Joyce. *Unsettling Gaza: Secular Liberalism, Radical Religion, and the Israeli Settlement Project*. Oxford: Oxford University Press, 2011.

Euben, Roxanne L. *Enemy in the Mirror: Islamic Fundamentalism and the Limits of Modern Rationalism: A Work of Comparative Political Theory*. Princeton, NJ: Princeton University Press, 1999.

Feige, Michael. *Settling in the Hearts: Jewish Fundamentalism in the Occupied Territories*. Wayne State University Press, 2009.

Ghandour, Zeina. "Religious Law in a Secular State: The Jurisdiction of the Sharī'a Courts of Palestine and Israel." *Arab Law Quarterly* 5.1 (1990): 25–48.

Habermas, Jürgen. "Religion in the Public Sphere." *European Journal of Philosophy* 14.1 (2006): 1–25.

Harding, Susan. "Representing Fundamentalism: The Problem of the Repugnant Cultural Other." *Social Research* 58.3 (1991): 373–393.

Keddie, Nikki R. "The New Religious Politics: Where, When, and Why Do 'Fundamentalisms' Appear?" *Comparative Studies in Society and History* 40.4 (1998): 696–723.

Kramer, Martin. "Coming to Terms: Fundamentalists or Islamists?" *Middle East Quarterly* 10.2 (2003): 65–77.

Mahmood, Saba. *Politics of Piety: The Islamic Revival and the Feminist Subject.* Princeton, NJ: Princeton University Press. 2005.

Mahmood, Saba. "Secularism, Hermeneutics, and Empire: The Politics of Islamic Reformation." *Public Culture* 18.2 (2006): 323.

Marty, Martin E., and R. Scott Appleby. *Fundamentalisms Comprehended.* Vol. 5. Chicago: University of Chicago Press. 2004.

Mouffe, Chantal. "Religion, Liberal Democracy, and Citizenship." *Political Theologies: Public Religions in a Post-Secular World.* Ed. Hent De Vries and Lawrence Eugene Sullivan. New York: Fordham University Press, 2006. 318–326.

Rawls, John. *Political Liberalism.* New York: Columbia University Press, 1993.

Rawls, John. "Idea of Public Reason Revisited." *University Chicago Law Review* 64.3 (1997): 765–807.

Sezgin, Yüksel. *Human Rights under State-Enforced Religious Family Laws in Israel, Egypt, and India, Cambridge Studies in Law and Society.* Cambridge, UK: Cambridge University Press, 2013.

Sivan, Emmanuel, and Gabriel Almond. "The Fundamentalism in the Wake of the 21st Century." *Alpaim (Two Thousands)* 22 (2001): 244–262.

Snow, David A., Sarah A. Soule, and Hanspeter Kriesi, eds.*The Blackwell Companion to Social Movements.* John Wiley & Sons. 2008.

Response
Strategies for Inclusive Conversation

Meagen Farrell

Lihi Ben Shitrit's inquiry about Israeli and Palestinian women on the religious right unpacks a relevant and uncomfortable theme within women's studies: The voices of politically engaged women in religious movements that explicitly reject and critique the secular agenda of liberal feminists. Her chapter offers several conclusions and implications for teaching, research, and activism that are worth summarizing before I respond:

- Replacing the pejorative term "fundamentalism" with the more accurate phrase "socially conservative religious-political movements."
- Recognizing the "powerful liberatory narratives" that such movements offer to women.
- Acknowledging that women do have agency and voice within these movements, particularly through emphasizing "the conscious choice and consent of the individual."
- The necessity of moving beyond Rawls's concept of public reason and Habermas's notion of the translation of religious narratives in order to find a "more honest secular liberal approach" to engage in conversation with those who reject pluralism.
- A model of "acting as if" one accepted the tenets of the religious movement in order to accurately represent a movement in research.
- The proposition that "acting as if" one were authentically engaged in the religious movement might be a tool to gain an authentic voice for the purpose of secular dialogue.

I embrace Ben Shitrit's concerns and balanced conclusions as someone who regularly struggles with presenting my perspectives in a way that is both *personally* authentic and is *received* as authentic by my dialogue partners. This includes those who identify with conservative gender norms and liberal feminist practice, and many who explicitly attempt both. While I was inspired to study religion by liberation theologians like Sallie McFague, Darby Kathleen Ray, Amina Wadud, Oscar Romero, Elizabeth Johnson, and Elisabeth Schüssler-Fiorenza, I struggled to translate my academic inquiries into practicable methods for engaging in respectful and productive dialogue on controversial social and religious issues.

Ben Shitrit modeled a potential solution to this quandary for researchers by introducing a method of "acting as if" one were personally authentic within the religious tradition, even if you're not. While I thoroughly agree with the rest of the chapter's conclusions about the respectful representation of conservative religious-political movements within feminist academic literature, this is where my enthusiasm for Ben Shitrit's conclusions wanes. I can certainly see how "acting as if" one were a member of the tribe, so to speak, does gain one access to otherwise closed realms. It also opens the researcher to a more holistic understanding of the research subjects' paradigms, which is beneficial for researchers, like Ben Shitrit, who aim to achieve a "fair representation of their worlds and commitments." I can also concur that this *may* be done with integrity if one is forthright about one's research goals and the process is undertaken with proper ethical oversight.

However, I don't think the approach of "acting as if" one were *personally* authentic in order to be *perceived* as authentic within a religious tradition is a workable solution for ongoing dialogue between disparate groups in secular discourse because without proper oversight, the approach carries the strong possibility of pushing the ethical envelope. The difficulty with this approach lies in the tenuous line between the salience of performed identity and coercive appropriation.

As an illustration of this difficulty, the author provides an interesting and unintended foil to the "act as if" method: The chapter itself. This is a well-written and researched contribution to an ongoing dialogue that gains its authenticity precisely by conforming to the expected norms and vocabulary of a tradition. This appeal to the tradition of academic literature allows the author to introduce a critique that will be deemed authentic *within the movement with which the speaker identifies*. The author's admirable fluency in the discipline demonstrates who is truly considered the peer group—not the research subjects, but the research consumers.

The congruence of both the *personal* and *perceived* authenticity of the author's identification with the liberal feminist audience is surely the strength of this chapter. However, this very authenticity, through mutual identification, highlights some of the inherent difficulties of the "acting as if" method. Internal critiques within any movement are most effective when the speaker demonstrates both fluency and authenticity within the group, whether secular liberal feminism or socially conservative piety.

So is there any hope for those who identify as liberal feminists to engage in productive research, education, and dialogue with conservative people who explicitly reject their secular agenda? I encountered methods during my work in the education and non-profit sectors that I have ultimately found effective, particularly initiatives to create trauma-informed environments. By contrast, I have observed or participated in post-secondary classes that were clearly not informed by the psychological research that confrontation, focusing on deficits, and inducing vicarious trauma activates a fight-or-flight response that leaves most people initially unable to engage in dialogue and inquiry.

For those readers who, like myself, are just as interested in methods for research and education as content and results, I would like to offer four additional methods for social change in response to Ben Shitrit's central challenge to find "a less domineering and a more honest secular liberal approach [. . .] to include rather than exclude those who reject pluralism." The benefit of these approaches is that they potentially offer both authentic *and* effective methods for people who do not personally identify with a religious movement or tradition to facilitate and engage in constructive conversations. As an added benefit, they provide a few new acronyms to memorize.

APPRECIATIVE INQUIRY

This method of positive organizational development was developed by Case Western Reserve University doctoral students David Cooperrider and Suresh Srivastva during a project with the Cleveland Clinic in 1980 (Cooperrider and Srivastva, 1987). Qualitative interviews and facilitated dialogue across multiple levels of an organization seek out positive, life-giving examples or visions to implement, promote, or take to scale for the improvement of the whole. Decades later, a body of research demonstrates that focusing on strengths and opportunities generates more resources for change than deficit-focused initiatives (Cooperrider, Stavros, and Whitney, 2008).

MOTIVATIONAL INTERVIEWING (MI)

MI is an evidence-based counseling practice used largely in the healthcare field. MI practitioners facilitate conservations to explore ambivalence about change in order to achieve a resolution. The MI approach focuses on deep listening, strengthening internal motivation, and celebrating incremental steps towards change (Miller and Rollnick, 2012). The method is both popular and effective because it achieves a balance between passive listening and direct confrontation. Co-founder William Miller has proposed that MI could have implications beyond individual change, into social justice efforts as well (Miller, 2013).

SUSTAINED DIALOGUE (SD)

SD was founded by Harold Saunders, whose deep knowledge of the Arab-Israeli conflict, gained while he was the Assistant Secretary of State in the Carter administration, is relevant to Ben Shitrit's research. Though SD has found the most traction on college campuses, it is a method of social change with applications from workplaces to international conflict resolution. SD is an evolving institutional process that transforms conflictual relationships by promoting ongoing dialogue about identity, interests, power, perception, and patterns of interaction (Saunders, 2001).

BUILDING A TEACHING COMMUNITY

Though not a formal method with international training institutes, I would like to highlight the practical work of teachers like bell hooks and Paulo Freire to create communities of practice for teachers dedicated to liberation. Freire promoted the politically controversial vocation of educators who humbly enter into dialogue with oppressed individuals to overcome the sources of their suffering (Freire, 1992). As a professor at Oberlin College, hooks facilitated peer dialogues about teaching in a multicultural setting. She also impacted Freire's thought by challenging him to overcome his male-normative worldview (hooks, 1994).

Whereas liberal feminists acknowledge the deep need for interpersonal and institutional change to build a more just and inclusive society, the process of change can be full of conflict and trauma. These methods share the common values of respect for the autonomy of one's conversation partners, building relationships of mutual trust, and uncovering internal motivation for change efforts. These answer Ben Shitrit's challenge to find "a less domineering and a more honest" method for inclusive conversation. Such methods allow practitioners to be authentic about their own identities by changing the focus of the conversation to the vast potential for change within each individual.

WORKS CITED

Cooperrider, David L., and Suresh Srivastva. "Appreciative Inquiry in Organizational Life." *Research in Organization Change and Development.* Eds. William A. Pasmore and Richard W. Woodman. Greenich, CT: JAI Press, 1987. 129–169. Print.

Cooperrider, David L., Jacqueline M. Stavros, and Diana Whitney. *Appreciative Inquiry Handbook: For Leaders of Change.* 2nd ed. Brunswick, OH: Crown Custom Publishing, 2008.

Freire, Paulo. *Pedagogy of Hope: Reliving Pedagogy of the Oppressed.* New York, NY: Continuum, 1992. Print.

hooks, bell. *Teaching to Transgress: Education as the Practice of Freedom.* New York, NY: Routledge, 1994. Print.

Miller, William R. "Motivational Interviewing and Social Justice." *Motivational Interviewing: Training, Research, Implementation, Practice.* 1.2 (2013): 15–18. Web.

Miller, William R. and Stephen Rollnick. *Motivational Interviewing: Helping People Change.* 3rd ed. New York, NY: The Guilford Press, 2012. Print.

Saunders, Harold. *A Public Peace Process: Sustained Dialogue to Transform Racial and Ethnic Conflicts.* New York, NY: Palgrave, 2001. Print.

Response: The Paradox of the Feminist Religious Radical

What kind of extremists will we be?

Megan T. Wilson-Reitz

"Who do you mean when you say 'we'?"

Every semester, I find myself posing this question to a student, and the answer is nearly always illuminating. To the Catholic student of Spanish descent who unthinkingly refers to "our" British Navy defeating "their" Spanish Armada, for example, I might pose the question, "Were *you* there in the 16th century? If not, then why is one historical group 'we'?"

These questions always unsettle my students, and for good reason—because when people use the term "we," they make a pledge of allegiance—often unconsciously—to a particular group. Those terms of allegiance are often buried among shifting layers of culture, identity, and privilege.

I find myself, like my students, unsettled by the question, "Who is meant by 'we'?" upon reading Lihi Ben Shitrit's chapter. Like many people, my many group identities represent a set of paradoxes: I am a feminist theologian who is alienated from secular political feminism, a religious activist within a conservative church, a political organizer who rejects many of the promises of representative democracy. I am, in short, much the sort of woman that Ben Shitrit studies. In the course of reading this chapter, I experience the familiar opposing pulls of these simultaneous identities.

The "we" of Ben Shitrit's conversation is clearly the "we" of feminist theorists, the Western academy, those of us whose privilege it is to examine "others" through the lens of field research. My training as an academic allows me to inhabit the world of that "we" quite easily. However, I also identify quite strongly with the "other" described here: The woman who rejects much to do with secularism, democracy, liberalism, and political feminism, in favor of religious movements that aim to do nothing less than rearrange the entire structure of human society. I am intensely aware that in that role, I am not part of the implied "we" of this text. Though Ben Shitrit entitles her chapter "Practicing Conversation," the truth is that the primary conversation here is a conversation *among* feminist academics ("we") *about* religious women (the "others"). These "others" do not, for the most part, serve as dialogue partners here; we are, rather, research subjects.

My "we" is, of course, deliberate. Certainly I cannot claim to speak for conservative religious women in Muslim or Jewish traditions, nor can

I claim any expertise in the Middle East. What I can do here, however, is to draw upon my own experience as a religious radical and activist to speak as a dialogue partner in this conversation, to expand the "we" who are included here. To that end, therefore, I will apply my own lens of interfaith dialogue to the exercise of "practicing conversation" between the secular and the religious; I invite the reader into my own experience to understand how someone with feminist sympathies might choose to engage in a conservative religious-political movement.

If the encounter between religiosity and secularism is to be treated as an interfaith dialogue, as I propose, we must first ask, is secularism a religion? The short answer is, of course, that it depends upon who is asked. However, Paul Tillich argues that everyone has a "faith" because everyone has an ultimate concern (Tillich, 18). Ben Shitrit's own worldview (educated, liberal, feminist, democratic, and secular) is, in its own way, a religious (or, at least, pseudo-religious) worldview, constructed of its own particular set of orthodoxies. This worldview is certainly as uncompromising in its demands, as dependent upon ritual, as rooted in myth, as any other religion (Tillich, 2–4). Therefore, I suggest that the encounter between Ben Shitrit's liberal secularism and the religious fundamentalism of her research subjects may be illuminated by examining it through the lens of interfaith dialogue.

For interfaith scholar Diana Eck, interfaith dialogue's transformative power rests in the fact that each participant must stand rooted in (and speaks from) her own tradition and religious commitment: "Pluralism can only generate a strong social fabric through the interweaving of commitments" (Eck, 195). Interfaith dialogue requires a balance: One must always balance openness to the other's point of view with a firm commitment to one's own faith foundation. Dialogue depends upon humility and listening. It requires a willingness to set aside judgments and prejudice, while holding fast to one's own beliefs.

When our cross-worldview encounter leads to a dialogue in which even the value of the dialogue itself is not shared, however, how do we move forward? In this chapter, Ben Shitrit includes an astute discussion of Saba Mahmood's argument, describing the long-standing problem of liberal secularism's violent dominance over the dialogue between secularism and religiosity (13). In my field as well as Ben Shitrit's, it would indeed be inappropriate to give credence to any interfaith dialogue that forces one partner to abandon a fundamental faith commitment as a condition of participation. Ben Shitrit's solution to this problematic power dynamic, however, appears to move too far in the opposite direction. By behaving "as if" she is willing to accept the claims of the religious conservatives with whom she is in dialogue, she affects an inauthentic position, which she describes as necessary to help convince others of her point of view (15). This represents a shift in rhetoric, rather than a genuine openness to other points of view.

There are times when "trying on" an unfamiliar religious practice may be an appropriate way to engage in dialogue, but it must be authentic in order to bear fruit—i.e., one must truly be open to the other's ideas, not just pretend at openness. I had never, for example, considered covering my hair to attend worship until I read another woman's reflection upon her own motivation for doing so.[1] It had not occurred to me before reading her article that covering hair for worship could be an autonomous choice born of religious desire and humility, rather than externally compelled by an oppressive tradition. Although for me (and most of my feminist peers), such a conservative act of piety was uncomfortable, even abhorrent, I wanted to listen harder and try to understand my sisters at the other end of the political spectrum. I decided to try it. For a year I covered my hair each time I attended church. Though eventually I abandoned the practice, I realized, over the course of the year, that despite its political baggage, this was a tradition that I appreciated for its own beauty, for the intensity of religious purpose represented in it, for the countercultural statement made by "covering up" to pray.

Was my year of head covering, in the end, a feminist or an anti-feminist experiment? Was it purely religious? Was it political? Perhaps it was all or none of the above. If nothing else, however, I believe that my small experiment with my own religion's tradition of modesty has helped me to engage more meaningfully with the practice of feminine modesty in other religious traditions. This engagement was an experiment of "trying on" the religious practices of others, but it differs from Ben Shitrit's practice of "acting as if" in two important ways. First, I adopted a practice already present in my own tradition, so the practice, while new to me, was authentic within my faith commitment. Second, this was a self-reflective practice adopted in order to deepen my own understanding of (and dialogue with) others, rather than a costume assumed for the purpose of convincing those others that I was an ideological ally.

Religious dress, like any religious practice, is important because it is part of the language that we use to express our convictions. Ben Shitrit describes the necessity of learning to speak in the language of religious, rather than secular, terminology, which is definitely a valuable skill for any ethnographer working in a religious context. The trouble, however, is that Ben Shitrit gives her primary reason for such "translation" as the desire for her own position to be accepted by the other: "I should translate my positions from a secular liberal language to one grounded in religious justifications that my interlocutor could potentially accept" (15). When read through the lens of interfaith dialogue, such motivation is troubling. In my field, this would be described as proselytism, rather than dialogue. The reason to learn the other's language should always be to gain understanding and build relationship, rather than convince the hearer of the rightness of one's own position. Of course, it can be difficult to engage openly with perspectives that seem abhorrent, but that does not mean that the openness is inappropriate. The hard work of pushing beyond abhorrence to real, rather than affected, understanding is the work of building real relationships and creating real social change.

Of course, the underlying question here is, "What makes for real social change?" For Ben Shitrit, the answer is obvious: The struggle for gender equality makes for real social change. However, there are other perspectives on what makes for social change, and this question, to my mind, is the unspoken part of the interfaith dialogue Ben Shitrit describes in this chapter. For members of religious sociopolitical movements, social change is always an imperative, but we have many ways of attempting to achieve that goal. I beg leave to serve as the "religious radical" half of this particular interfaith dialogue for a moment.

My primary faith community—the Catholic Worker—is a community of witness and resistance: Witness to what we believe to be the fundamental truths of the Christian Gospel (and, to a degree, their articulation in the body of Catholic social teaching), and resistance to those elements of our culture that reject those Gospel truths. Politically, we can be considered neither purely liberal nor conservative, but certainly radical and profoundly religious. One popularly stated aim of the Catholic Worker borrows from the Industrial Workers of the World (IWW) slogan, "To build a new world in the shell of the old," as Peter Maurin's "Easy Essay" explains:

> The Catholic Worker believes in creating a new society within the shell of the old with the philosophy of the new, which is not a new philosophy but a very old philosophy, a philosophy so old that it looks like new.
>
> (Maurin)

The narrative of all sociopolitical religious movements is largely the same: We engage in these particular social, political, and economic struggles because we believe that they are demanded of us by our religious commitment. Our struggles to change society are guided by, and serve, this highest of purposes. It should not be surprising that these movements are successful at gaining adherents. Human beings are, as Viktor Frankl says, made more human and freer by dedicating ourselves fully to a greater and higher purpose. "Self-actualization is possible only as a side-effect of self-transcendence" (Frankl, 133). What these movements offer to their participants is a form of ultimate self-actualization.

Those of us on the radical ends of these sociopolitical movements generally interpret our religious traditions in such a way that we see extremism, not only as self-actualization, but as the purest expression of the tradition itself. As Martin Luther King, Jr., famously asked, "[T]he question is not whether we will be extremists, but what kind of extremists we will be. Will we be extremists for hate or for love? Will we be extremists for the preservation of injustice or for the extension of justice?" (King) It is in homage to Dr. King that I adopt the term "religious extremist" with pride here.

The more of a commitment we make to this struggle, the more we become labeled "radicals" or "fundamentalists" by a culture that fears extreme positions. The difference between a "radical" and a "fundamentalist" is, in fact, more a matter of connotation than content. A "radical," from the Latin *radix*, "root," wishes for a dramatic return to the roots of a tradition, embracing the original purity of purpose. A "fundamentalist," similarly, desires the simplicity of a tradition's "fundamentals." Whereas "radical" is a word most commonly applied to left-leaning movements and "fundamentalist" to those leaning right, the words—and the movements—are very much alike. The labels—and the politics—are immaterial: The point is that it is religious extremism *itself* that poses a challenge to the culture.

When understood through the lens of the deeply religious person, the categories of "progressive" and "conservative" are frequently downright meaningless. The question is not, "Are you left wing or right wing?" but rather, "How serious are you about living the beliefs you profess?" There is tremendous common ground and room for dialogue, even at the far ends of the political spectrum, among those who are religious, but that dialogue— and the positions taken on them—can be mystifying to those whose activism stems from political convictions, rather than religious.

As a feminist, there are certainly many things I will disagree with the religious right about. However, I often find myself adhering more to their ideology than to that of secular liberal feminism, because of the ultimate goal we share—that of building the Kingdom of God. I admire their courage and their willingness to reject certain very strong messages of the culture in favor of following the Law of God as they understand it. The reason should be easy enough to understand: Regardless of how one expresses the nuances of one's political convictions, the true motivation for the life of a religious extremist is the desire to live out the commandments of God in a deep, radical, and sacrificial way.

The religious extremist often shares John of Patmos's contempt for the moderate. "I know your works; you are neither cold nor hot. I wish that you were either cold or hot. So, because you are lukewarm, and neither cold nor hot, I am about to spit you out of my mouth" (Revelation 3:15–16, NRSV). I find that I have little in common with those who pay lip service to the ideals of the Gospel but refuse to commit time or money to those ideals, for example, or those whose faith falters when they are asked to take a risk to stand up for the beliefs they profess. The extremists take those risks because they are convinced of the greater Truth they follow.

The Gospel of John says that "you will know the truth, and the truth will make you free" (John 8:32). Does liberation automatically follow from religious conviction? While we know that this is frequently *not* the case, Ben Shitrit does point out that conservative sociopolitical religious movements do, in fact, "offer women powerful liberatory narratives" (6). This insight is an important one that deserves more attention from liberal Western feminists, who tend to behave as though they hold the monopoly on liberation.

These movements also provide something more important than "liberatory narratives." They provide for their adherents—male and female alike— a practical path of resistance to a global culture that is, by any standards, increasingly destructive, avaricious, and hedonistic. For religious extremists participating in sociopolitical movements, the movements present a clear set of practices, based upon shared values, which represent a real alternative to the status quo. Adherents believe that these practices, when observed assiduously, will contribute to the larger work of conforming the entire culture to the values of the religion. In Christian terms, for example, we might articulate this ultimate goal as "the building of the Kingdom of God on Earth."

It is this goal—i.e., bringing the culture into line with religious ideals—that gives these movements their strength. Gender equality may be a valuable end goal for a secular movement such as liberal feminism, but those of us working in religious-political movements see ourselves as working towards a much greater purpose than individual (or even collective) liberation. This is not to say that certain secular, progressive movements are not valuable or important—of course they are, and we all benefit from many of them. But to a religious activist, the goals of these movements are always limited by comparison with the ultimate goal.

To put this in starkly religious terms: We who are considered religious extremists are attempting nothing less than bringing the entire culture into alignment with God's greater purpose for humanity. This ultimate goal is given priority over, or even rejects, self-interest or individual liberation, in service to the higher cause. Furthermore—and this is important—I would add that if this realignment is done correctly, most of us believe that the liberation, mercy, and love of the Divine Plan will not allow for the continuation of any human injustice. To put it another way: If we can actually achieve our goal of a fully thriving human family, there will be no more need for any other social movement. Of course, this is a lofty goal, and to a moderate, it would appear to be impossible or absurd. But to be called absurd for such a goal is no insult—it is recognition of the importance of the work. "For God's foolishness is wiser than human wisdom, and God's weakness is stronger than human strength" (1 Corinthians 1:25). That is why we are considered extremists.

Therefore, while progressive, secular feminist movements may provide more explicitly liberative narratives for women than those of religious movements, I do not share Ben Shitrit's puzzlement that feminism continues to enjoy less support in some areas than conservative religious-political movements (3). As long as these movements can provide a place for women and men to work towards the ambitious goal of transforming the earth to be more like heaven, they will maintain their hold on the popular imagination of many. Certainly there are many variations on this theme, and some versions of "heaven on earth" seem very foreign indeed to secular activists, or incomprehensible to a Western feminist ethic. However, it is incumbent upon all of us to remember that "we" are all engaged in this work together—and to remember that none of us can achieve our ultimate goals without achieving genuine relationships through dialogue with the Other.

NOTE

1 The article in question is a blog post entitled, "Notes from Beneath the Veil," by popular conservative Catholic blogger Jennifer Fulwiler. I recommend it. The post is a few years old, but is still available online.

WORKS CITED

Eck, Diana. "Is Our God Listening?" *Encountering God: a Spiritual Journey from Bozeman to Banaras*. Boston: Beacon Press, 1993.
Frankl, Viktor. *Man's Search for Meaning*. New York: Washington Square Press, 1985.
Maurin, Peter. "What the Catholic Worker Believes." *A Collection of Peter Maurin's Easy Essays*. The Catholic Worker Movement. N.d. Web. 13 July 2015.
Tillich, Paul. *Dynamics of Faith*. New York: Harper, 1957.

8 Voices of Administrators

*Cantice Greene with Beverly Guy-Sheftall,
Julie Hartman-Linck, Stanton Jones,
and Scottie May*

In a book that examines how women's studies courses are offered and received in conservative environments, it is also important to hear from administrators who have accomplished the task of creating a women's studies program to see how the programs and courses were envisioned and how the program progressed from idea to reality. To get that information, I settled on interviews because they provide an apparatus for repetition and duplication from person to person and because they provide room for a speaker to insert the details of a story as those details seem appropriate. This survey was not meant to be exhaustive or rigorous in terms of research methodology. In fact, some of the participants were chosen due to my familiarity with the program and or based on the recommendations of colleagues. Those who agreed to be interview participants include Dr. Beverly Guy-Sheftall, director of the Comparative Women's Studies Program at Spelman College; Dr. Julie Hartman-Linck, coordinator of the women's studies minor at Frostburg State University, who was recommended to me by an early participant in this project; Dr. Stanton Jones, provost of Wheaton College; and Dr. Scottie May, associate professor of Christian formation at Wheaton College.

Many of the introductions to the interview participants came about organically. For example, as I was discussing the book with a colleague in pregnancy care, she shared her experience taking courses at Wheaton, which immersed her in women's issues within a program of Christian education. Based on those conversations and Wheaton's presence in a survey of top Christian schools, I targeted Wheaton.

I assumed that the program directors at secular schools with a women's and/or gender studies program would be more liberal on the continuum from progressive or liberal to conservative or traditional. For the conservative counter perspective, I chose to target Christian schools. In my preliminary Internet search of top Christian schools, their majors and program offerings, I hadn't found any one that had a women's studies program. The ranking of top Christian schools was based on Forbes' 2010–2011 "America's Best Colleges" report. All schools were members of the Council of

Christian Colleges and Universities and included Wheaton College, Westmont College, George Fox University, and Gordon College, among others. Later, in my interview with Stanton Jones, he informed me that Wheaton does have a women's and gender studies program, which I had missed in my online review of the school's program offerings. After noticing the limited sample of women's studies programs, I wondered how Christian colleges meant to have a voice in the shaping of policies that affect women, family, the understanding of race, gender, sexuality, and power systems if they failed to engage these topics with their students—students that could potentially shape these discussions and make significant contributions. Given a Christian school's attention to restorative and therapeutic practices, attention to scripture, ecumenical action, and church history, I considered them to be well positioned to speak to women's studies issues. Another reason I chose Wheaton College is because it was ranked highest in the Forbes survey.

Three major findings resulted from these interviews. First, conservatives are generally supportive of women's studies programs insomuch as they seek to promote or broaden opportunities for women (Hartman-Linck, Guy-Sheftall, Jones). Second, conservatives showed resistance mainly to information in women's studies that treats sexual orientation and abortion, as noted in the comments of Guy-Sheftall, Hartman-Linck, and Scottie May. Third and finally, religious conservatives engage women's studies by advancing women's scholarly and career advancement (Jones, May).

What follows are excerpts from my interviews. Many of the excerpts substantiate the summative findings I've listed above. Other comments generally discuss the nature of the programs, how a specific course is taught, or additional information that I found enlightening to the discussion of teaching women's studies. I've chosen to keep some in the original interview format and to paraphrase other comments for ease of reading.

Dr. Beverly Guy-Sheftall
  Founding Director of the Comparative Women's Studies Program at Spelman College
  Selected Books: *Sturdy Black Bridges: Visions of Black Women in Literature, Words of Fire: An Anthology of African American Feminist Thought*
  http://www.spelman.edu/academics/majors-and-programs/comparative-womens-studies

Dr. Beverly Guy-Sheftall is the director of the Comparative Women's Studies Program at Spelman College in Atlanta, GA. The school is in the Bible Belt and has conservative roots, dating back to its founding by missionaries Sophia Giles and Harriet Packard, with funding by the Rockefellers.

Dr. Beverly Guy-Sheftall is the founding director of the women's studies program, which started in 1981 with a handful of goals: Community outreach, or to bridge the gap in the academy and spaces outside, to publish a journal (which became SAGE—A Scholarly Journal on Black Writing), research, and "mainstreaming," which involves mainstreaming women's studies with other disciplines. Dr. Guy-Sheftall noted that in the beginning, the program "didn't have as much student activism as we've developed over the years. The Toni Cade [Bambara Conference] and Audre Lorde papers came a little later." Though it was imagined in 1981, they operationalized it more over the years.

Regarding the uniqueness of a women's studies program at Spelman, a historically Black college for women, Guy-Sheftall remarked,

> I wouldn't say that our program is different from all other programs. I would say that Spelman is a Black college. I would say that there are some commonalities between our program and other women's studies programs. There are some ways in which we may be different. We have a strong activist component to our program. We are very committed to issues having to do with women of color and women of African descent globally. There are other women's programs that focus on race, class, gender, and sexuality. At Spelman, there may be a greater focus on women of color and women of African descent.

Elaborating on the activist component of the major, Guy-Sheftall noted that the program has an activist practicum course where students can collaborate with one of several women's organizations. Dr. Guy-Sheftall noted that resistance to the program since its founding has been "very minor. There were some faculty who didn't vote for the program," and it "is perceived by some as more radical." She finally noted that "there is resistance around issues of sexuality," which she perceives to be ideological.

In an effort to directly confront ideas about conservatives and conservatism, I read her a quote on conservatism by Rush Limbaugh:[1]

> Conservatism is all about people being whatever they want to be, using whatever ambition, talent they have, to be the best they can be. That's what we want for people. I think that scares a lot of people, because I think to people who are not conservative, the whole concept of self-reliance scares the pants off of 'em.
>
> We want people to be the best they can be. Conservatism is established so that people have the freedom to be the best they can be. Most people [who are] not conservative do not believe people can be the best they can be without help, which in this day and age translates to government help, which translates to some form of government assistance.
>
> Well, there's no question that one of the characteristics that irritates a lot of people is when you are dead certain you're right, that can be

threatening to some people, it can be off-putting, because a lot of people are not that sure of themselves, and they think that somebody who is, is a little strange. And they almost take that as being closed-minded. Being sure of yourself, being confident in your beliefs, has morphed into closed-mindedness. Being undecided and open-minded about everything means you're brilliant.

Dr. Guy-Sheftall responded this way:

I'm an academic and a scholar. I don't respond to the Rush Limbaughs of the world. In the academy, the notion of right and wrong is problematic. There are some issues that are in the realm of right and wrong. If the Rush Limbaughs of the world say women don't have a right to an abortion, there's no rational response to that. If someone just says I'm right and you're wrong, there's no response to that. I can say that there are a range of opinions around this issue.

There are certain things that are verifiable, and we can make a distinction in the classroom about what's verifiable. [For example,] Black people were enslaved. I have problems with the Rush Limbaugh arguments because they are purely ideological. You can't argue with people whose agenda is arriving at a truth that doesn't align with reality, and I don't waste my time with those kinds of arguments because they don't get you anywhere and these are people who are not engaged in any scholarship.

In our discussion, Dr. Guy-Sheftall later expounded on her role as a scholar:

When students come into the class, they have a huge range of positions. My goal is to expose them to the best research in the field. Some of them become women's studies majors. I would say a professor's goal is to expose students to knowledges.

When I enter [a] class, I don't think about who in here is conservative or liberal. Most of them know what they were exposed to for 18 years. What do most people know at 18? Most Black people who come into our classes don't know anything about African American history or women's history and it doesn't matter if they're conservative or liberal. They don't have much information. They haven't heard of Seneca Falls. . .

Finally, when I asked Dr. Guy-Sheftall to address conservatives, telling them how they could support the mission of the Comparative Women's Studies Program at Spelman, she remarked,

I have seen that these classes make a huge difference in my 44 years of teaching. It makes a huge difference. I also know people who are unwilling to change their attitudes about things, not willing to open their minds. That's a huge disadvantage. I've had students to say, I can't read anything about sexuality because that's against my religion.

I also have people say, you opened my thinking to a range of things that I knew absolutely nothing about . . . I didn't know anything about arranged marriages, female genital mutilation . . . That's why you go to college, and Black studies does the same thing for White students.

I've gotten letters from students that say, now I see what you were trying to say . . . I've had some life experiences . . . I can't tell you how much those classes have an impact on their thinking about women.

I asked her if she had any additional comments about this book project or the subject of teaching women's studies in conservative environments. She responded with,

These courses have the potential of having even more impact in conservative environments. We're not talking to a Republican or liberal audience. These alternative ways of seeing the world have the potential to have more impact here [in Georgia] than in California, for example.

You can be conservative and not talk nonsense. There are conservatives who can engage you in an intelligent conversation. Conservative doesn't mean stupid.

Dr. Julie Hartman-Linck
   Coordinator of the Women's Studies Program at Frostburg State University
   Authors Used in Class: Tracy Ore, Maxine Baca Zinn, Stefanie Coontz
   Sample of Courses Taught: Marriage and Family Relationships, Social Inequality
   Program Overview: http://www.frostburg.edu/dept/womn/program-overview/

Dr. Julie Hartman-Linck is the coordinator of the women's studies program at Frostburg State University in rural Maryland. The program has been in place at the university since the 1970s, and she has coordinated the program for more than five years. Dr. Hartman-Linck and I discussed program offerings, responses from the community, and her approaches to teaching. A sociologist by training, Dr. Hartman-Linck teaches all of the sociology courses within the women's studies minor and the Intro to Women's Studies course with a feminist approach. She places herself to the far left in terms of political ideology, and identifies most with the Green Party on social and economic issues. When I asked her about opposition to the program, she responded:

Overall, I would say the university, in terms of the administration and those I work with, have been pretty supportive. When we do get resistance it tends to either come from students who are resisting within the course or community members when we have campus events that aren't well understood or aren't well received. So the university as far as administrators go tends to be supportive. We get resistance more from the local community or from students who don't always embrace some of the topics we talk about.

We've been producing *The Vagina Monologues* for 11 or 12 years, but there are a few businesses in the community that won't put up the monologues [signs]. Overall, the people who come to the show, which also includes community members, are very supportive. We also have a group that has a slut walk and I got calls from some of the community members. They won't put up a flyer.

When I asked her to comment on the idea that some conservative opposition to women's studies is opposition to its viability in the marketplace, she remarked,

> We don't have a major in women's studies. We only have a minor, which sort of helps me sidestep the issue because I tell students you can major in something mom and dad like and minor in things you like. But, I do think that it is more marketable than people realize. I think you just have to know how to market yourself. The reality is we live in a very diverse world where you have to know how to get along with different kinds of people, and having a degree that shows some interests and some strengths in understanding human beings is, I think, a great skill to have and then in fact people can go into a lot of different fields with a degree in women's studies. It isn't just what you think of—like you can only be an academic or a women's studies professor. You can go into a lot of jobs; you just need to know how to market yourself. A lot of our students, depending on what their major is, go into various helping professions. Whether its addictions counseling, or preventing violence against women and children, or the criminal justice systems, they used their women's studies degree to show their interest in those various fields. The skills they develop are really important too. Women's studies tends to be a very writing-intensive major or minor, and I think a lot of times people don't realize it, but when you hone those skills, you can find yourself in a job. The specifics of the degree itself isn't going to help you as much as what's in that degree—thinking critically, writing, speaking, being able to do those things really well.

As in my interview with Dr. Beverly Guy-Sheftall, one of my exchanges with Dr. Hartman-Linck focused on a quote by Rush Limbaugh. I chose to quote and include Rush Limbaugh as part of my interviews because he is one of the most outspoken public personalities on the subject of conservatism. While, as Dr. Guy-Sheftall pointed out, Limbaugh is not an academic, he is widely recognized by conservatives and progressives as representing a large conservative constituency. After I read the quote (see the interview with Sheftall), I asked, "To what degree would you say this characteristic is true of the conservative students in your classrooms, and how do you respond to the assertion that being confident in your beliefs is considered closed-minded and being open-minded means you're brilliant?"

Some of it comes from our misunderstanding of what confidence and open-mindedness might be. Sometimes people act really confident in their beliefs because they aren't actually that confident in their beliefs. They express it very strongly because they're afraid that if they gather new information, that belief might be shaken. In a classroom, I try to present information. The textbook presents information. When it comes to applying information to their lives, they're the experts and we can learn from each other. And so usually, when I do have students who are reluctant—and some students are reluctant because it's kind of scary to think about inequality and to realize that the world isn't always sunshine and roses, but other students don't believe that there is inequality at all in our society and I think sometimes are really firm in that belief because they don't want to uncover what might be there if they really took a closer look or listened to other people's experiences. Usually in the class, we'll have enough students that have experienced discrimination, if not by gender by race, or by some other factor, and they'll go, oh I can't deny this experience and if they really listen, they learn something that maybe informs their opinion. I find that often-times it's more like a façade of confidence, because they're not actually that confident in their opinion. When you're open-minded, you're less attached to views. So if it turns out that something they think is wrong, it doesn't destroy [them] or it doesn't destroy who [they] think [they are]. And so I think that's something that can be cultivated. It's harder perhaps. It's one of those really difficult things that we try to teach students in college—to be confident in themselves and what they think but also open so that they're not rigidly attached to a particular view.

And that's one of the things I try to introduce in the class Intro to Women's Studies. We talk about what they have heard feminism is and we talk about what other information might be out there, and a lot of times students who think feminism is bad realize that they really don't know what feminism is. In talking about it they can get a better sense of how it isn't as scary or threatening as they thought, and they develop more confidence in what they think and also are more open to hearing what other people think.

When I asked her how students and instructor/scholars who identify as socially, religiously, and/or politically conservative could support the mission of women's studies at Frostburg she replied:

We are in a conservative area. As I mentioned, some of my colleagues are far more conservative and several of my colleagues are more religiously conservative and do support women's studies. I think because at the very basic level of what women's studies is about, equality, not having your gender determine what opportunities you have in life, those are things that most religions, most conservatives, I think, can get behind. So the very basic ideas of women['s] studies I think are things that people can support. You know, we might disagree about how we feel about abortion rights and how we feel about sexual orientation, but I think people can support some of our issues pretty easily. Some people don't like to hang up [*The Vagina Monologues*] posters, but we tend to get a lot of support for that event because it's about violence against women and supporting a local battered women's shelter. They might not think of it as a feminist cause, but they certainly like the idea of ending violence against women. So I think I would encourage people who are conservative in various ways, whether it's politically or religiously or in other areas, to really investigate what women's studies is all about. At the end of the day, the basic principles of feminism is that your gender should not determine your life, whether that's involving your pay or other issues we talk about in women's studies, and I think that's something that most people can get behind regardless of ideology.

One of the final comments she left me with about this book project is:

I think it's a really good topic to talk about because there is a huge difference for teaching women's studies—whether it's [to] a conservative audience or at a religiously affiliated school, or a major metropolitan area, or like in my case, where I'm in the middle of a very rural, conservative area. I think it's a really interesting topic because it's not something where people automatically support women's studies from all kinds of contexts. It can provide a really interesting opportunity for some coalitions to form. Oftentimes, those of us who are left-leaning just kind of automatically assume that if somebody's conservative, they're just going to be sexist and racist and bigoted and homophobic, you know all of those stereotypes that go together. Where I live, they talk about people being a redneck. Well, it's not quite so simple. You know oftentimes we find that when we talk to people and allow people to have conversations, there's a lot more support there than people realize.

Dr. Stanton Jones
    Provost and Professor of Psychology at Wheaton College
    Selected Books: *Homosexuality: The Use of Scientific Research in the Church's Moral Debate, Psychology and Christianity: Four Views*
    Most Recent Publication: "Same Sex Science" in *First Things*

Dr. Stanton Jones was recommended to me by another Wheaton professor. After a cursory overview of his background, I learned that Dr. Jones had written extensively on sexuality and psychology. During our interview, he sent me his recent 2012 article, titled "Same Sex Science," which was published in *First Things*, a print and online ecumenical journal on religion and public life. In our discussion, we discussed the book and other questions. I began our discussion by asking him to situate Wheaton's conservatism.

> Dr. Jones-That's a complicated question. On the theological spectrum, we're fairly conservative, but not on the farthest end of the conservative scale. Within Christianity broadly, we're in the conservative half. Within the conservative world, there are some very strict biblical literalists, folks that fashion themselves as fundamentalist, and Wheaton has for decades and decades and decades not counted itself in that group. I would say the driving force behind Wheaton's conservatism is a theological conservatism, but it's a moderate conservatism. There are of course correlations between political conservatism and social conservatism of various kinds, so I would say in the mind of some of our constituencies, there's a presumption that theological conservatism should go along with, for instance, family or conservatism on women's roles, whereas that's not always the case with the institution. We're working hard to recruit more female faculty, more female leaders on the campus. And so not all of our faculty, by their very natures, are prone to recommend full-time mothering and homemaking as the primary role that a woman should fill. Some of our most conservative constituency doesn't feel really good about that. So the conservatism is expressed explicitly on our campus by having an institutional Statement of Faith, which is focused exclusively on theological beliefs, and our Community Covenant, which is a general theological grounding with moral implications. Those things ground us, and conservatism is expressed more implicitly in other ways. Our Community Covenant commits us to the sanctity of life from conception. There's room for some debate about what that means, but that's something that grounds us in terms of a certain swath of what it means to engage in women's studies.

To turn our conversation toward women's studies as a field and on campus I asked Dr. Jones how students, faculty and administrators typically engage in women's studies on campus.

> Dr. Jones-We have a gender studies certificate at Wheaton that's been championed by a number of our female faculty. I've supported the approval of that certificate program, so we have a number of gender studies courses. Quite a number of our female faculty would describe themselves as feminist[s], and I've tried to serve as an advocate to the conservative part of our constituency that would see that as somehow contrary to conservative Christian values. Our gender studies certificate is a primary example of our engagement with women's studies. Another

example is that we're just in the process of revising our general educa-tion curriculum, and gender is a diversity variable on which we want to encourage students to study issues of power and exclusion.

Shifting our conversation to the narrower subject of sexuality, I asked Dr. Jones what led him to write a book on the subject of the use of scientific research in the Church's moral debate on homosexuality.

Dr. Jones-Thanks for asking. What led me to write it is by training, I'm a clinical psychologist. My training was in the more scientifically driven aspects of the clinical psychology field rather than the purely clinical, so I try to stay attuned to how scientific research drives clinical practice and so forth. In [the] 1980s, I was a member of the Episcopal church, and there was a very strong sort of advocacy movement for full acceptance of lesbian/gay/bisexual/transgendered persons. So I was lis-tening to arguments, these moral arguments, and many of them invoked science as part of the reasoning, [for example] you know science says blank and therefore the church's views about this issue are invalid. It was a trope to argue that of course, sexual orientation is genetically determined; therefore, you can't hold a person morally accountable for how they live out their sexual orientation. I just felt like all too often, the scientific evidence was being misappropriated in those arguments, so I tried to make an argument that bringing scientific arguments to bear on these moral issues was much more complicated and needed much more nuance than what had previously been done.

Considering the circumstances, I felt it was important for me to speak into that conversation within the church. So that book was an attempt with a former student to speak to those issues, and I've continued to speak on those issues since that time.

When I asked how he might revise the book today, he said,

Today I'd be writing about gender and sexuality. I would need to do a whole new chapter on transsexuality, transgender . . . whether sex as male and female is a real thing. That matters a lot and the answers there are much more complex from a theological standpoint.

Our discussion about his book and recent article in *First Things* eventually ended, and I returned to the subject of his role in making women's studies an area of study. Specifically, I asked him to explain the variables involved in mak-ing a decision to include or not to include women's studies as an area of study.

At Wheaton, we would ask, is this consistent with our core? Is this problematic? Part of the conservative constituency would say women should not be senior pastors. They would be complementarians, but a majority would be egalitarians. We intentionally don't take a stand on that issue on campus, but we are also very clear that our campus is not a church and we are open to women's leadership on campus. Wheaton has never had a female president. We're all White males. I saw as problematic all White males reporting to me. So I've worked hard to have women represented in the leadership. We've increased from 24–35% female faculty.

Finally, I turned my attention to Wheaton's Center for Multicultural Development. Insomuch as women's studies aims to point out the intersections of multiple systems of oppression including race, gender, class, sexuality, and others, I wondered how the center has shared the mission of women's studies. Dr. Jones responded this way,

> The office is looking at [the] issues [of] race first, class second, and gender only much less so. Their large focus is racial and ethnic identity. Where that [is] getting attention is in general studies, with a required two courses: Diversity in the U.S., and global, multiple systems that influence oppression.

GENERAL EDUCATION REQUIREMENTS: ESSENTIALS OF A CHRISTIAN WORLDVIEW (WHEATON COLLEGE)

Studies in Diversity—Two Courses (4–8 hours)

> *Diversity courses substantively interact with one or more of the following: races, genders, ethnicities, religions, and cultures other than Anglo-American and white majority European as their major content or subject matter.*
>
> *Student[s] will grow in their ability to a) Identify the role of plural races, genders, ethnicities, religions, and cultures in shaping human knowledge; b) gain an understanding of their perspectives and attempt to "see" the world through another's eyes; and c) experience engagement with, concern for and commitment to the worth and welfare of those from diverse ethnic, racial, religious and cultural heritages.*

Scottie May
   Associate Professor of Christian Formation, Wheaton College
   Influential Authors Mentioned: Kathleen Norris, Cathy Stonehouse, Ann Voskamp
   Courses Taught: Personal Spiritual Formation, Family Studies

Dr. Scottie May describes herself ideologically as "middle of the road." In practice, she says she leans to the left, but in theology, a little to the right. Dr. May acknowledged that because she teaches Christian formation, women's studies is not her focus; however, she also acknowledges that many women, her students, come to her to discuss their career paths in ministry and at these times, she points them to women leaders in ministry as well as the more classic women's studies scholars.

Our discussion was very conversational. As I mixed in questions during our talk, it felt mainly as if I was wondering aloud. For example, it seemed to me that the formation of or expression of gender would enter into a discussion of Christian formation in the family. So I asked, In what ways do you address gender, or race, or specifically women when you teach family studies?

> Dr. May-I teach a course called Personal Spiritual Formation. And in that course, I intentionally assign readings by males so that they can see a male perspective and include readings by males that bring in more of feminine attributes and feminine leanings. And I have two or three articles on women's spiritual formation and what uniquely characterizes the way women tend to connect with God. And here, again, that's painting with a broad stroke. But I think Kathleen Norris's writing and some of those people are very helpful for evangelical women to read on how they can broaden themselves from their early church experiences which tend to be quite conservative, somewhat narrow, and homogenous. When it comes to the course on ministry with families, I don't focus specifically on women. I focus on parenting and every aspect of parenting and use case studies going into even same-sex marriages and same-sex parenting much more that way than specifically women as parents.

Next, I wondered how Dr. May's understanding of a woman's Christian formation in and outside of the family had guided her.

> Dr. May-My initial guides are males, Henri Nouwen and Brennan Manning, who influenced me to stop being so active in Christian religious activity and start being willing to be still in the presence of God. And once I got over that hurdle, I began to read others. I mentioned Kathleen Norris. I enjoy Ann Voskamp. I have read African American women and their passions. I read global voices of women and their practices in other cultural settings. One of the really strong books for me was *Motherless Daughters*. That had a profound impact on my thinking. Even though I had a mother, I was motherless in a way because she was so busy in ministry. So, those have been some key voices. And the other thing that has been so highly significant for me is what Cathy Stonehouse and I call reflective engagement practice with children,

and carrying those practices into groups of women and adults. Silent retreats, spiritual direction for women, [have been] very, very influential in my life. Some of my early heroines were pioneer missionaries who opened up unexplored countries like the Baliem Valley, part of Irian Jaya in Papua. The first women to go in there, I knew them well. I knew them deeply. They had an impact on my life. So I have been very shaped by strong women and people in ministry throughout my life. I just put all that together against trying to overcome that activist mode and finding a more content, consecrated mode, which has enriched my soul beautifully. It has been a journey for me which has just been wonderful.

. . . and it's very good for me to talk about this because I had never seen that trajectory before. I have very, very rich evangelical heritage, and so some of the key women's voices have had a profound shaping on me.

I asked if she would say that she has consciously tried to either engage or avoid feminist teaching or women's studies and what theories, ideas, or approaches attracted her to the field or repelled her away from it.

Dr. May–What repels me is the radical feminists of the 60s elevating females as better than males in every way. That's what repelled me and so it took me a while to engage in the more balanced ideas that all people are made in God's image and yes, women are equal to men and [as] gifted as men are. That has been much more attractive and helpful . . . that we are superior in some areas, but we are inferior in other areas, and that varies by individual.

After our rich discussion and my final probing on the topic of teaching women's studies in conservative contexts, Dr. May remarked that she thought there would be "less interest" in the topic in Wheaton's student body as a whole "because of the conservative background that so many of them come from." She added that students' positions "are not often reflective of the positions of the faculty."

NOTE

1 "Millenials Haven't Experienced Conservatism." The Rush Limbaugh Program. Archives from 14 April 2015. Rushlimbaugh.com

Contributors

Lihi Ben Shitrit is a former Colorado Scholar of Harvard University's Women's Studies in Religion Program. Her research is on women's activism on the Israeli and Palestinian religious right. Her book *Righteous Transgressions: Women's Activism on the Israeli and Palestinian Religious Right* (2015) was published by Princeton University Press. She is an assistant professor of political science in the School of Public and International Affairs at the University of Georgia.

Amena Brown is a spoken word artist and author of *Breaking Old Rhythms: Answering the Call of a Creative God*. She has participated in many live recordings, including two poems on Gungor's album *A Creation Liturgy*. She is the author of the spoken word CD *Live at Java Monkey*. She also hosts a regular open mic night every fifth Thursday with her husband (DJ Opdiggy) at Urban Grind in Atlanta.

Cecili Chadwick received her master's degree in women's studies in 2007 from Claremont Graduate University. Most of her research interests center around reproduction, identity politics, pornography and prostitution, and violence against women. Currently, Cecili teaches a variety of women's studies courses at California State University San Marcos, which cover topics ranging from the history of the feminist movement to reproductive rights.

Latona F. Disher is the CFO of a non-profit organization in metropolitan Atlanta, Georgia. Her career in higher education as a student affairs professional, which spans more than a decade, and her post-graduate studies in higher education administration/leadership are areas of reflection and research. She earned her Doctorate of Strategic Leadership in organizational leadership from Regent University, Virginia Beach, VA.

Monica Carol Evans earned her Master of Divinity from Emory University, where she focused her studies on womanist and queer theologies and spiritual formation. Her writing and teaching lives at the intersection of personal development and womanist spiritual praxis.

Meagen Farrell is an author, teacher trainer, and instructional designer specializing in adult literacy. She holds an A.B. in religion from Oberlin College, an M.A. in theology and religious studies from John Carroll University, and a certificate in distance education from Penn State University. Meagen is a blogger by hobby, teacher by vocation, and married with kids by the grace of God.

Veronica N. Gravely is a writer, worship artist, engineer, and theologian residing in the greater Atlanta, GA area. She obtained her Bachelor of Science in chemical engineering from the Georgia Institute of Technology, and her Master of Divinity from the Interdenominational Theological Center. She is a married mother of two who believes in the reconciliation of all created things to their Creator in such a way that shows the power of Jesus and the cross.

Cantice Greene received her B.A. from Spelman College and her Ph.D. from Georgia State University in English, specializing in feminism and composition. She has been consistently engaged in women-centered work, including women's spiritual development at her local church and in local non-profits, especially Cobb Pregnancy Services in Marietta, GA. Cantice is an assistant professor of English at Clayton State University.

Beverly Guy-Sheftall is the director of the Comparative Women's Studies Program at Spelman College in Atlanta, GA. She is the author of several books. Among them are *Sturdy Black Bridges: Visions of Black Women in Literature*, and *Words of Fire: An Anthology of African American Feminist Thought*.

Julie Hartman-Linck is the coordinator of the Women's Studies Program at Frostburg State University in rural Maryland. She is an associate professor of sociology, and her areas of interest include gender, sexuality, inequality, and feminist and queer theory. She received her Ph.D. from Michigan State University.

Judy L. Isaksen, professor of media and popular culture studies, teaches and researches at the intersection of rhetoric, critical/cultural theory, media studies, and matters of gender, race, and sexuality. Her recent publications have focused on the rhetoric of Barack Obama through the lens of Black masculinity, and the rhetoric of Black masculinity within hip-hop culture.

Stanton Jones is the provost and a professor of psychology at Wheaton College. He has written extensively on sexuality and psychology, including his book, *Homosexuality: The Use of Scientific Research in the Church's Moral Debate*. His most recent article, "Same-Sex Science," appeared in *First Things*.

Maria Lastochkina received her B.A. in literature and languages from the Russian Orthodox University of Saint John the Divine and her M.A. in theology from the University of Durham, UK. She is a freelance translator working in Moscow, Russia, and pursuing her interest in Christian bioethics by acting as a liaison between a number of institutions and individual scholars.

Scottie May is an associate professor of Christian formation at Wheaton College. She teaches the classes Personal Spiritual Formation and Ministry with Families; in the latter, she focuses on parenting. She is the author of *Listening to Children on their Spiritual Journey*, co-authored with Catherine Stonehouse, and a contributing editor of *Children's Spirituality* (2004).

Jennifer McWeeny is an associate professor of philosophy at Worcester Polytechnic Institute. Her research and teaching interests are in the areas of feminist philosophy, phenomenology, philosophy of mind, ontology, de-colonial theory, and Asian and comparative philosophy. McWeeny is co-editor, along with Ashby Butnor, of *Asian and Feminist Philosophies in Dialogue: Liberating Traditions* (Columbia University Press, 2014), and her articles have appeared in the *Continental Philosophy Review*, *Hypatia*, *Journal for Critical Animal Studies*, and *Simone de Beauvoir Studies*.

Le'Brian A. Patrick is an assistant professor of sociology at Xavier University in Louisiana. His research areas of specialization are crime and social justice, and women's and gender studies. His variety of works have been included in both academic articles and books such as *HyperSexual HyperMasculine: Gender, Race, and Sexuality in Contemporary Black Men* (2014). He also has an artistic background in which he uses artistry to focus on bringing awareness to social injustices.

Megan Wilson-Reitz is a long-time member of the extended Catholic Worker Community of Cleveland, an urban community dedicated to radical Christian discipleship. She is a regular at community protests and prayer services. She is a lecturer in the department of theology and religious studies at John Carroll University, where she also supports the Honors Program and the Office for Institutional Diversity and Inclusion.

Index

For Product Safety Concerns and Information please contact our EU
representative GPSR@taylorandfrancis.com
Taylor & Francis Verlag GmbH, Kaufingerstraße 24, 80331 München, Germany